A Restless People

A Restless People

Americans in Rebellion
1770—1787

Oscar and Lilian Handlin

Anchor Press/Doubleday
Garden City, New York
1982

Library of Congress Cataloging in Publication Data
Handlin, Oscar, 1915–
A restless people.
Includes bibliographical references and index.
1. United States—Social life and customs—Revolution,
1775–1783. 2. United States—Social conditions—To
1865. 3. United States—Social life and customs—1783–
1865. I. Handlin, Lilian, joint author. II. Title.
E163.H36   973.3
ISBN 0-385-06102-1   AACR1
Library of Congress Catalog Card Number 79-8432

For Emily

Contents

All that has happened to you is also connected with the details of the manners and situation of a *rising* people; and in this respect I do not think that the writings of Caesar and Tacitus can be more interesting to a true judge of human nature and society.

(Benjamin Vaughan to Benjamin Franklin,
Paris, January 31, 1783)

A Restless People

A Place of Big Spaces

In the United States there is more space where nobody
is than where anybody is.
This is what makes America what it is.

GERTRUDE STEIN,
The Geographical History of America (1936)

Carpenters' Hall in Philadelphia was the scene of an unusual
gathering on September 5, 1774. The craftsmen who ordinarily
assembled in the building had yielded it up for use by strangers.
At ten o'clock the delegates from eleven British mainland colonies had met at Smith's Tavern, then walked over to inspect
the hall. Joseph Galloway of Pennsylvania expressed a preference for the more imposing State House, but the others judged
the room good enough—and there they remained, to be joined
nine days later by representatives of North Carolina, one of the
two missing provinces.

The men who took counsel in the hall had come to the city to
consider their common grievances against the Crown. The chamber resounded during their sessions with affirmations of loyalty
to Britain. But sensitive observers smelled rebellion in the air.

The action taken was mild enough. But from it proceeded active measures of resistance—then, within a year, war—and fifteen months thereafter the Declaration of Independence that established the American republic.

The individuals who arrived wearily in Philadelphia that morning were not members of any recognized body. They were emissaries dispatched as ambassadors by the assemblies that governed the thirteen distinct provinces. They referred to themselves, therefore, as the Congress, a term applied in Europe and in America to such extraordinary conclaves. The men who met in Carpenters' Hall, and who in time learned to act as a unit, became generally known as the Continental Congress; and so the title has been fixed in the memory of succeeding generations.

The adjective was as important as the noun. The word "Congress" described the function of its members: they gathered to consult and negotiate. The word "Continental" set this gathering off from other extralegal bodies that had sprung up in individual provinces for the same purpose. But it also expressed a sense of the vast area for which the delegates in Philadelphia presumed to speak. In a sense that challenged the imagination, they assumed that the people of a whole continent could freely cooperate and act together.

The distances staggered those who thought by European standards. Some members had come five hundred miles or more —the distance from Charleston to Baltimore as the crow flies. Five hundred miles from London took an Englishman to Kirkwall in the Orkney Islands, Copenhagen, Hamburg, Geneva, or Bordeaux. Boston and Savannah were fully a thousand miles apart; and the Londoner who traveled that far came just short of Iceland or beyond Trondheim, reached Stockholm, Warsaw, Budapest, Naples, or Lisbon. Americans developed a new mode of thought to bring into focus the great spaces of their country.

And then, the delegates did not travel as the crow flies. They came in sailing ships, making their way at the mercy of wind and tide, down the coast and up the river's tortuous passages. Such voyages were preferable to travel by land, even where roads existed. The choice of bone-rattling coaches or ambling post-horses subjected the traveler to prolonged discomfort under the best of circumstances, for the rutted roads were but a slight improvement over the trails that had served the Indians. The less fortunate voyagers were at the mercy of delays caused by snow, storm, or flood. In some places riders found shelter in an inn or tavern, but often they had to seek the hospitality of the nearest farmer when the sun set.

For this was, even in the most densely settled areas, a land of immense emptiness, holding perhaps two and a half to three million people in all. The tiny clusters of population that punctuated its great distances only emphasized the long stretches in between.

The population hugged the coast. As one moved into the interior, signs of human habitation thinned out. For more than a hundred and fifty years the arriving Europeans had beaten against the wilderness that once reached to the very ocean's edge. Their efforts had taken them, by 1774, only a short distance inland. The line of settlement followed the Maine shore, cut across New Hampshire and southern Vermont, ran through eastern New York, central Pennsylvania, and western Virginia, then turned back eastward in the Carolinas and Georgia. But the very concept of such a solid line is misleading; for frontiersmen had only recently drifted into much of the area within it. Their number grew sparse away from the coast; few settlements had yet taken hold beyond the mountains, which formed a temporary barrier to further advances. People in Massachusetts and Virginia knew vaguely that, deep in the interior, virgin acres lay ready for exploitation, and their imagination leaped to the great western river and its tributaries, flowing through fertile lands that awaited only the arrival of families to give them life.

The Americans formed a society with a long and variegated history. Europeans had been bringing this part of the continent under cultivation for 170 years. Diverse causes drove them across the Atlantic, and they brought with them diverse heritages. They lived, therefore, in diverse communities sharply differentiated from one another by ethnic antecedents, cultures, and economies. These distinctions long endured.

Nevertheless, when in 1776 delegates to the Second Continental Congress signed their names to the Declaration of Independence, they found no anomaly in the statement that they acted as "one people." They recognized a social reality. They had become one people—the Americans.

That one people, the Declaration pointed out, was separating from another people, the British. Paradoxically, Yankees and Virginians, Yorkers and Georgians, though quite different from one another, had become aware of a collective identity, different from that of their ancestral peoples. As a motto for the new republic they chose E pluribus unum; they had been many, then had become one.

The Revolution demonstrated the capacity to act; it did not, however, eliminate differences. Indeed, the prolonged crisis that sealed the separation from Britain exposed the economic, regional, and social lines that set groups of Americans apart from one another. Yet the same crisis also revealed the cultural and social bases of the nationality that unified them. In the course of becoming independent, conflicts between the rebellious colonies and the Crown, and among the colonists themselves, tore provincial society apart; but the same process also furnished the unifying elements that made the nation a whole.

Many yet one, divided but united, separate but attached—Americans frequently encountered the contradictions in their own lives. In their aspirations, in their attitudes toward their families and their own bodies, in the willingness to take risks and the value placed on security, they felt the pull of polar forces which the Revolution only partially reconciled but which did much to shape their national character.

In hindsight, the Revolution consists primarily of changes in government; political grievances, independence, and the composition of constitutions dominate the events of the entire quarter century after 1763. Regarded in the perspective of the times, however, the Revolution comes into focus as an incident in the life of a people occupied with many more matters than politics. Events on the battlefields and in the debating chambers did not at once alter the ways in which farmers and townsfolk worked and prayed, married, reared families, and passed to their rewards. No point in the calendar, however later generations would celebrate it, marked the clear divide between colony and republic, between British subjects and American citizens.

Americans of the 1770s shared with the Britons of their time and with other Europeans common ideas, many cultural traits, and significant economic and political characteristics. The Atlantic was as important a means of uniting as it was of dividing the continents. The people, however, were different—not by blood or by heritage, but by a style of life that subtly altered ideas, culture, economy, and government, and that shaped the New World revolution and the republic to which it gave birth.

That style of life, the subject of this book, became clearly visible in the 1770s, although evidence of it appeared a decade earlier and persisted a decade later in the modes of production that sustained Americans, the communities in which they lived, their social organizations, and their familial patterns. A harsh existence, particularly on the frontier, developed habits of risk taking that made possible the plunge into war and independence; but it also shaped ideas and beliefs that justified the chances taken. People who survived these conditions longed for means to express lofty aspirations yet spoke most eloquently of hard reality; they devised ingenious schemes for self-government but fell short of their own definition of a virtuous society; and they yielded readily to the temptation to postpone for the indefinite future problems they could not solve in the immediate present.

"We live, my dear soul, in an age of trial," John Adams wrote to his wife, Abigail, in May of 1774. What would be the consequences he did not know. He and his wife never doubted that "the cause of truth, of virtue, of liberty and of humanity" was at stake. Yet they soon observed a "spirit of avarice, and contempt of authority, an inordinate love of gain" around them. The longing for virtue and the temptations of gain complicated the lives of their countrymen and countrywomen who explored the conditions of freedom in the pursuit of happiness.

The American Revolution was the product of subtle yet profound changes that formed the life of people made aware of their distinctive attributes and determined to create a new society in accord with habits and beliefs shaped by the New World environment. The signers of the Declaration of Independence were trying, not to overturn their government or transform their society, but to preserve both against external threats. Often they used the word "revolution" in the sense of a return to a starting point, as of the earth about the sun or the moon about the earth. Only later did the idea of a new order of things spread.

Jefferson and his collaborator John Adams lived fifty years from the date on which they signed the Declaration. Their notable longevity was the product of robust constitutions, personal and political—for the settlement they contrived endured without such purges or liquidations as elsewhere in the next two centuries destroyed revolutionaries. The founders of the American republic moved peacefully in and out of office in the decades after 1776 because their handiwork rested not simply on political programs or arrangements but on the character of the people whose work it was.

1

Rural Life

"For my part," explained the popular writer who used the pseudonym "An American Farmer," "I had rather admire the ample barn of one of our opulent farmers, who himself felled the first tree in his plantation, and was first founder of his settlement, than study the dimensions of the temple of Ceres. I had rather record the progressive steps of this industrious farmer, throughout all the stages of his labors and other operations, than examine how modern Italian convents can be supported without doing anything but singing and praying."

The American Farmer was a native of France, and he did not remain in the idyllic setting he described. In 1780 fear of disorder drove Crèvecoeur to a refuge in England. But he had worked in America long enough so that his lyric celebration of rural life rang true to thousands of readers on both sides of the ocean. The greatness of the New World, he explained, stemmed from the opportunity it afforded every man and woman to live a virtuous life on the soil, dependent on no one, holding no one in dependence, bringing forth their own means of sustenance in close communion with nature. For decades this recurring theme reverberated in the thinking of the citizens of the Republic and of the Europeans who aspired to join them. Americans were seen as a people of cultivators without aristocratic families, courts, kings, or bishops—and without factories. They had turned a savage wilderness into a glorious empire by honorable conquest—not by destroying but by promoting the wealth, the number, and the happiness of the human race.

This idyllic portrait of the American yeoman contained a measure of truth. But the whole truth was more complex than the farmer-writer Crèvecoeur implied. The limitations that deprived toilers in the crowded Old World of the ability to lead a happy life here dropped away. Continental abundance opened opportunities to all. But not all could grasp them; and those who did often found themselves dragged away from the virtuous existence they avidly desired. Hence the contradictions characteristic of rural life in America.

Land was abundant. Whoever wished to work could build a home and put a plow to the soil. If the price of the desired acres was high in the eastern counties, it was low in the western; let the seeker go but far enough and he would find a place in the woods, his for the taking. To those who measured by the standards of crowded European holdings, America was abundant almost beyond belief. Not land but labor was in short supply. Such was the value of work that even the penniless—those who arrived from abroad as indentured servants or children bound as apprentices—gained freedom after a few years of service, and with stakes large enough to start as masters in their own rights. Independent proprietorship was within the reach of all.

Crèvecoeur did not, however, understand that Americans worked under tremendous pressures and that immense variations of wealth and prestige divided them. Colonial farmers were not all alike. Nor were all Americans cultivators of the soil. And none led the carefree, independent, and secure existence of which the American Farmer dreamed.

The Yankees were a breed unto themselves, heirs of the seventeenth-century Puritan migration. In the 1770s many were fifth-generation Americans and all had developed a distinctive character in their corner of the continent. They had fastened to the coastline of Massachusetts, to Narragansett Bay, and to Long Is-

land Sound and thence had moved up the valleys of the Mer-
rimack, Charles, Connecticut, and Housatonic rivers. From time
to time fresh arrivals from England, Scotland, or Ireland or a
handful of French Huguenots had added to their strength. But
the original Puritan impulse still shaped the culture of the New
Englanders.

From the start, the Church had been important in the life of
this region. A yearning for purified forms of worship had been
one motive for the original migration. Learned men, swayed by
godly ideals, continued to command respect, and church membership remained connected with property and political power.
Periodic religious revivals kept zeal alive and reinvigorated the
rigid discipline that regulated the entire life of the community.
Throughout New England, faith linked the minister to society
and impinged upon government, economic attitudes, and family
relations.

So long as this was the case, people remained in towns within
reach of the meetinghouse. Early on in the course of settlement,
when the Indians and the wilderness were a double threat, everyone lived within sight of one another around the green or
common. Once the danger from the Indians abated, people
drifted apart and built their homes in the midst of the plots upon
which they worked. Nevertheless, they did not go off by themselves, and to a remarkable degree the town still held its coherence in the 1770s.

Most New England farmers, therefore, were not isolated; the
community maintained rigorous control over everyone in it. In
the 1770s the selectmen of Fairfield, Connecticut, were not unusual in dealing severely with idle persons who misspent their
time and neglected their families; towns did not hesitate to warn
out vagrants, giving legal notice that the community would not
assume the obligation of supporting a new arrival who became
dependent. Others prosecuted idle strangers and those who entertained them.

Society favored those willing to work. Off in the hills and in
backward corners the shiftless or unfortunate planted what they
needed for subsistence alone. But access to markets opened op-

portunities for raising crops for sale. The chances of finding
nearby buyers, of producing goods for the cities or for Europe
and the West Indies, tempted all but the most lethargic.
Such pursuits enriched a few large landowning families
with aristocratic pretensions. Along the Connecticut River the
Dwights and others exploited substantial estates with the aid of
numerous tenants. The Narragansett region of Rhode Island
raised sizable herds of cattle and horses, and especially the valuable breed of pacers exported to the West Indies. These plantations used tenants and Indian and white servants as workers, but
also about a thousand black slaves.

The great landowners were gentry mostly by comparison with
less fortunate neighbors. The largest houses rarely reached fifty
feet in any dimension, and the rustic furnishings offered little
scope for the display of wealth. Since others did the labor, and
managerial chores consumed but a few hours, the masters sought
relief from boredom in hunting, fishing, hospitality, politics, and
speculation.

A short way back from the valleys, stony hills encumbered the
tasks of cultivation. Few settlers in these areas remained lethargic long. Survival called for unremitting labor. To break the soil
with the wooden bull-plow, to sow broadcast with repeated
sweeps of the arm, to cut the grain with a scythe, and to thrash it
on the barn floor with a flail took heavy toll in human energy.

Neither soil nor climate was congenial to a life of leisure.
Harsh winters, relatively short growing seasons, and unpredictable weather demanded constant vigilance. Once the husbandmen had stripped the forests away, they discovered the deficiencies of the land. And since only hard labor could win a
livelihood from the earth, most farmland remained unimproved.
No matter how extensive his holdings on paper, a man alone
could manage to cultivate only three or four acres. In the absence of sons or servants it was more prudent to devote large
tracts to meadows or woodlots, for it was easy to raise livestock
so long as one let the beasts feed and breed as they would.
Hence, too, the preference in the region for corn, which kept
better than wheat, required relatively little labor, and left stalk
leaves and husks to feed the animals.

Families content to live off pickled pork and clothe themselves in plain homespun textiles tolerated the indolence of adults and the idleness of children. But anyone who wished to do more than barely hold on worked hard to hoe the vegetable garden, gather nuts, and tend the poultry and the apple trees.

The unending struggle shaped Yankee character. The lesson that life was a battle against uncongenial elements, learned early in life, trained people to strive lest they go under. The failures plunged into poverty, a sign of personal defeat that brought with it the additional degradation of relief from public charity, or open auction for support by the best bidder. The old and the disabled as well as widows and orphans fared badly in rural New England, dependent as they were for aid on relatives with limited means, or on towns which resented every charge that increased taxes in a society always short of funds.

The need for some cash pushed everyone toward money-making ventures. Every husbandman had somehow to earn the means of paying taxes and dues to the church and of making occasional purchases—of guns or powder, of pots, axes, saws, salt, rum, and other goods he could not himself fabricate. And some went beyond rudimentary needs to set aside a margin against future hard times. They yielded to the temptation of commercial crops, raising tobacco or onions for export in Rhode Island and Connecticut, flax and hemp there and in Massachusetts, and, almost everywhere, working up timber into shingles, clapboards, and barrel staves.

These pursuits bred discontent, for they deepened dependence upon the market, increased risks, and diminished stability. Production for sale cut into the farmer's time for feeding and clothing his family, forced him to buy more—and therefore created a need for additional cash. Furthermore, once he ceased to think only of providing for himself, he was inclined to expand. Ambition made Yankees great swappers of land. A high rate of turnover was one measure of their restless temper. Always they considered the plots where they were inadequate; any move would better their situation. That periodic shuffling around, from the center to the outskirts, from one town to another, from south to north and from east to west, was a sign not of lack of space but of the inextinguishable desire for improvement.

Arrivals and departures were commonplace in the Yankee towns. Many were the complaints against intrusive strangers outlandish in habits, unfamiliar presences in the meetinghouse, who would perhaps even in time become charges on the public purse, given as they were to crime and prone as they were to poverty—else why would they not stay in the places they had left? The outlanders, of course, were rarely foreigners. Although not natives of the particular locality, they usually came from within the region, frequently from within the colony, and often even from the same county.

Farm families that stayed where they were displayed a similar restlessness. Not satisfied to plow the same furrow, they diversified their activities. The flocks of geese they kept, though their cackling heard miles away drowned out the minister's sermon, three or four times a year yielded up feathers for household use or for sale. Levi Dickenson of Hadley, Massachusetts, planted half an acre of broom corn. Scraping away the seed with a knife, he first scrubbed the corn, then combed and tied the brush, then sewed it, pressing the needles with a "leather palm." He successfully peddled two hundred brooms around the countryside and the following year planted an acre. Where they could, innovative people expanded their output; they converted pasture into tillage, or they took fish when the season permitted, and salted and packed it; or they used moments of leisure to whittle shingles, cobble boots, cut nails, press cider, or distill vinegar. Near the seacoast they signed up "on shares" in fishing voyages, so that the farm itself became a side activity, entrusted to other members of the family. Those who went whaling from Nantucket left for months on end.

Now and again a bold spirit laid in a stock of goods, opened a shop, and began trading with his neighbors. Another took advantage of a favorable site to build a mill, to grind grain or saw timber. Many people were borrowers and lenders—often the same person, giving and taking in multifarious operations. Peter Hitchcock, a farmer and carpenter in Wallingford, Connecticut, died in 1774 leaving an estate valued at £330 2s. 6d. He owed twenty different creditors a total of £10 6s. 9d., while twenty-five debtors owed him £35 16s. 5 1/4d.

Early in life, Yankees learned the merits of long-term investments and became avid speculators not only in land but in commodities of every sort. The fool and his purse were soon parted. None challenged that wisdom. But he who was unwilling to take a chance would never improve himself. That, too, was wisdom. The ministers, observing these calculations with dismay, denounced the sin of avarice, by which they meant the incessant efforts of men to better themselves at whatever cost to community welfare. The sermons were in vain. The call to self-improvement evoked a greater response than that to patience and pious perseverance.

By the 1770s generations of experience had validated Yankee individualism. Neighbors resented the charges paid the miller and the blacksmith, grumbled at the shopkeeper's hard bargains, and hated the squire who made usurious loans. But all of them knew that they would do the same were the position reversed; even men of God, like John Gorton, the Baptist minister of Warwick, Rhode Island, combined business and preaching with no sense of incongruity. Yankees accepted sharp competition and respected those who came out on top. Though the share of the wealthiest farmers grew, the incomes of the less fortunate also rose and eased their acceptance of inequality.

People driving to get ahead repeatedly ran into the economic constraints of numbers and space. The population of rural New England continued to grow at a spectacular rate of about 2 percent a year, which inevitably meant that sons could not expect simply to inherit holdings as good as those of their fathers. Yet no one wished to divide estates into tiny plots after the European fashion. Sooner or later, either the parent or the child had to strive to increase the patrimony. The felt lack of room in a country of great spaces drew some people onto the roads; vagabondage increased.

Yet, paradoxically, the colonists considered both labor and land to be in short supply. The number of hired hands and indentured servants did not increase, and may actually have declined after 1750, because more attractive opportunities else-

where on the continent drew immigrants from the region; and
while few towns were overcrowded, most had reached the limits
of their good arable fields and their desirable mowing and marsh-
land. The pressure of numbers did not, however, create an agricultural proletariat, for yeomen not content with what was at
hand turned elsewhere for opportunity.

At first the restless migration from one spot to another very
much like it did not sever the links with a known neighborhood.
But, increasingly, impatient men took their families with them in
departures that cut them off entirely from the past. The first
thrusts had been northward along the coast of Maine, or up the
river valleys through central and western Massachusetts and on
into New Hampshire. The pioneers were rarely content just to
lay out farms for themselves. They wanted former neighbors to
come along, both to raise the value of land and to help support
the church, school, and roads a proper town required. Captain
Jonathan Willard of Colchester, Connecticut, thus established
the settlement at Pawlet in what would later become Vermont
and then went back to the old home to persuade others to mi-
grate with him.

In time the flow took a southerly and a westerly direction. In
the winter of 1773–74 Rufus Putnam, from Massachusetts, and
Phineas Lyman, from Connecticut, led four hundred Yankee families to west Florida. Others had drifted into the area along the
unsettled border with New York; many looked still farther west
to the Ohio Valley, once the French and Indian War extended
British sovereignty over that region. The latter area, already
known for the wealth of fur extracted from its forests, promised
still greater riches from its fertile soil. Hence the fury with which
rural New Englanders reacted to their exclusion from that promised land by the Quebec Act of 1774. For the residents of these
not quite peaceable kingdoms, the Revolution, in addition to
other things, meant opportunity. In consequence, farmers from
the region supplied about half the soldiers for the Continental
Army.

When they moved outside their own provinces, the advancing
Yankees encountered agriculturists of quite another sort. In New

York, New Jersey, Pennsylvania, and parts of Delaware and Maryland, settlements were more recent than in New England and of a different origin; neither the soil and climate nor the social context were the same.

Heterogeneous antecedents gave the middle colonies an eclectic character, yet each was distinct from the others. The Dutch had been prominent in the settlement of New York and had left visible marks upon the culture of the province. The English and German Quakers who had first come to Pennsylvania now mingled with clusters of Ulster Scotch-Irish, Irish, and Welsh but shared no unifying heritage with them. These provinces contained no equivalent of the New England town, no social or cultural focal point to bring together the spreading farms. Each family occupied its own home on its own holding detached from all others, with churches and other institutions hidden in villages, necessarily remote from one another.

History gave each colony a distinctive social system. New York's heritage of large landholding went back to the Dutch patroonships, and throughout the eighteenth century its internal provincial politics encouraged the pretensions of a few great aristocratic families. Liberal grants by the royal governors preempted some of the very best areas in the Hudson and Mohawk valleys, where their favorites developed extensive estates using a combination of hired and tenant labor. Robert Livingston, for instance, an ambitious newcomer from Scotland, met and married a Rensselaer girl, then judiciously used political connections to develop a holding of well over 100,000 acres, complete with a manor and its privileges. Large landholders also played a dominant role in New Jersey, Pennsylvania, and Delaware. True, in those provinces yeomen owned farms similar in size to those in New England, and many laborers and tenants were younger sons, saving their gains for the stake with which to establish themselves, and by no means destined for poverty. Nor were the anachronistic quitrents (payments for the use of the land in some colonies) serious burdens. Nevertheless, the gentry exerted heavy social and political influence.

The environment was more favorable for agriculture here than in New England. The land was better and the climate more benign, the crops more varied and numerous. The abundance of cherries, strawberries, and green peas near Philadelphia three weeks earlier than at home surprised John Adams. That was due, he thought, to the warm, sandy soil of New Jersey—not at all like the cold clay of Massachusetts. Good navigable rivers reaching deep into the heart of the middle colonies offered easy access to the market towns. Along the Hudson and the Delaware, through New York and Philadelphia, the products of the farms moved in mounting quantities to consumers in all the continental cities and to the West Indies and Europe as well. As trade grew and settlement took hold, the local authorities improved roads to serve the traffic; and after 1760 the Conestoga wagon appeared in the Pennsylvania interior.

The farmers of the middle colonies harvested corn, rye, oats, and barley. Like the Yankees, they tended livestock and raised poultry. In addition, New York and Pennsylvania produced substantial crops of wheat for export either as flour or baked into biscuits; such sales grew dramatically after 1768. Colonists there could pay for agricultural improvements—for oyster shells used as fertilizer, for big barns, and sometimes for permanent floors on which the oxen or horses trod the grain. Many households engaged in domestic manufacturing on the side; and the more enterprising launched a variety of grist, saw, and tanning mills. Such families could afford an indentured servant; in these areas the trade continued until the Revolution.

A steady stream of arrivals moved into the same ports through which exports flowed in the reverse direction. The newcomers brought with them labor, sometimes capital, always the desire for cultivated lands, a demand that raised the value of existing holdings.

The strain of the month-long crossing, the miseries of seasickness, even the dangers of disease and shipwreck did not slow the movement to America. Instead, the number of immigrants increased to about 20,000 a year in the third quarter of the eighteenth century. Nicholas Cresswell, a young Englishman who toured the colonies in 1774, reckoned that a person could live better and make greater improvements in America than in Europe, especially as a farmer, so that many almost from infancy entertained some thought of moving to the New World. Some British soldiers, discharged after the end of the French and Indian War, stayed on to take up the bounty lands they received as rewards. Hard times and crop failures in the German Rhineland, the disruption of the traditional Scottish clans, a slump in the Irish linen industry, enclosures in Yorkshire and other parts of England: all kindled a rage for emigration, with the goal America—more specifically Pennsylvania, New York, and Maryland. People responded not only to the puffery of guidebooks, tracts, and agents, but to the factual record. Men like George Taylor and Charles Thomson, both members of the Continental Congress, had demonstrated that a humble indentured servant could rise to wealth and respectability, even to political power. America exacted no tithes of the yeoman and subjected him to no overbearing social hierarchy. The arrivals of the 1760s and 1770s therefore included not only servants and laborers, but also independent craftsmen and husbandmen of some means, as well as members of religious sects for whom freedom of worship was a primary goal.

The middle colonies had room for all and the presence of the newcomers caused few complaints. Thousands of Presbyterian Scotch-Irish as well as German Pietists added to Pennsylvania's population. The industry and skill of the newcomers were sources of pride in the province; visitors to Bethlehem invariably had to tour the tannery and the carpenter's, cabinetmaker's, and blacksmith's shops. With few exceptions the immigrants took up the cause of revolution, not only the Irish—for many of whom it was enough to know that England was the enemy—but others who resented restraints upon the New World's opportunities.

In New York the land-hungry pushed westward along the Mohawk, renting for a while from the magnates before taking up holdings of their own. Tenancy was a temporary arrangement advantageous to both parties. The renter paused to gather the capital that would make him an independent proprietor or enable him to expand an existing farm; the landlord profited not so much from the immediate income as from the rising value of his property. In Pennsylvania few large estates barred the way to expansion; yeomen moved unimpeded toward the mountains, then down the great valley into western Virginia and the Carolinas.

There they met the southern yeomen. In the seventeenth century the great chartered companies and quasi-feudal establishments that had founded the colonies had disintegrated. Thereafter small-scale husbandmen sustained the economy of Virginia, Maryland, and North Carolina. In raising tobacco the large estates had no advantage over the small; and much of the region depended on mixed, diversified farming. Although plantations dominated the tidewater, family-size holdings spread rapidly over the uplands. In North Carolina and Virginia they remained preponderant until the Revolution.

The Shenandoah Valley, open to settlement in the 1730s, forty years later was a region of rich, well-stocked farms. Its population grew by heavy infusions of Germans and Scotch-Irish, many of whom came as indentured servants and struck out for themselves as soon as they earned or seized their freedom. After 1770, however, more numerous arrivals from the east gave the valley a distinct Virginian character.

In some places the economy remained close to subsistence level. Tough, aggressive southern farmers survived less by work than by chance and the gun. In this country, a Maryland minister wrote, the boys, as soon as they could discharge a weapon, spent their time fowling or hunting. The great quantities of game made them excellent marksmen, and thousands supported their families in this way. Where deer and turkey were abundant for the shooting, the plow offered few attractions.

Yet the South also provided opportunities for the ambitious. Daniel Dulany, Sr., an Irish immigrant, arrived in Maryland as an indentured servant, his services sold aboard ship. In the course of a spectacular professional career the penniless youth became a prominent lawyer and acquired wealth and political power. Few Virginians matched in influence Edmund Pendleton, grandson of an indentured servant and himself apprenticed to a clerk. Scores of others who started from lowly beginnings advanced to respectable yeoman status. Much of the region's wealth lay in its small estates.

The Chesapeake colonies had been accustomed to production for the market since the seventeenth century, when tobacco dominated the economy. In the decades before the Revolution, the prospects for that crop had somewhat leveled out. Tobacco had taken a toll of the depleted soil and energies shifted to other salable staples. Virginia and Maryland became exporters of grain, beef, and pork. North Carolina more fully exploited its resources for naval stores—pitch, tar, turpentine, and timber. In the 1770s a drop in tobacco prices hastened the shift; and in 1774 politics added to the motives for change.

The grazing of livestock had been important from the earliest days of settlement and remained so in the 1770s. Stock ran loose, either on the open range or in disregard of fence laws, despite the hostility of the planters and the danger of infection. Some herds in that decade ran upward of 1,500 head, a few as high as 6,000. Scottish Highlanders and German Salzburgers brought the cattle-raising techniques of their homelands to Georgia, rounding up their beasts twice a year for branding, as at home.

Great variety thus characterized southern yeoman society. Travelers often noticed log huts, the chinks stuffed with clay, the windows without glass, filled with furniture rudely made at home. The rarity of plows and dependence upon hoes from the local smithy, handles made of saplings with the bark still intact; a wheat field left one-fourth uncut; and grain harvested with the sickle, thrashed by horses in the open field, and ground with pestle and mortar: all these were evidence of slovenly occupants. Hogs, poultry, and sheep left to care for themselves and stunted cattle were also signs of rudimentary agriculture. Yet other observers in the same colonies noted neat farmsteads on which fruit trees and gardens of turnips, cabbages, and potatoes offered evidence of a bountiful diet. There substantial husbandmen carefully and prudently made the most of their holdings, and some Virginians in the 1770s were tinkering away at machines to improve their farming.

In the southern colonies, and in Delaware, the yeoman society overlapped that of the plantation and large estates mingled with smaller ones. The density of the slave population varied from one section to another, as did the character and scale of agriculture. Fewer than 1 percent of the people in Augusta County, Virginia, were bondsmen, compared to more than 64 percent in Warwick County and fully 80 percent in some parts of South Carolina.

Only in eastern Georgia and in South Carolina was the plantation dominant; this area had become the scene of the first large-scale agricultural enterprises on the continent. On the eve of the Revolution, however, the populations of South Carolina and Georgia still included modest farmers who raised cattle, produced naval stores, and dabbled in the fur trade; and in both colonies, frontiersmen led their own lives in the West. Both had also received and assimilated influential groups of Germans, French Huguenots, and Jews.

Opportunities created by expanding markets for staples and by royal bounties to stimulate production for export fostered tropical agriculture. The great inland swamps reaching southeast from Charleston were ideal for raising rice, a valuable crop that required enormous amounts of labor—to clear the land, to dig and clean the ditches, to cultivate the plants by hand, and to harvest, thresh, and pound the seeds. The indigo fields also called for intensive cultivation. Gangs of black slaves supplied the need; and the plantation introduced by settlers from Barbados and other West Indian islands furnished the form of organization which, after 1750, dominated the region.

Year after year, the great estates exploited with bond labor gained importance, while their masters in Georgia and South Carolina increasingly controlled the politics and the society of the two provinces. The plantation owners, newly arrived and newly enriched, aggressively and vociferously sought to preserve and expand both their holdings and the bond labor force that cultivated them.

By contrast, the older settlements in Virginia and Maryland in 1774 were midway in a transitional process. Population continued to rise but did so despite an unstable economy. Black slavery had developed in the seventeenth century on a small scale, as a supplement to white indentured servitude in the cultivation of tobacco. In the early eighteenth century, plantation size increased in imitation of the South Carolina pattern, although with less advantageous results. Tobacco growing did not require large amounts of servile labor, and many masters piled up debts in the effort to maintain unprofitable estates. Those with cash or credit added slaves to augment production, preferring predictable though limited returns to the risks of experimentation. Tools and methods remained unchanged; the author of *American Husbandry* derided the lack of innovation or rational principles in the planters' adherence to the ways of their fathers. In the 1760s only one planter in twenty owned a plow, an instrument Colonel Landon Carter of Sabine Hall, Virginia, believed yet another means of making slaves more indolent than they already were. Dreamers thought of raising silk or sheep for wool that their bondspeople could spin in factories. Robert Carter of Nomini Hall, Virginia, built salt works, grain mills, and bakeries to supply his own and his neighbors' needs. He also forged and repaired farm implements for himself and others and invested in a Baltimore plant that produced bar and pig iron. But few among his neighbors had the means or inclination to do the same.

Despite local variations, common features distinguished the plantation from other agricultural forms. Everywhere production was on a large scale, whether on extensive unified estates in South Carolina or on scattered holdings in Virginia. Everywhere links to overseas markets tied the plantation to a network of factors and merchants who sold on consignment, so that returns fluctuated with perilous unpredictability. No planter knew until months after he sent the crop off whether he had gained or lost by it. Most overvalued their prospective incomes and lived according to their expectations without providing against calamities. Extravagance diminished the estates of even the best families, so that their members never thereafter eluded the shadow of insecurity. George Washington's mother ended her life obsessed with fear of want, although rent from her plantation guaranteed her a fixed income. Still she complained to all and sundry, soliciting gifts from compliant friends—to the fury of her son.

Slaves, male and female, did the work. A few favored women, perhaps one in twenty, had places in the household; a few men, perhaps one in five, acquired a skill and became drivers, carters, plowmen, or house servants. All others toiled in the fields. House servants formed intimate relationships with the family, received better clothing and food, and set themselves apart from slaves in the quarters. Artisans, acculturated and educated, dealt with whites outside the plantation and spent time away from home while hired out. Opportunity and a sense of worth and dignity made them the largest group of runaways. Conditions also varied according to the district, the prosperity of the enterprise, and the benevolence or whim of the owner or overseer. In some places the blacks earned occasional tips, enjoyed enough leisure to work on their own plots, celebrated holidays with gunfire and carousing, and held a recognized place in society. Elsewhere harsh treatment bred sullenness, idleness, and disobedience among bondsmen and -women, kept under control by fear of the lash and other forms of torture.

Masters almost everywhere felt the tug of opposing forces. In this society of sharp disparities and conflicting ideals, many a planter saw himself as the leader of a small self-sufficient tribe, a patriarch surrounded by family and dependents, ruling benevolently but with a firm hand, and managing the estate in his own and thus in everyone's interest. The wise, humane, kind father, responsible for the welfare of his children, treated the sick slaves and attended to their needs—but also corrected rather than punished, making an example of some as a deterrent to others. Yet the plantation was an economic enterprise, designed to maximize income, and driven by uncontrollable forces such as the market and the weather. When considerations of efficiency outweighed those of benevolence, the patriarch found himself an exploiter, driving his charges to their duty. Some planters had therefore begun to feel qualms about the propriety of slavery.

New World conditions and humane ideas frustrated their efforts to imitate the English gentry or to preserve the gracious customs of the Old World. Travelers misled by accounts of southern hospitality sometimes discovered that their hosts expected remuneration. Hugh Finlay learned in 1774 that a South Carolina house had no food for its own inhabitants and certainly none for strangers. Johann Schoepf a decade later in Virginia found lodging grudgingly made available only "after prolonged counsel between husband and wife." Near the North Carolina border, Elkanah Watson called at the home of a wealthy planter in rain-soaked and soiled clothes and, though he had been hospitably entertained there several years before, was coldly received because of his appearance. A planter who casually ordered the hospitality of the house kept up, so that no one would go away hungry, could not make the calculated decisions the running of his estate required. The strain of sustaining the style of life that justified slavery raised doubts about the worth of the institution.

The absence of commonly accepted standards put unwelcome responsibility for judgment upon the individual planter. Conditions varied: some travelers saw slaves well treated; others found black children stark naked and adults poorly clothed, meagerly fed, frequently beaten, and harshly worked. Some planters perceived the contradictions that bondage created for them. Those who regarded their property as human tried in more gentle ways to extract labor from their slaves, always suspecting, however, that the lash would yield more results than kindness. Something was wrong in a system that penalized the virtuous and rewarded the abusive.

Furthermore, many yeomen farmers now disapproved of bondage. The planter aristocracy still commanded the deference of inferiors, but political control was uncertain in the absence of such patronage as the gentry in England wielded. Small farmers did not scruple to take advantage of the blacks when they could. But increasingly they questioned the future, in their country, of slavery. In the 1770s Virginia and Maryland encouraged the shift from tobacco to grain and tried to halt the inhuman trade in Africans—only to encounter vetoes by the Crown. This became one of the counts in George III's indictment by the Declaration of Independence. Yet the separation from Britain made emancipation no easier. Many Americans understood the problem: how to escape this heritage of the past; few knew how to resolve it.

Commercial concerns influenced agriculture in all the colonies. Prices climbed in the early 1760s, then fell late in the decade, only to rise and fall again in the 1770s. Depression, in 1773, drained the provinces of specie so that only stay laws that postponed repayments relieved many landowners of the consequences of debt. The upward and downward movements influenced rural attitudes. New World yeomen could not live with the self-sufficiency of European peasants, could not escape the necessity of calculation. *American Husbandry* in 1775 warned its readers that they would remain dependent, helpless victims of world trends as long as they relied upon abundance of land instead of upon good industry and management.

Commerce also had an impact upon the composition of the population. The residents of the countryside were not just tillers of the soil. Craftsmen, traders, intermediaries in litigation, and healers of the body and soul served the agriculturists with other skills.

The most important artisans performed tasks the individual farmer or planter could not do as well himself. Millers with the necessary capital harnessed the power of flowing streams to grind grain into flour and saw logs into timber. Fewer communities enjoyed the services of a tanner to turn the hides of local livestock into leather, for the skill and equipment of these craftsmen enabled them to charge fees that only the well-to-do could afford. Blacksmiths fabricated or more often repaired the articles made of iron that every household needed. To supply the numerous forges, enterprising landowners dug so much ore out of their bogs that, on the eve of the Revolution, the colonies produced 30,000 tons of crude iron a year, or one seventh of the world's total.

In some places, local shoemakers or cordwainers provided footwear for the neighborhood and also did some farming on the side. Elsewhere, itinerants took the family's measurements and made up the season's boots. Carpenters, weavers, and coopers were less common because many people knew how to provide for themselves. The South enjoyed the services of fewer craftsmen than the North. James Murray, a North Carolina planter, had to offer forty pounds sterling and a house, garden, and passage for a skilled tanner, and a tenth part of the lumber sawn for a good sawyer to tend his mill.

Trade, in the countryside, was less a separate calling than the occasional pursuit of many yeomen. Sometimes one undertook to act the drover, another the wagoner, delivering the neighborhood livestock and crops to market. From serving merely as agent, one such man occasionally began to buy and sell on his own account or to bring back goods or keep a shop, moving gradually into commerce, yet often retaining the farm as well. A sprinkling of country traders, at the crossroads or the village green, stood ready to turn any service to account.

In the rural areas, lawyers with or without formal legal training were on the watch for opportunities to become rich, by picking up land and mills and by going into politics. The position of justice of the peace brought with it local power and income from fees. Those who did not enjoy superior backgrounds by birth married into the local elite groups, or wriggled in through efforts of their own. Jonathan Grout of Petersham, William Jernegan of Edgartown, and William Starkweather of Lanesborough, in Massachusetts, were among those who simply practiced without either a formal education or an apprenticeship. Thomas Burke of North Carolina, Patrick Henry of Virginia and John Sullivan of New Hampshire began as lawyers and became governors at the time of the Revolution.

Ministers in the rural areas were in a bad way, their status and income both in decline. Where they were spokesmen for the Crown, as in New York or Virginia, the debate that led to independence hurt them. But even in New England, where they assumed intellectual leadership and articulated the grievances and viewpoints of the farmers about them, their social position and their salaries grew feebler by the year. Often they made ends meet by taking in students, for schools were few in the country; and the experience of many a master demonstrated that no one did well by teaching alone. Hercules Mooney of New Hampshire, Irish-born participant in the French and Indian War and sometime representative in the general court, desperately needed the income that came with the rank of colonel in the revolutionary army. And John Sullivan, a New Jersey teacher, eked out his earnings by sweeping the town meetinghouse.

Formally qualified and educated doctors almost never settled in the rural areas. The few exceptions, in the South, were also planters and slave owners. Charles Drayton of South Carolina and William Jones of Virginia had studied at Edinburgh, but medical practice was not the chief source of their income; they were slave owners, associated with the upper level of society. Other physicians who made homes in the country were usually either self-trained or had learned by apprenticeship, although some were respected and influential men who went into politics, as did Colonel John Brooks of Medford, Massachusetts. Having served an apprenticeship with Dr. Simon Tufts, the town physician, Brooks joined the minutemen, became a member of Washington's inspector general's staff, and went on to prominence in state affairs. Apart from such exceptions, however, physicians were so rare that they easily found more advantageous positions in the cities.

An attentive observer in 1774 might well have asked, "What, then, is the American farmer?" The delegates to Congress who met in Philadelphia that September represented a variety of constituencies with different agricultural bases. The economic system that supported the Yankee farmer and the Hudson River magnate, the yeoman of Pennsylvania and Virginia, the trans-Allegheny frontiersman, and the Carolina planter was far from homogeneous. Yet a shared set of attitudes had made all these people Americans.

Less than two years later, the men who signed the Declaration of Independence recognized the nature of the values they shared in one of those inalienable rights to which the document referred. By "pursuit of happiness," they did not mean the hedonistic quest for pleasure. "Happy" referred rather to a condition that was apt or felicitous—as in a happy achievement, a happy conjuncture. Happiness was that state of well-being the yeoman enjoyed beneath his own vine and fig tree, subsisting from the fruit of his own labor. Dr. Benjamin Rush, a signer of the Declaration and professor of medicine in Philadelphia, easily demonstrated that contented agrarian employment led to mental and physical health.

For more than a decade, political orators and essayists from James Otis to Josiah Quincy, James Wilson, and John Adams had explained that "the end of government" was "the happiness of society," that is, "above all things to provide for the security, the quiet, and happy enjoyment of life, liberty, and property." Jefferson borrowed the words he used in the preamble of the Declaration of Independence from George Mason's formulation of the Virginia Declaration of Rights. Mason had equated happiness with a quiet life in retirement, modest but independent, replete with contentment. To Jefferson, happiness implied harmony instead of discord, individual satisfaction enhancing the common good. Those who labored in the earth, he wrote in *Notes on the State of Virginia*, were "the chosen people of God," and corruption of morals among them was unthinkable. Felicity, John Adams believed, called for awareness that any person's share of earthly bliss would be minuscule, so that each had to accept as they were things they were powerless to alter. Benjamin Franklin sometimes used the term "happiness" to mean resignation, contemplation, and the solitary pursuit of truth. No one disagreed with those exemplary sentiments.

Unfortunately, Samuel Adams explained, people often confused true and false happiness. The former required moderation, fortitude, prudence, and Christian bearing in the face of the world's vicissitudes. The latter led men on in relentless pursuit of delusive dreams.

And as he well knew, the wraith of false happiness led all too many on. When he set forth to attend the Continental Congress in 1774, one friend rebuilt his barn, another repaired his house, a third bought him a new suit and wig, and a fourth gave him a "little purse" for expenses. The substantial estate inherited from his father had long since slipped through his fingers. In their gainings and losings, restless Americans drifted away from the true happiness of contentment, gave dogged chase to achievement. They did not surrender the common idyllic yeoman's faith, but space and opportunity drew them away from it.

The gentlemanly owners of great estates gave achievement and happiness another name. When young George Washington forced his way into the savage wilderness toward Fort Duquesne, he hoped for more than the additional acreage a claim to western lands would bring. Fame was the spur that drove on such men as him; great deeds, readers of the classics knew, made

individuals happy in the benefits brought to the state. In this
view, too, the New World proffered opportunity.

Jefferson copied from *Paradise Lost* the lines in which Milton's
apostate angel defied God. Lucifer's heroic defiance portended
his downfall. Stretching forth beyond his reach, he toppled, and
the depth of his plunge measured the height of his audacious
lunge. A land of great spaces was a place of extraordinary temptations in which the attractions of achievement and fame constantly lured people devoted to contentment and moderation.

Through the whole period of his public service, George Washington complained that the burden of office tore him away from
his vine and fig tree. In 1783, having a firm hold on military
power, he relinquished his command, and in 1796 he turned his
back on the presidency—in each case, returning to cultivate the
soil. Avoiding thus the satanic error, he implanted an enduring
image in the imaginations of citizens unsettled by a country that
ever diverted them from the pursuit of true happiness.

Planters and yeomen everywhere agreed that a secure economic existence and a productive life on the soil were essential
to the pursuit of happiness. But acquisitive, expansive impulses
often revealed the inadequacy of the ideal. Constant insecurity
was a condition of freedom. For the pursuit of happiness implied
individual choices between contentment and ambition. And the
contradiction that tormented farmers gnawed at other Americans
whose pursuit of happiness also shaped revolutionary society.

2

The Stress of City Life

The attractions of town beckoned people eager to improve themselves. John Hancock called it fame, John Adams called it public service, others called it wealth—that glittering opportunity flashed from the places where commerce and power converged. The ambitious shouldered their way forward; the defeated lingered for want of alternative.

Americans hastened to these centers although the learned Dr. Benjamin Rush of Philadelphia and many others warned that endless hours of sedentary work in stifling air and crowded quarters would leave them easy victims to deadly disease. They knew well the deleterious effects of city life in Europe, but continued to come to Philadelphia, New York, and Charleston. They reasoned that no colonial metropolis approached the great transatlantic ones in size and doubted that any London or Paris would ever appear in the New World. Free institutions and abundant space would instead foster neat, orderly, stable, and urbane communities such as John Winthrop and William Penn had long before conceived.

The outcome in the 1770s was not quite as expected. A placid scene greeted visitors coming in pilot boats up any of the coastal harbors. Yet a closer approach revealed a restless, frenetic shuffling about not only in the back alleys, but even more in the homes of well-to-do merchants and artisans.

Each provincial town differed from the others and also from those of about the same size in the mother country—Bristol, Edinburgh, Glasgow, and Belfast. Philadelphia, Boston, New York, Newport, and Charleston held about 4 percent of the colonial population, with about 30,000 people in Philadelphia, the largest, and about 14,000 in Charleston, the smallest of them.

Overseas trade was the lifeblood of all the seaports. Hence the physical similarities among them—the small area, the spatial orientation toward the rivers and bays, the prominence of wharves, ships, and seamen, and the presence of forts and military installations. Philadelphia's neat rectangular blocks lay between the Delaware and the Schuylkill rivers, so that an hour took the walker from one end of town to the other. The tree-lined streets bore names, but no one needed numbered addresses; everyone more likely than not knew everyone else. Most Boston buildings huddled north of the simple State House on King Street; few residents lived in the still rural South End, cows roamed the common, and only the rope walks and copper works lay in the west. Settlement in New York had hardly straggled north up the Bowery Lane to Broadway and the open spaces around the college, the prison, and the poorhouse. Newport's homes crowded around the harbor, with only a few built up the hill, studded with windmills. And Charleston extended only a short way inland from the row of bridges or wharves along the Cooper River, where the trading vessels came in.

The differences among the towns originated in the circumstances of settlement. In Philadelphia, signs on the posts and shops written in German as well as in English reflected a heterogeneous population. Germans, Irishmen, and other immigrants lived here; Catholics and Jews worshiped in their own fashion. Nevertheless, descendants of the Quaker founders, while no longer in undisputed control, set much of the city's tone. Profits from rising real estate values prudently reinvested in trade brought them handsome returns, sustained their local political power, and preserved attitudes that valued and rewarded sobriety, honesty, and industry.

By contrast with Philadelphia, Boston was narrow, insular, its constricted topography singularly appropriate to the city's character. The regular rise of tides inundated the narrow neck that connected the peninsula with the mainland. But the isolation inconvenienced few; ferries carried travelers to neighboring Charlestown and Cambridge, and little overland traffic moved even to nearby Roxbury and Dorchester. No one needed to spread out. Rapid growth was not characteristic of the place; its population had remained stable, at about 15,000, since 1750, and some industries, such as shipbuilding and distilling, had actually declined.

Like the site, Boston life was enclosed and self-contained. Since everyone lived within range of their tolling, church bells regulated the pace of communal activity, calling people to worship, opening and closing markets, and marking a fire to fight, a law to protest, or the passing of a neighbor to mourn.

The old-time religion had suffered reverses since the days of Mather preeminence in Boston. An Anglican chapel rose within sight of the First Church; Baptists and Quakers, even Catholics and Jews, enjoyed some tolerance; and one compromise after another had softened the austere features of seventeenth-century Calvinism. Still the Church remained powerful, not only for the revolutionary rhetoric frequently uttered by the ministers, but also for its intellectual and social leadership and influence upon daily life. Puritans set the tone for Boston as Quakers did for Philadelphia.

Dutch antecedents shaped the character of New York. Far-flung trading activities and a heterogeneous population, about 15 percent of it black, reached back to a time when the town was New Amsterdam. As the seat of the command that conducted military operations during the French and Indian War, the city boomed. But by 1770 it had stabilized at about 18,000, a curious amalgam of British institutions implanted in soil originally Dutch.

Newport was cosmopolitan in another fashion. There tolerance was a principle derived from the first founding of Rhode Island by Roger Williams. The town, about 10 percent black, held a total population of about 15,000. It had grown wealthy through the freedom and enterprise of merchants whose social and political primacy the loose government of the colony never disturbed. Between May and October fashionable visitors from the Carolinas and the West Indies, who came to enjoy the cooler air in rented houses and apartments, contributed to the town's gracious living and increased its income. The farmer-writer Crèvecoeur, impressed with the beautiful gardens and summer climate, called Newport the Montpellier of America.

Close links with the West Indies from which some of its first settlers had come gave Charleston, the most substantial southern city, a unique tropical quality, with relationships between town and country more intimate than elsewhere. Slaves outnumbered whites. Merchants bought plantations. And planters spent the summer months in the city.

Different as they were, all the colonial communities in the 1770s seethed with uneasiness. Each looked enviously and anxiously at the others, fearful of being outdone; and within each, men and women engaged in an unending struggle for position. All the cities grew, although not at the same rate and none steadily, but rather by unpredictable fits and starts. Each therefore suffered some degree of economic, social, and political instability.

The flow of population measured relative prosperity. Movement was free. Some places continued the practice of warning out strangers, but the towns rarely required those warned to leave; residence was open to all willing to support themselves. No formal decision by a governing body established that policy, completely at variance with the prevailing practice in Europe. It was, rather, a practical response to the wilderness need for hands. Benjamin Franklin, a native of Boston but Philadelphian by adoption, was not the only ambitious young man to move where opportunity lay.

No large American city was free of competition or able to relax in enjoyment of a dependable flow of trade. All fought for expanded shares of a common business. The same ocean lapped against their shores and carried their vessels to the harbors of England, the Indies, and Europe. The depth and wealth of the hinterland and ease of inland access by river helped New York and Philadelphia. The post office, directed by the postmaster general in London and operated in the colonies through a monthly transatlantic mail service to New York and to Charleston, favored their merchants. But ingenuity and enterprise could offset these advantages; and hopes of future greatness beat in the hearts of traders all along the coast.

Challenges from numerous smaller but no less ambitious places sharpened the rivalry, for Newport worried about losing business not only to Boston and New York, but also to Providence and New London. Schemes abounded to develop scores of little harbors into new cities. The possibility was not unrealistic. Baltimore, with fewer than 500 residents in 1750, had increased to 5,700 in 1776—almost the size of Norfolk, Virginia. Providence, Rhode Island, grew as rapidly. It had become the seat of a Baptist college, and its merchants frequently considered the possibility of improving the Blackstone River to extend their operations in the interior. Portsmouth in New Hampshire, Salem in Massachusetts, New Haven in Connecticut, Newcastle in Delaware, Alexandria in Virginia, and Savannah in Georgia also buzzed with plans to profit by growth. Some young towns would indeed match or outdistance the older ones. Others would see their dreams fade and the flush of early optimism give way to stagnation. The fickle economic situation, combining instability and opportunity, left none utterly secure, none altogether hopeless.

Inland, too, numerous trading centers linked the interior with the sea. Albany, New York; Lancaster, Pennsylvania; Fredericksburg, Virginia; and Hartford, Connecticut, were points of transshipment and exchange for goods moving to and from the coast. These were therefore convenient locations for meetings of the county courts and other administrative bodies. There and in smaller places like Frederick and Hagerstown, Maryland, retail facilities for the neighborhood appeared. Speculatively-minded proprietors in many a rural community schemed to turn abundant space into villages, towns, cities; by the quiet river shore, undisturbed as yet except by an occasional canoe or skiff, they envisioned a future stretch of wharves and piers, markets, town houses, shops, and manufactories—for by such means the world's fortunate spots had always enriched themselves. The few communities that made it were more important than the many that never shed their rusticity.

No town could relax in the expectation that it would grow solely by performing administrative functions. Williamsburg, the site of Virginia's government, remained tiny because it never acquired the economic role of a big city. Annapolis, Maryland, seat not only of the provincial bureaucracy, but also of the naval office, and therefore a necessary stop for all vessels on the way to Baltimore and other Maryland towns, likewise remained small. Such places served officials and visitors who did business with them, but lacked any broader economic base.

Differences in size, regional peculiarities, and instability of both economic functions and political power scrambled the urban population, preserving its diversity and preventing it from settling into rigid patterns. The larger the town, the more frequent the rivalries among trades, neighborhoods, and sects. On Pope's Day, for instance, November 5 of every year, the anniversary of the Gunpowder Plot, Boston's Northenders fiercely battled Southenders, in a struggle of uncertain origins. In New York, conflicts between city watch and foreign sailors were common. Everywhere High Church men looked down upon dissenters, and both united in condemning Methodists. Rich merchants and lawyers styled themselves the gentry but were rogues and thieves to less affluent neighbors. Such divisions shook even the smaller places.

Social distinctions lacked neatness and changed rapidly and therein differed from those of Europe. The vagueness of the lines that set off merchants from artisans from servants disconcerted visitors accustomed to precise Old World groupings. Outsiders often perceived a leveling principle at work, for ease of access to property seemed to establish a common condition among all townsfolk. There was a grain of truth in these observations: occupational boundaries did differ from those of Europe, and rest-

lessness drove individuals on in the quest for better conditions.
But the population did not share equally in the wealth or power
of American cities.

Merchants played the key roles. The success or failure of their
enterprises determined whether a town prospered or decayed,
and they usually exerted as decisive an influence in government
as in trade. But they were neither a coherent unified group nor
fully in control.

By 1770 established families long in the mercantile business
dominated the most important and the most reliable lines of
commerce, those involving the direct exchange of goods with
Britain. Command of time-proven connections in the mother
country and adequate capital set them apart from less fortunate
competitors who bought and sold by whim or guess. But even
the best-entrenched merchants, unable to relax, yearned for stability that would reduce risks and permit them leisurely enjoyment of their wealth. The security derived from royal appointments that carried status and income had disappeared after 1765,
when the Stamp Act riots turned crown favorites, merchants
among them, into objects of the mob's wrath.

European ways of safeguarding wealth did not work in the
New World. An unstable society prevented traders from using
the same business practices for very long or from relying on personal, family, and political connections. New opportunities arose
frequently, while old ones, once profitable, dried up, making
constant adjustment and manipulation essential. Local government failed to respond to merchants' wishes. However much
commerce would have profited, counties refused to improve
wretched roads; and canal projects, such as that to link Chesapeake Bay with the Delaware River, remained idle dreams. Political boundaries meant little. Goods moved in utter disregard of
province lines; wheat from Maryland passed through Philadelphia and corn from western Pennsylvania through Baltimore.
Whoever wished to remain solvent had to keep on his toes.

Furthermore, the subordination of colonial interests to those of
the mother country unsettled the mercantile community. The
damaging results of British policy ran far beyond the acts of
trade. Parliament forbade the creation of banks and other finan-

cial institutions, choked off provincial efforts to emit paper money, and prohibited the chartering of corporations, thus inhibiting all large-scale use of capital and making insurance outrageously expensive. American ingenuity discovered ways to circumvent some of these restraints, which nevertheless diminished the security of all investments and exposed the economy to sharp fluctuations. But then statesmen in London paid slight regard to the interests of Boston or Philadelphia. The colonists had no voice at all in shaping declarations of war, treaties of peace, or acts of trade and navigation, although those measures vitally affected their welfare.

The instability of trade permitted interlopers to break in. Without banks or other institutions behind which to entrench themselves, established merchants had few advantages over later comers. And British colonial policy actually tilted the odds against those who depended upon routine. Newcomers, like the old-timers, operated within the imperial system when they could, but also outside it if there were enough prospects of large return. According to the loyalist Peter Oliver of Massachusetts, smuggling was an accursed vice, destroying all moral sense. Cheating became standard practice and business "a school to teach the art of trickery and foreswearing." Running molasses in disregard of the 1764 Sugar Act was merely "cheating the Devil." New Yorkers easily evaded customs officials to trade in forbidden goods with Hamburg and Holland. And contraband destined for Philadelphia went through Wilmington, taking advantage of the creeks and tributaries on the Delaware. "No country is better calculated for Running Goods than this," commented a dour inspector of the Southern Customs District. Rhode Islanders, many knew, resorted to bribery when all else failed. Some covered illegitimate cargoes of wine and silk with legitimately imported salt, and a certain collector in Newport raked in six thousand Spanish dollars a year by neglecting the duties for which he received an annual salary of one hundred pounds. Periodic sweeps by racketeering customs officials sometimes caught the unprotected, but the inconsistent enforcement of cumbersome regulations allowed long-term profits to offset occasional losses. Daring intruders, with less to lose and more to gain than the well established, grasped every opportunity and made the most of changing circumstance, as when poor harvests opened new markets for wheat in southern Europe after 1765.

Colonists engaged in trade differed widely from one another. The old families were no more like the new than the wealthier were like the less wealthy. Those occupied mainly in overseas transactions stood apart from local retailers who earned their bread by a trifling business. Some indulged in speculative flyers; others cautiously put their funds into urban real estate. Some got lush government contracts; others dreamed up industrial experiments. Charleston people did not do business in precisely the same way as Bostonians; Quakers did not operate as Jews or Huguenots or Yankees did; and only in the South did resident factors or commercial agents accept goods on consignment for English firms. All who described themselves as merchants were alike in facing general uncertainty but diverged profoundly in interest and outlook.

The people who provided the various goods and services on which the city depended were no more immune to anxiety than the merchants with whom they shared space in the city. Numerous, politically influential, and sometimes wealthy, artisans owned their own tools and labored on their own account. Almost everything in the towns was their handiwork. They made up perhaps two thirds of the population of larger places, perhaps one third of the smaller ones.

New and rapidly growing communities required a great deal of building; masons and carpenters did the work. Seaports needed many complex services to keep vessels going: not only scores of shipwrights, sailmakers, and caulkers who built or repaired the vessels, but also rope makers and outfitters, and coopers who made the casks to convey the goods. Furniture was so bulky that only the wealthy imported tables, chairs, or cupboards from abroad; cabinetmakers on the spot put together what most householders desired. Tailors, boot makers, and hatters provided the town's clothing. Printers furnished the town with newspapers and other reading material.

The degree of skill, education, and capital required in each craft was a rough index to the esteem in which the town held its practitioners. Goldsmiths, silversmiths, clockmakers, and printers were people of substance, position, and influence. Shipyards, rope walks, and distilleries called for considerable investment and also for managerial adeptness in running large enterprises. Tailors, shoemakers, and carpenters possessed commonplace skills, earned little, and ranked relatively low in town society.

Differences in condition further divided the artisans. Although the general standard of living rose in the decade before the Revolution, some remained journeymen all their lives, working by the day or the season. People who never advanced became, in effect, permanent wage laborers rather than temporary members of a master's household. Other craftsmen acquired the means to handle an expanding volume of business by increasing the number of apprentices, servants, and slaves; half the Charleston artisans held bondsmen. A few produced stocks of finished goods for sale in their own or nearby shops or for export by enterprising merchants. Stockings made in Germantown and shoes shipped from Lynn and Philadelphia found markets in the West Indies. But even well-trained newcomers learned about the elusiveness of fortunes in America. Peter Hasenclever, a British subject born in Germany, plunged into bankruptcy despite the substantial resources of his company, formed to establish manufactories in New York. Christopher Ludwick brought to Philadelphia gingerbread molds, forms, and other baking equipment unavailable in America. An advantageous marriage gave him a start; by 1775 he owned nine houses, a farm in Germantown, and 120 acres in Lancaster County. As superintendent of bakers, he set up ovens wherever the Continental Army passed, paying from his own pocket when Congress refused to remit. In 1781 he tried unavailingly to resign, for his efforts had achieved only a ruined fortune, impaired health, and loss of his right eye.

Others were more fortunate. A poor cordwainer might begin by working in the homes of his customers, acquire a faithful following, then open a shop of his own so that buyers came to him. Able tailors, smiths, and cabinetmakers followed the same course. And no trade could bar access to outsiders; indeed, the foreign-born trained by European masters sometimes had an advantage. Nor did custom or law set off the categories of crafts sharply from one another. Tradesmen of the middling sort dabbled freely wherever opportunity presented itself, or entered a variety of other businesses, or kept shop.

In comparable European towns, strict regulations prevented individuals from shifting about or changing occupations. But the colonists lacked the one ordering element familiar across the Atlantic, the guilds which in the Old World still prescribed who could practice and under what conditions. The absence of such corporate organization created opportunity and encouraged social mobility.

Not all artisans had the right to vote, but some rose to political prominence, thus weakening the sense of stability and place. A brickmaker, a sugar refiner, and a shipwright sat in the Pennsylvania assembly; a gunsmith and a mason, in New York; a carpenter, a blacksmith, and a mason, in South Carolina; and a mason and rope maker, in Massachusetts. Politically ambitious people sometimes appealed to the solidarity of the leather-aproned folk; and revolutionary rhetoric often made much of the "mechanical interest," that numerous portion of the community styled "the people." Since the distinctions among them, though real, were not rigid, the artisans were conscious of their identity as a group. Certainly they knew who they were by contrast with the merchants above and with the lower orders below.

Artisans and merchants, despite their great variety, shared an unstable, dynamic economic situation, the cardinal mark of which was total immersion in a pattern of credit. It was possible, then and later, to consider some individuals creditors and others debtors, in the sense that the balance of obligations fell in one direction or another. But more realistically, the absence of banks and the shortage of currency compelled everyone engaged in any form of trade both to borrow and to lend. Every significant exchange required credit and depended upon contingent transactions; the expectation of future payment qualified all gains and losses.

Periodically, obligations crested, both for individuals and communities, and paying-up time revealed disastrous shortages of cash. The British determination to limit colonial currency had

thwarted desperate efforts to create a circulating medium in
1764 and had left bitter memories in America. On the personal
level, credit stringency ruined even those who worked assid-
uously sixteen and eighteen hours a day. Richard Sheepshanks,
applying for a position as clerk in Baltimore, explained his reduced circumstances this way. Having come from Scotland to
this Garden of Eden, he found himself, on the eve of the Revolution, with a large warehouse in Philadelphia and money owed
him in New York, New Jersey, and Pennsylvania that would
have made him comfortable for life, had he been able to collect.
Inability to do so reduced him to teaching school, "an honorable
employment but a bare Existance as the Custom of this Country
makes but little difference betwixt an Ignorant and a Compleat
Teacher."

For everyone the decisive consideration was depth of protection against the unforeseen—against the ship that never returned,
the cargo arrived to find a glut in the market, or days stretching
by with no callers at the shop. Mechanics and retailers living on
daily earnings were more vulnerable than those who reckoned
profits by the week or month or year. In the nature of the case,
those long in business had more opportunity to accumulate a
saving margin than the young just starting out. People who
could rely on extensive family connections were better off than
loners remote from kin; the prudent, than the lavish livers;
holders of urban real estate, than plungers in distant lands; and
the husbands of rich widows, than romantics beguiled by a
pretty face. But none could put out of mind the possibility of
failure.

Dependent persons, parts of someone's family, possessed no
such autonomous status as merchants and artisans enjoyed.
Wives and children fell into this category. But so, too, did the
journeymen and apprentices who worked and resided within artisan households, subject to the parental discipline of masters.
These temporary members of the family moved off on their own
at the close of the service period. Servants, whether free or indentured for a term, occupied a similar status with comparable
opportunities but could not expect to acquire the skills of a trade

—although James McCullough, an Irish weaver who settled in Hackensack, New Jersey, was not alone in the rise to prosperity and respectability. Ronald McDougall arrived in New York from the Hebrides and worked all his life as a milkman. His son, Alexander, would become first a privateer, then a merchant, general, and politician.

Opportunities varied considerably from one place to another. Boston had fewer indentured servants in its labor force than Philadelphia. In both cities, apprenticeship tended to break down into a form of hire. Young men not ready to strike out on their own extended their terms for a secure wage and for freedom from the burden of managing their own families. They joined similarly situated journeymen in a pool of restless men without steadying stakes in the community, ready to participate in politics, fun, games, or mischief when employed, more ready when not.

A clear line divided all such people from the dependent slaves who were also members of a master's household. In the eighteenth century all earlier ambiguities vanished. The numerous unfree Negroes—bound for life, they and their descendants in perpetuity—served in a variety of jobs, having in some places acquired skills equivalent to those of white artisans. Most slaves outside the plantation South resided in cities, where they formed a turbulent and unstable element of the population.

British troops from the garrisons stood outside American society. Increasingly, in the decade before 1774, they reminded annoyed colonists of the power of imperial authority. The common soldiers with time on their hands competed for jobs with civilians; resentment of the bored officers rose with occasional instances of misbehavior and deepened with the visible contempt of the Britishers for "mohairs," the term by which they designated all not in uniform.

Crowds of transients shuffled through the streets, and though some departed soon, others found reason to remain behind. Immigrants, debarking from ships just arrived, paused to recover before moving to a final destination. Those coming under indenture awaited sale to a master. Young men from the country scouted about for opportunity. Farmers in for the market or for attendance at court added to the throng.

The cities also housed many placeless people who fitted into no familiar civic category. Sailors of diverse origins passed through the seaports, some on shore leave or for temporary stays while they waited for new berths, others for lengthy periods, although never settling down. Victims of tyrannical officers on board ship and of press gangs while on land, fleeced by sharpers and tavern keepers, they could turn to no one for protection or counsel; desperation made them ever ready for trouble. An indistinct line separated them from the laborers, men without fixed occupations or skills, not part of any household or attached to a master. Impressment gangs from the Royal Navy, sweeping through the alleys in search of bodies, paid no attention at all to that line but snatched up any likely unattached male.

The stratagems of the poor, by which all these people lived, defied statistical calculation. By any reckoning of average income they should all have perished, or they should have fled the cities, or they should have risen in desperate rebellion. In fact, they did nothing of the sort, for the untidy structure of colonial urban life enabled them to get by except in periods of unusual economic stringency. They survived through odd jobs, underconsumption, and the ability to make do with hand-me-downs and leftovers. But an uncertain marginal existence exposed them to temptation, and they yielded to the drink and sex their social superiors defined as vices; now and again they joined in the volatile crowds and mobs that rioted, sometimes to express grievances, sometimes for excitement.

The presence of a placeless rabble heightened the pervasive concern about the security of residents in the little urban communities. Without a dependable social order, the power to govern wavered unpredictably; and growth compounded the daily problems of town life, through difficulties both real and imagined. Harried householders worried about fire, about interruptions in the supply of the necessities of life, about the filth and noise in their streets, and about eruptions of crime and violence. Unable to count upon the formal political system, the colonists slowly improvised new communal means of coping with their problems.

Fire was a constant threat to every city; flimsy construction, carelessness with foot warmers, open fireplaces, and lack of any speedy or safe mode of kindling increased the hazards. A blaze, once started, spread rapidly among houses crowded one up against another. Disaster followed when flames got out of hand. In the early morning of Saturday, September 21, 1776, a conflagration touched off at Whitehall Slip in New York progressed furiously up Broadway to College Green, destroying almost five hundred houses, one third of the town. Newport had suffered ten years earlier, as had Boston in 1760.

Efforts to limit the danger reassured few townsfolk. Massachusetts towns long required inhabitants to keep appropriate ladders in their homes. Norfolk, Virginia, put a prohibitive tax of five shillings a month on wooden chimneys and penalized the owners of those "blaised out." New York enacted ordinances to regulate fireplaces and stoves, to ensure the proper care and cleaning of chimneys, and to appoint fire wardens who would supervise the bucket lines. Not a head rested easier for the legislation.

No eighteenth-century community enjoyed an adequate or healthful water supply; all relied on what nature put close at hand. New York's only tolerable drinking water, distributed in a cart, sprang from the Tea-Water Fountain. In Charleston all the wells were bad (and the cellars full of rats, the garrets of bats). In 1777 John Adams, after complaining about the foulness of Boston's water and the frequent shortages, suggested a windmill to pump a supply to the top of Beacon Hill, whence gravity could distribute it to the whole city. Nothing happened, there or elsewhere.

Population growth made every city vulnerable to interruptions in the supply of food and fuel. Patches of garden away from the town centers provided some vegetables, but any break in the flow of wagons and coastal vessels that brought provisions and wood from the country immediately raised prices and threatened the health of all. Hunger and cold then made the northern winters, difficult under the best of circumstances, intolerable.

Narrow, unpaved, poorly drained, and dirty streets offended
all the senses. In New York the changing seasons dotted the
roadways with mud holes, ice rinks, or dust bowls; and a good
rain raised or leveled hills. Everywhere carts carrying produce
from nearby farms rumbled through the ruts, pedestrians picked
their way around puddles, and pigs feasted off the garbage habit-
ually thrown out through the windows. Clouds of dust forced
Philadelphians to keep their doors and windows shut, while in
wet weather the wheels of heavy carriages plowed the streets
into quagmires. Artisans who disposed of wastes in the roads
contaminated whole neighborhoods with foul and stinking liq-
uids. Dock Creek became "a receptacle for the carcasses of
dead dogs, and other carrion, and filth of various kinds, which,
laying exposed in the sun and air," putrefied offensively to the injury of health.

Endless controversy retarded efforts to deal with these problems. New York divided into two camps. One group considered
pigs beneficial—they kept the city clean by eating the garbage.
To others such reasoning was beyond comprehension. They
pointed to the obvious mess and accused the hogs of upsetting
the neat piles citizens gathered for their servants to remove. Not
until 1790 would the municipality outlaw the roving scavengers.

Attempts to establish order in other matters also bogged down.
Norfolk appointed a surveyor of streets, but the townsfolk ig-
nored his instructions for repair. Laws to "prevent filth and so
forth being hove into the streets" did not keep refuse from piling
up in the alleys. Salem, seeking to improve its main street, raised
funds to fetch cobblestones from the beaches at Baker's Island,
taking into consideration the fact that the sale of manure left by
beasts passing on the pavement would offset the cost.

New York's sidewalks by no means assured pedestrians of safe
passage. In the absence of clear uniform building lines, steps
sometimes stretched across to the road; and low projecting bay
windows, unexpected pumps, trees, stumps, hitching posts, and
refuse piles made the stroll hazardous, especially at night. The
gutters slanting toward the street often spilled their content on
unsuspecting walkers. Dainty slippers were safe only when
shielded by goloshoes, clogs, or pattens. In the summer, Phila-

delphia householders affixed canvas to two poles to shade passersby; and the city began to pave its streets, not unexpectedly turning first to those paralleling the homes of the gentry. Some, such as "Tom Trudge," an anonymous correspondent of a Philadelphia newspaper, never saw the dung cart come or heard the paver's sound. Though their lean kitchens produced little that would not conveniently mix with the manure of the cow, these citizens wallowed in filth and their wives waded to the knees while carrying a loaf of bread to bake.

The inability to do much about traffic and noise left residents' nerves on edge. Legislation in Norfolk aimed at curbing unruly oxen and forbade servants or slaves from riding horses "faster than a foot a pace." Hoping to curb the din in the streets, New York banned iron-shod wheels and did not allow drivers to sit upon their wagons while in the city. Another ordinance forbade carters and water carriers from moving faster than a walk, to give pedestrians a chance to evade the spattering mud. Boston, too, tried unsuccessfully to quiet the noise. The law prohibited coaches and carts from passing by the general court while in session, forbade the shooting of pigeons from rooftops, and barred sleighs from coming into town "with the beat of drums . . . at unreasonable times of the night."

The racket nevertheless continued. Before sunrise barking dogs chased squealing goats and pigs, signaling the successive cries of the milk carriers, chimney sweeps, and purveyors of various other services: knife grinders, woodcutters, vendors of straw (for restuffing mattresses), of beach sand (to cover muddy floors), and of yeast ("'East . . . here's 'east"). Meanwhile the town crier made himself heard. Tolling church bells announced funeral processions, and the buzz of horseflies and mosquitoes pervaded the air.

The cities learned to live with the din of crowds assembled for various patriotic enterprises; to Judge Peter Oliver of Boston their uproar was a signal whistle which, like the Iroquois' yell, forever echoed unpleasantly in the ears of whoever heard it. However cozy and intimate Boston and its rivals seemed in retrospect, in the 1770s residents who could afford to do so moved

out to the country, where they slept quietly at night and where
taxes were lower.

Americans knew the hazards of violence well enough to heed
the warnings. Frequent complaints about theft and vandalism
and about the tumults that served after fires as a cover for stealing revealed the widespread fear of disorder. Alert neighbors in
Boston thoroughly plundered the home of Tory Peter Oliver
when it went up in flames. Robbers and prostitutes dared show
themselves in the City of Brotherly Love; and Madam Juniper, a
black woman, operated a notorious and thriving brothel in Newport. Such establishments multiplied, as did liquor shops, wherever troops were garrisoned.

On the fringes of society in every town, criminals, male and female, thrived on violence, thievery, or simply a general disregard
for the law. Restless men, women, and children, denizens of the
back alleys and uninvolved in the town's organized life, occasionally played an important part in the riots of the decade before the Revolution; and New York's semimilitary gangs, the
Skinners and Cowboys, easily assumed a political guise as Patriots and Tories.

Dread of the mob and repeated complaints about vice, whoring, drunkenness, impiety, and fraud arose from concern lest the
authority of government prove too weak to head off a war of
plunder and a general dissolution of the distinction between rich
and poor. The signs were ominous in Boston when Negroes and
little boys, black and white, denied bonfires and crackers for a
celebration, broke the Town House windows; and Philadelphians discovered with dismay the sons and relations of respectable burghers among the vandals who slit gowns, broke
knockers and bells, and cut spouts.

The means of law enforcement fell far short of the need. New
York's sheriff and his deputies chose juries, issued legal notices,
and tried to prevent looting. These officials, however, were not
beyond corruption; numerous statutes punished their more common offenses—cheating during elections, accepting bribes, allow-
ing prisoners to escape, and padding expense accounts. New
York also had a constable and elected assistants, unwelcome

honors despite lucrative rewards for the apprehension of vagrants, a duty shared with twenty-five marshals and a chief.
These, however, all spent much of their time keeping hogs off
the streets. The militia was available for serious emergencies.

A paid force to police the city was unwelcome both as a threat
to liberty and as a drain on town resources. Norfolk citizens preferred to make the rounds themselves in turn at night, gun in one
hand, lantern in the other. Bad weather kept shirkers indoors,
though fines penalized those who refused to serve.

A hired watch created other problems. The watchmen were
sometimes drunk and often asleep when they should have been
out on patrol. The doors of the Boston watchhouse were stolen
twice in 1742 while the guardians of order snored within. Fines
for napping improved vigilance, but not enough; the job attracted those least likely to perform it properly. The "better sort"
often suspected night watchmen of complicity with arsonists and
looters.

Fear of ridicule and an overwhelming concern for public opinion made people sensitive and touchy. Neighbors seeking redress
for slander crowded the courts; and guardians of public morals
and peace exploited this extraordinary sensitivity in the punishments imposed. Since considerations of costs counted for more
than the criminal's well-being, penalties humbled the transgressor and provided exemplary warning to others. Confinement
in stocks, the pillory, or the ducking stool, in which the culprit
was tied and plunged into water, exposed the individual to deri-
sion and contempt; branding marked the guilty with the symbol
of crime for life. Newport, Rhode Island, in 1771 condemned the
counterfeiter William Carlisle to stand for an hour in the pillory,
have both ears cropped, and be branded on each cheek with the
letter *R*, in addition to a fine. The community readily heaped
abuse upon such unfortunates—rotten eggs, stones, oyster shells,
and bats flew freely. Murder, arson, robbery, and forgery were
among the score of capital crimes that led to public executions—
events of great excitement that drew huge crowds.

Jails were an unnecessary expense and deemed useless as punishment. The largest group subject to prolonged incarceration
were the miserable debtors; and their frequent escapes testified

to the desperation of men and women abandoned to rot and disease in cold, dark, dank prisons.

The weight of the tax burden blunted public concern for the orphaned, the ill, and above all the poor. Resenting the worthless vagabonds who depended upon the common purse, the townsfolk everywhere held costs to a minimum, yet could not avoid the responsibility altogether. When a severe winter reduced the amount of outdoor labor available and, at the same time, raised the cost of firewood, or when an epidemic incapacitated large numbers, the taxpayers met the cost, resentful or not. The charges rose during the decade before the Revolution, though not at a startling rate. To avoid direct outlays, the towns apprenticed youngsters, indentured adults to masters who exchanged support for labor, and auctioned paupers to the lowest bidder: "Rattle his bones over the stones, only a pauper that nobody owns," one tombstone proclaimed. Recurrently, towns sought "some suitable Methods of employing the Poor," but nothing came of those endeavors.

Outdoor relief—payments to the dependent in their own homes—was meager. In the worst of times, between 3 and 6 percent of the population of large cities drew support from public funds; and that included the aged, the infirm, and the ill as well as the poor. By contrast, about one third of the populations of Paris and London was then destitute.

The social problems of the cities evoked inadequate responses. People who worried about the dangers of fire or shortages, about personal and mob violence, and about crime and pauperism regarded urban places as dangerous to health and morals. But uncertainty about political controls prevented them from dealing with these sources of concern.

The inherited system of municipal government varied from city to city, but was everywhere a feeble instrument for the exercise of power. New England contained, properly speaking, only towns ruled by meetings and elected officials, like those in the rural regions. In form, Boston was identical with Deerfield or Bellingham. Loose suffrage requirements, resistance to privilege, numerous offices, one-year terms, and open debates left management of affairs diffuse and unstable. By contrast the middle colonies and the South adapted English municipal arrangements to local circumstances.

Everywhere the residents expected control to rest in the hands of the wealthier, better-educated, and more influential men with the leisure and inclination to devote themselves to public affairs. The less wealthy, less educated, and less influential accepted those arrangements partly out of habit and the inability to conceive of an alternative state of affairs, and partly out of the conviction that opportunity and mobility in this society did make riches, learning, and success valid measures of character and ability.

In smaller cities where political and social relations were intimate and personal, the ruling cliques wielded power successfully so long as they were flexible enough to make room for rising outsiders. Places that thrived accommodated themselves easily to this necessity; those that did not grow failed to attract newcomers and lost their most enterprising youngsters, so that the problem solved itself. The small scale made political stability possible.

In larger cities, however, where government arrangements were less personal, elite groups, lacking the respect accorded an inherited aristocracy, could not maintain control. Even in New York and Charleston the great merchants and the governor's cronies, incapable of excluding outsiders totally, squirmed beneath the necessity of sharing power. Those who wished to govern Boston, Newport, and Philadelphia felt even greater pressure. Local officeholding there was often an unrewarding duty, less an honor or a privilege than a burden, and willingly left to whomever the title would gratify. The comparatively low correlation between officeholding and wealth after 1760 permitted a good deal of rotation despite the influence of oligarchic dynasties.

The obligation to share authority grew more compelling as relations with the mother country deteriorated in the 1760s. Merchants, artisans, and storekeepers joined informal groups like the Sons of Liberty in New York, Baltimore, and elsewhere to shape decisions. In Boston, since the middle of the eighteenth century, organizations known as caucuses had met secretly to decide on common action and to vote as a bloc in town meetings. In 1774 artisans, tavern keepers, and petty traders, along with some merchants, together debated the issues and selected candidates for office. By then the propertyless in Boston attended meetings and held minor offices. Such laxity undermined the control of the well-to-do; what transpired in the Bunch of Grapes and other inns was more important than what went on in meeting. Unwittingly, community leaders had encouraged the tendency by using crowd action to resist the Stamp Act, the Townshend Acts duties, and the East India Company tea, thus giving unexpected meaning to the concept of consent of the governed. To some extent, other cities witnessed a similar diffusion of power.

Yet urban problems did not dismay the townsfolk. Their government was mild, tolerant, and chaotic; but a broad sense of community permitted action effective enough to cope with the most important difficulties. In the absence of clear guidelines, improvisation was the rule. Without alteration in the charters or laws, often without debate or even reflection, colonists reshaped the formal structure to fit novel circumstances and subtly modified urban institutions familiar to Europeans. Even before the Revolution transformed local politics, city government imperceptibly but significantly changed. The colonists did not abandon the inherited structure; indeed, Boston retained the town meeting until well into the nineteenth century and Philadelphians in 1783 resisted incorporation lest that subject them to an aristocratic police force. The adjustment was more subtle, but effective.

Though between 1763 and 1774 no issue was in general more important than taxes, it evoked no controversy on the local level. Men and women whipped into a fury by the Stamp Act or by levies on tea accepted much larger municipal charges with equanimity or at least with resignation, and the elected assessors and collectors served long terms. Their popularity stemmed from the ability to adjust the letter of the law to practical necessity. Leniency and inefficiency were rough means of sparing the hard-pressed; and assessment practices shifted a large part of the burden to the merchants best able to afford it. Such variable application of the rules also ensured reelection.

Other half-conscious understandings eased the pressure of numerous traditional practices. Viewers of fences, sealers of leather, and other inspectors continued to take office but tempered the rules by judicious laxity in performance. The assize of bread, an effort to apply communal standards of a just price, broke down and became perfunctory, as did old regulations that fixed the place and time for holding markets. On stated days, farmers from the surrounding countryside still entered town and schools closed. But there were no means of preventing private and unauthorized trading. At Boston's Faneuil Hall and at New York's Fly (fish) and Oswego (country produce) markets, housewives made purchases any morning, while peddlers and retailers picked up what remained. Wartime shortages further encouraged uninhibited enterprise.

Adaptation to necessity varied from city to city. The prospect of long-range economies in some places at times justified immediate expenditures. In the hope of reducing the cost of outdoor relief, New York thus built a poorhouse in 1736 and thereafter crowded it with inmates whose feeble labors contributed to small savings. The same prudent hope led the city in 1775 to erect a Bridewell, or house of correction, within which to put criminals to work. Sooner or later, other cities erected almshouses, shaped to their own needs. Calculation, civic pride, and the desire to improve business conditions persuaded Philadelphia not only to pave but to light some streets, to provide markets where buyers and sellers could meet, and to separate hospital from poorhouse. It was practically alone in these respects.

More often, communities encouraged individuals and groups to develop amenities in ways that required no outlay from tax revenues. To build and operate a wharf vital to commerce generally strained the resources of single individuals. An incorporated company gathered the capital and provided the management of Boston's Long Wharf. No place enjoyed the means to construct a substantial bridge. It was more convenient, as in Europe, to li-

cense a ferry to convey traffic across the river; the privilege
brought freedom from competition in return for an obligation to
furnish service. The same device encouraged innkeepers to provide facilities for travelers and for the conviviality of neighborhood residents.

Municipalities unable to supply needed facilities encouraged
the appearance of voluntary institutions. Nothing came of the
suggestion in 1746 by its mayor that Philadelphia erect a merchants' exchange. Instead, eight years later the city's traders
began to meet in William Bradford's London Coffee House,
where they got the latest news and found an active market in
bills of exchange. When Bradford left to join the revolutionary
army, operations shifted to the City Tavern.

Associations filled other gaps as well. Private collections supplemented relief from Boston's Overseers of the Poor to the victims of the earthquake of 1760. The sermon at that city's quarterly charity meeting regularly moved listeners to contribute
voluntarily. Self-help organizations sprouted to protect their members from the hazards of life. The Philadelphia Society for
the Relief of the Poor and Distressed Masters of Ships, their
Widows and Children tried to mitigate the effects of losses at
sea, of unemployment, and of excessive drinking. Dues and do-
nations provided the funds. By 1773 the society was paying out
regular sums, including annual pensions, but it did not hesitate
to instruct one recipient to move into more modest quarters, for
its purpose was not to subsidize luxurious living.

Hospitals in Philadelphia after 1754 and in New York after
1771 sheltered the helplessly ill, although government subven-
tions helped build them. Virginia in 1772 established a refuge for
idiots and the insane; but Boston did nothing despite Thomas
Hancock's bequest of £600 for the purpose. In 1774 fear of the
disease persuaded some Philadelphians to propose the formation
of a society for inoculating against smallpox.

Fire companies had greater success because they united practicality and conviviality: they both extinguished conflagrations
and sustained good fellowship. Members undertook to keep
bags, buckets, and ropes ready for use, identifying one another

by secret codes and competing fiercely for the bonus that rewarded the most successful. In the 1760s Philadelphia boasted fourteen societies. Some clubs kept an engine in readiness—a tub constantly refilled threw water on the fire by means of an extended arm. More specialized groups, like New York's Hand-in-Hand company, removed valuables from burning buildings for safekeeping. In 1774 Salem, Massachusetts, had three fire clubs, two engines, and many buckets—and a huge fire that burned down the church and twenty-five large buildings.

When the delegates to the Continental Congress arrived in Philadelphia, they received gracious permission to use the books of the Library Company, another kind of voluntary association. Benjamin Franklin, a member, was also instrumental in founding an academy, a fire company, and the American Philosophical Society Held at Philadelphia for Promoting Useful Knowledge. A host of societies served smaller groups, drawn together by common antecedents, like the Germans and Scots; by trade, like the carpenters; or by humanitarianism, like the participants in marine societies. By 1774 the townspeople voluntarily did for themselves much of what government would not or could not do.

Some by then had learned to ease life's tensions. Philadelphians could attend a theater, and Newport welcomed David Douglass' dramatic troupe. In Fredericksburg the jockey club arranged races. In any city a well-off man met with his club in the tavern, sailed his boat for pleasure in the river or bay, and took his family for outings to the harbor islands or to a country teahouse. A boy growing up in Philadelphia paused regularly on his way to school to watch a game of rackets on the tennis courts or peep at the racehorses kept during sporting seasons in the Widow Nichols' stables. In summer he observed the rowing, sculling, sailing, and swimming on the river; and among the winter ice skaters he knew that Massey the biscuit baker was as good as General Cadwalader, and that a certain black Othello had no competitor when it came to swiftness. Apprentices and mechanics could use the libraries and clubs to improve themselves or they could tipple and game their time away. There was a choice, and size of income was no indication of either wisdom or folly in spending it.

The long conflict that led to revolution shifted influence to the fluid and adaptable elements of the urban population. The struggle with Britain legitimized some types of violence, as against taxmen and Tories, but without plunging society into chaos. For a decade after the Stamp Act the established leaders, the men of substance who led the protest movement, either used or tolerated extralegal action to resist British policies. On the night of August 26, 1765, the attack on Lieutenant Governor Thomas Hutchinson's mansion in Boston foreshadowed the events of the next decade. Excited by agitation over the Stamp Act, stirred up by the Reverend Jonathan Mayhew's fiery sermon and by wine from the cellar, gangs from the North End and South End joined to destroy the building and furniture and to appropriate cash and clothing. This initial act of vandalism shocked even Hutchinson's bitter foes. The elected town officials certainly sympathized with the protest, but feared the consequences of unrestrained tumult. By repetition, riot became a familiar means of political action, although never on the scale of European cities and usually circumscribed by cautious pleas for the safety of the lives and properties of even the most inveterate enemies.

The removal of royal authority and emigration of the loyalists did not plunge the cities into chaos. For a generation or more the towns had learned to function without strong government controls, without even a police. In some places the leadership remained intact through the 1770s and 1780s; elsewhere new people came to power. In either case, persuasion, voluntarism, and restrained use of force remained the important instruments of politics, a development that put lawyers and other professionals in a strategic social position. But fear of the mob and of anarchy lingered, for this society of striving men and women longing for change and achievement functioned without the stabilizing influence of a hierarchical social order.

3
Status in the New World

Americans, impatiently on the move toward fame, achievement, wealth, and comfort, often brushed aside custom, habit, and tradition only to discover that they missed the guidance of those restraints. Opportunity drew people on, but brought them to a hard life and left them longing for the security forever left behind.

The ability to move and rise testified to the fragility of social control everywhere in the colonies. Remote from British sources of authority, unstable in population, the New World lacked institutions to ensure tranquillity through the familiar means—a hierarchical organization of power that provided those with most at stake the force to protect it. The Revolution and the Republic that grew out of it did not remedy the deficiency. Neither before nor after 1774 did social groups possess enough continuity, coherence, or awareness of common interests and identity to fix every individual's place, rights, and obligations. Society remained fluid because groups formed and reformed as their members broke away or moved upward or downward.

Only the masters of great landed estates possessed some of the attributes they and Europeans recognized as aristocratic. The Livingstons, Carters, and Wentworths were by no means part of a stable homogeneous class; they, too, were subject to changes of fortune and had to make room for newcomers. But their homes and the extensive acreage about them provided a setting unique in the New World for the assertion of superiority. In Virginia, gentlemen waited until after the service began, then entered church in a body, and left as one; and they enjoyed private buryings, unlike the lower sort accommodated in the graveyard. The wealth drawn from plantations and the political power associated with officeholding commanded deference.

No one else was similarly situated. The tillers of the soil and the townsfolk followed personal rather than class interests. And while the slaves were a group apart, bondage deprived them of the ability to act and made escape from their condition the sole desirable goal.

Mobility, however, was not the product of egalitarian theory. In the colonies, as in Europe, every individual wished to know where he or she stood in relation to the whole community; and most believed that neatly calibrated gradations along a recognized economic, political, and social scale, defining interests and obligations, advanced everyone's welfare. But unstable conditions obscured the definition of such a scale.

Fortunate individuals who gained some wealth in the cities puffed themselves up to play the parts of gentlemen; they reached for social prestige and political power. But the putative urban aristocracy never acquired the authority or influence of the great European families after which it modeled itself, or of the possessors of landed estates.

Insofar as it did exist, the urban aristocracy depended upon the favor of governors who rewarded services with lucrative positions and substantial land grants and dominated provincial society; their mansions were its visible centers. Thomas Hutchinson of Massachusetts, Cadwallader Colden of New York, John Wentworth of New Hampshire, and William Bull of South Carolina were local people of influence, closely allied to the dominant families of their provinces. Titled Englishmen, such as Lord Botetourt, who came as governor to Virginia from the House of Lords, enjoyed additional prestige. Shortly after his arrival in the same colony, Lord Dunmore had two counties named for him, began to build an appropriate residence, imported great stocks of furnishings, collected a library, and assembled valuable paintings, none, however, guarantees of prestige.

The governors were not free agents; to rule, and in some cases even to collect their own salaries, they depended upon a network of alliances in assemblies and among local influentials. Political considerations circumscribed the freedom to act. Governor Francis Fauquier of Virginia supported the populace against the clergy, entertained local notables lavishly, and incurred the wrath of London for too often taking sides with the Americans. Although deference to superiors was habitual in this society, so that officials, as a matter of course, commonly addressed the rabble from above, their offices alone rarely earned the governors enough respect to ease their tasks. Whether natives raised to power by usefulness to the Crown, or ministerial favorites sent over for a few years of enrichment, or even noble lords, they attracted a circle of cronies but did not endear themselves to the populace. Often a haughty demeanor earned contempt rather than admiration. When the wife of Maryland's governor Robert Eden suffered a miscarriage in the ballroom during a drunken party, that was just about what was expected of the dissolute hirelings of proprietors and Crown. Elected republican chief executives after 1774 knew they had to behave prudently.

The inability of the governors, before and after independence, to provide a suitable model hampered the efforts of all would-be aristocrats to set themselves apart. True, John Cadwalader of Philadelphia commanded the city's elite in a silk-stockinged militia company, which had counterparts in the Charleston Artillery and Boston's Ancient and Honorables. Parading in their gaudy uniforms, the gentlemen soldiers felt and were superior to the excluded populace. Some churches still assigned meetinghouse seats by rank or willingness to pay; and appropriate forms of address (Sir, Esquire, Mr., Goodman) continued to distinguish social ranks. Bostonians just before the Revolution tried to catch up with the fashions of England; expensively dressed young ladies, dancing at the assembly in winter and feasting in country parties in summer, often did not return to their homes till daybreak.

The taste for luxury as a symbol of status survived the war and flourished in peacetime. Hairdressing was a serious and time-consuming business. Men attended to their locks or wigs daily, some putting their curls up at night in paper and using curling tongs the next morning. By the 1780s the pigeon's wing and the comet had given way to a more natural style, which in turn would yield to cropped hair—"à la Brutus" or "à la Titus." Ladies had other choices. Elaborate structures of feathers, lace, cambric, gauze, or fringe provided foundations; pads, cushions, and puffs gave the arrangements height; jewels, pins, or pearl ropes embellished them; and creams and powders held them in place. William Lang, a barber in Salem, Massachusetts, used special wiring to help his clients "raise their heads to any pitch they desire." After 1776 the "Dress à l'Indépendance" became popular, thirteen curls at the neck in honor of thirteen states.

Women had other causes for concern. They worried about the softness of their hands, the smoothness of their complexion, the color of their teeth, and the wrinkles on their faces. A vast array of cosmetics helped them improve on the work of nature. Beautifying Ointment safely removed pimples and eruptions; and, worn during sleep, "chicken skin gloves" made of strong, thin leather, dressed with almond oil and spermaceti, left the hands "plump, soft and white."

No sooner did wealth provide the margin for expenditure than dressmakers and tailors made an appearance. The hoop skirt touched off a mild controversy about its beauty, comfort, practicality, and effect on health. Factions divided pro and con, newspapers carried articles for either side, and whoever could and dared, wore it.

Men of wealth had their clothing in a variety of colors (queen's drab, sea-green, mouse's ear, new brown, and London smoke) and materials ("jeaunets, muslinets, worsted florentine cotton denim, jeans, gold tambour muslin"). Patterns came from London. A proper riding coat, "made full like a bomb or globe," jockey hats, muslin cravats, and muffs of black bearskin were almost obligatory. Mather Byles, about to be dismissed by a congregation tired both of puns and Tory leanings, presented himself at the hearing in ample, flowing robes and bands, a full bush wig recently powdered, and a large three-cornered hat. Republican virtue and simplicity did not inhibit John Hancock from appearing in 1782 in a red velvet cap, "a blue damask gown lined with velvet, a white stock, a white satin embroidered waistcoat, black satin small-clothes, white silk stockings and red morocco slippers." A fashionable New Yorker in 1789 wore "a light French blue coat with a high collar and broad lapels," a double-breasted Marseilles vest, nankeen-colored cashmere breeches, shining pumps, full ruffles on the breast and at the wrists, and "a ponderous white cravat with a pudding in it." Many a smart fellow little more than five feet high swaggered about in a huge coat with cuffs to the armpits, "the shoulders and breast fenced in against the inclemencies of the weather by a monstrous cape, a rather short cloak, shoe toes pointed to the heavens in immitation of the Laplanders," and buckles of harness size.

Earnest republicans like John Adams grew censorious when they thought of the young gentlemen who played cards, drank punch, swore, and smoked tobacco night after night, still dependent on parents at the age of twenty-three. Seduced into unmanly pleasures, the idlers dissipated their time prattling of poetry and love and forgot the dictates of conscience. Widow Dorcas Griffiths, everyone knew, kept a grocery shop as John Hancock's tenant; the other relationship between them was a subject for lively gossip. Newport people justified horse racing by arguing that the contests improved the breed, but deceived no one into forgetting that they also served as vehicles for gambling. Many realized that a horse cost as much as several months of an artisan's wages and had to be fed and cared for. The Charleston enforcement committee added fuel to the fires when, in 1775, it exempted from the nonimportation agreement the racehorse that Robert Smythe brought back from England. Repeatedly, town meetings heard protests against wicked extravagance; in the cities, angry crowds demonstrated in violence the conviction that these monstrous developments were incompatible with republican society.

Important as the symbols of distinction were, they provided their possessors neither assurance of stability nor the genuine ability to command. Underlings, encouraged to sauciness by the abundance of chances elsewhere, simply would not stay in the positions assigned them. People who had a choice of places of worship gave little heed to who sat in which pew. Those not invited to the exclusive Boston assembly set up a Liberty Assembly in opposition. It was therefore hard to keep anyone out of anything. The exclusive merchants' club of Boston back in 1763 had 146 members, almost 7 percent of the city's adult male population. There never were enough servants in the city for true elegance; and those available were an unruly lot, given to wandering off when it suited their convenience.

The social context was unpropitious to aristocracy. Visiting French officers praised American women not for artifice but for nature's plainness, despite all the primping dictated by fashion. The finicky lady, reluctant to eat corn that grew through manure, trudged through the unpaved streets in embroidered shoes by the light of a lantern carried by a half-naked black wench. Even the finest mansions were not so fine as to awe ordinary burghers; the Morris family home on a 1,920-acre estate in Westchester boasted nine rooms; that of the customs official Hallowell in Boston, which cost £2,000, was no larger. The Carters' Nomini Hall failed to accommodate the whole household. Little structures used as counting rooms, schoolrooms, kitchen, and sleeping quarters for the boys surrounded the main house.

In the last analysis, a musket in the hands of a leather-aproned artisan did as much damage as that carried by a gentleman, creating a rough sense of equality. Fortunes came and went in a generation or two, making social demarcations provisional, except when based on land. Although youths taking their degrees in Cambridge still entertained lavishly, Harvard College in 1770 gave up the practice of ranking students according to the supposed dignity of their families. The closest approximations of aristocracy were urban clans like the De Lanceys and Livingstons of New York, the Manigaults of Charleston, or the Brinleys of Newport, sustained by great estates in the hinterland.

New World spas and watering places therefore struggled in vain to emulate the fashionable life of Bath and Tunbridge Wells in England. Stafford, Connecticut, rose to fame in 1765 when its waters healed the sufferer from a chronic disease. The town acquired a reputation for "curing the gout, sterility, pulmonary, hysterics, etc.," and earned the praise of Dr. Joseph Warren of Boston and Thomas Clap of Yale. Soon warm springs in Pennsylvania and Virginia promised relief from rheumatic fever. Their true purpose, however, was social: visitors came to see and be seen. But the crowds amusing themselves at balls, cards and gambling, singing, and dining were never far enough from the wilderness to make aristocratic games authentic.

Colonial townspeople knew that the opportunity to rise had greater worth than social eminence unaccompanied by political power or material gain. Differences in wealth were significant, as they had been earlier and as they would remain; the most consistent correlation of riches was with age, older people possessing more than younger. But far from witnessing a significant increase in the number of poor and of economic stratification, or an economic polarization of propertied and propertyless, colonial society in the 1760s and 1770s lacked the institutions to preserve inequalities or to defend the status quo. In England, monopolies or other incorporated privileges buttressed the patrimonies of fortunate families. In America, by contrast, inheritance laws and practices that provided for equal division among the heirs dissolved old business arrangements and broke up accumulated stores of capital.

Furthermore, unstable economies accelerated upward and downward movement. Trade fluctuated from decade to decade, even from year to year, so that the wealthy could not endow their fortunes with permanence. The absence of banks or other secure forms of investment put all earnings at hazard and subjected even the greatest stocks to loss or diminution. Investment in land, the only shelter that seemed at all durable, involved speculative risks. Yet the instability that threatened those already arrived opened opportunity to newcomers and outsiders. As some declined in status others rose, and constantly shifting positions agitated the social order.

The development of those callings known as professions demonstrated the difficulty of defining rank. In England, as in other

European countries, divinity, medicine, and law stood apart from other kinds of work not simply by virtue of earning power and social esteem, but also by distinctive modes of entry. The right to practice followed passage through a well-defined course of preparation, officially certified; and the title and privileges established the status of those who succeeded. By the 1770s significant differences had set the American ministers, physicians, and attorneys apart from their European counterparts. The colonists were substantially worse off in terms of Old World power, position, and the ability to keep out unauthorized outsiders. But as they lost the old familiar role, professional men gained a new and unexpected one. Deprived of the ranks Europeans enjoyed, Americans acquired new means to make their influence felt and thereby gained prominence in the unfolding events of the Revolution.

The men of the cloth were notable persons in rural as well as in urban places, in the South as in the North, on the frontier as on the coast, whether their incomes were large or small. In England, association with the state and with the aristocracy explained some of the esteem accorded them. Though the royal court and the great estates were rarely models of piety and virtue, the King's ministers, the members of Parliament, and the gentry understood the utility of a pious populace and expected the clergy to invigorate religion by external ordinances, by stated calls to worship, and by the salutary influence of example. The established Church served as a necessary instrument of social discipline.

Ministers of the Church of England were servants of God but also of the Crown and perhaps of a nearby patron. Entry upon a clergyman's career followed a regular pattern. Studies in a neighboring school prepared the aspiring youth for one of the universities, where he read in the classics as well as in theology, before taking his first degree. Further preparation might or might not be necessary before ordination; there followed a period of greater or lesser duration as a curate, until age or connections made the cleric vicar of a parish. A favored few advanced to the dignity of higher ecclesiastical office as bishops, canons, or deans. Some wandered off into teaching or public service. But usually the parson settled into a community and remained in one place for a lifetime.

Catholics, Jews, and other dissenters had their own ways of choosing ministers. But these were tolerated sects on the periphery of society. Their clergy, however respectable, did not command the position or the perquisites of a priest of the Church of England. The latter succeeded not of his own will but by following a course prescribed by authority, and by conforming to the rules that made ordination the culminating act of recognition.

The European pattern did not cross the ocean. Much of the colonial population retained its allegiance to the Church of England. As the established Church, that of which the King was head and the governor his representative, it carried great weight, even in Boston and Philadelphia, where the law did not give it a preferred position. Yet somehow the context was wrong. Although this was an episcopal Church, no bishop resided in America, and occasional suggestions that one might do so stirred up outraged protests. The American colonies remained subject to the nominal oversight of the Bishop of London. Nor were there means of training and educating an adequate corps of native priests. Neither the College of William and Mary in Virginia nor King's College in New York helped much, so that the churches depended on ministers sent over from the mother country. Now and then an individual of genuine distinction turned up in America: the philosopher George Berkeley had spent time in Newport, and President Samuel Johnson of King's College had made up in learning for what he lacked in tact. But the ablest divines preferred to stay in Britain while the least fit wandered to the colonies, there to acquire reputations for avarice and loose living.

Despised, neglected, and discontented, they preferred to mingle with the gentry and aped their vices. To augment their income, clergymen became schoolteachers and clerks. The more successful in the South acquired plantations run by overseers and stocked with slaves. Others married well, procuring wife, wealth, and position in one swoop. Defense of their privileges

and incomes involved the clergy in politics, and greed drew
them into land speculation.

The result, occasionally, was a religious vacuum. One thoughtful Virginia youth went less than once a year to church. Had he
gone more often, he believed, he would not have been much the
wiser. The parish minister was a poor preacher, nearsighted yet
lost without the written copy upon which he fixed his eyes—so
closely that what he said seemed addressed to the cushion rather
than to the congregation. Too often, journal entries read: "The
parson is drunk and can't perform the duties of his office," or
"The parson is too lazy to preach." Hungry worshipers, unfed, at
times felt awful forebodings of death and of the judgment to
come. They knew they were not as good as they ought to be, and
wished to be better. But what real goodness was, or how to at-
tain it, they knew not and therefore, though they shrugged off
the alarms, longed for something more.

New England suffered no shortage of preachers, but they, too,
could not sustain their social position. The Puritan settlers had
set high standards for the learned ministry and had founded
Harvard College to train the divines. In the seventeenth century,
Yankees accorded great prestige to the graduates, who remained,
until the Revolution, dignified, respected, and influential per-
sonages in the communities. Jonas Clark (Harvard 1752), who
long served the First Parish in Lexington, mounted the pulpit
garbed in gown, cassock, and bands and wearing a great white
wig. But as the years passed, the display of regalia ceased to satisfy his flock, and his colleagues in other parishes discovered a
disconcerting weakening of the ties to their churches. Dismissals
and departures converted the relationship of pastor to his flock
into a job, much, though not altogether, like any other.

The essential element in the polity of the New England
churches was congregationalism. The ministers were not ordained by a bishop—there were no bishops—but, rather, called
by a congregation. As a result, local variations appeared early,
and neither clerical nor legislative efforts in the eighteenth century succeeded in limiting the congregation's free choice.

Dependence upon popular grace imposed constraints upon
ministers in all sects and in all provinces. Henry Melchior

Mühlenberg, a learned and godly preacher, had to take a wife at thirty-three, although he would have preferred to remain single. A married man was less prone to become the subject of unseemly gossip, and Mühlenberg needed a housekeeper. His seventeen-year-old wife proved an ideal woman—"pure of heart, pious, simple hearted, meek and industrious." He set no store by the "shapely limbs and comely appearance" that attracted some of his colleagues, although eleven children rewarded his marriage.

But Mühlenberg frequently complained of the incompatibility of his duties as husband and father with study, meditation, prayer, and other parochial functions. A pregnant wife made additional demands, and her physical attractions always threatened to distract the pious divine, however often he directed her devotion to her true bridegroom, Christ. Worst of all, marriage did not prevent malicious gossip: a deranged parishioner spread the story that Mühlenberg kept two whores in Philadelphia.

The unease of the learned clergy mounted, for, by the 1770s, raucous dissenters challenged the whole concept of a prescribed course of training and ordination. The Great Awakening earlier in the century sent scores of unauthorized preachers through the countryside; and laws to exclude the unlicensed proved ineffectual. Strengthened by the spiritual turmoil of the revolutionary decades, the Baptists, who disdained more orthodox education, added to the number of ministers not qualified according to law.

The qualities Americans valued in the preacher had subtly changed. The figure in the pulpit no longer represented an institution, which supplied his credentials and prepared him properly for his post. Ever since the great revival movements of the 1740s congregations had expected acts of devotion to stir them in another way. They rejoiced, as Abigail Adams did, in a minister who had some warmth, some energy, some feeling. "Deliver me from your cold phlegmatick preachers, politicians, friends, lovers and husbands," she exclaimed. Bostonians who heard the Reverend Jonathan Mayhew call them unto liberty enlisted in God's service even in the act of rioting.

Stress upon the spirit diminished the importance of formal training; God moved the simple, honest soul as readily as, or

more readily than, the head stuffed with Latin phrases. Only the
listeners were competent to pass judgment on a man's fitness for
the pulpit. Any individual who wished to do so and could persuade his audience was free to declare himself a preacher.

Substantial differences set the ministers who served wealthy,
established congregations apart from those who traveled through
the backwoods or preached in the small towns. But everywhere
the calling ceased to be one permanently designated by the community and more often became an occupation the individual
practitioner chose by which to serve whoever would listen.

The approximation of European standards proved no more
successful in other professions. In England a society recognized
by the state certified physicians who had passed through a long
course of training. Few such men came to the colonies; the dy-
namics of selection kept the ablest at home, sent the less successful across the ocean.

The more usual American procedure, in medicine as in other
crafts, transmitted available skills by apprenticeship. The aspiring young man entered the family of an older doctor and learned
by observation and practice, picking up experience while sweeping the floors, handling drugs, and collecting bills. By the 1770s
such a person could also, if he wished, attend collegiate lectures
in New York and Philadelphia. The learning thus harvested was
meager. Thomas Parke read and worked under the direction of
Dr. Cadwalader Evans. He also enrolled for medical lectures in
the College of Philadelphia, taking Dr. William Shippen, Jr.'s
anatomy, Dr. Adam Kuhn's materia medica and pharmacy, Professor John Morgan's theory and practice of medicine, chemis-
try under Dr. Benjamin Rush, and practical midwifery under
Thomas Bond—earning a bachelor of medicine degree. Having
absorbed the best America offered, Parke went abroad in 1770,
only to find much of his previous learning put to shame in London and Edinburgh.

In the largest cities, some formal procedures tested the
aspirant's competence; and New York, New Jersey, and Connecticut began to license physicians. But even there the right to set
up for oneself did not await governmental approval. Elsewhere

anyone who could make a pill or compound a drug freely did so. Lack of social recognition of their qualifications and status particularly irritated surgeons. John Jones, trained in Philadelphia and in a host of European universities and first professor of surgery at King's College, defended his profession against those who regarded it as "a low mechanical art . . . taught to a butcher's boy in a fortnight." He argued that knowledge of ancient and modern languages and of anatomy, hydraulics, and physics was as important as "a firm steady hand," good eyesight, and "a mind calm and intrepid." During the Revolutionary War his *Plain Concise Practical Remarks on the Treatment of Wounds and Fractures* guided the treatment administered on many a battlefield.

Some branches of medicine remained outside physicians' control. Midwifery was almost exclusively a women's profession, most practitioners compensating with experience for what they lacked in scientific training. They not only assisted at childbirth, but also verified parenthood, testified in court concerning bastardy, and examined female prisoners who claimed pregnancy to escape punishment. In their presence women felt comfortable enough to speak of matters "too shameful" for the ears of male doctors.

In urban centers after 1770 ladies sometimes turned to university-trained obstetricians, at first only in anticipation of the use of instruments, later in normal deliveries as well. But opposition to doctors lingered out of fear of a hasty recourse to forceps, which in the past had served to dismember the child in order to save the mother. Moral considerations intensified the aversion to a male presence during childbirth. In 1772 the *Virginia Gazette* attributed adultery in England to the employment of men at deliveries. Even Professor William Shippen, Jr., of the College of Philadelphia lectured his students on the impropriety of examining a vagina until absolutely necessary and then only without looking. The best obstetrician, according to one medical manual, was blind. With the room darkened and the patient entirely covered, gentlemanly physicians—behaving with perfect decorum and talking, preferably of the weather—became tolerable, especially after the "daughters of Eve" ceased to believe that the

pangs of childbirth were their inescapable curse. The prospect of
lessening pain and anxiety and of increasing the survival chances
of mother and child subdued concern about ancient scriptural
admonitions.

At no time, before or after the Revolution, did physicians control medical care. The mass of the population got along without
their services, relying upon remedies inherited from family or
traditional lore, on compounds purchased from an apothecary,
chemist, or merchant, or on the advice of knowledgeable ministers, innkeepers, schoolmasters, barbers, and Indians. Doctors
could not establish a distinct line of demarcation between themselves and other healers.

Lawyers were officers of the courts, which determined who
could appear and plead. In England that power established rigid
qualifications. The colonies never used that potential for control.
No matter what the judges or legislators ruled, Americans in
effect allowed anyone to practice. On the eve of the Revolution a
sympathetic Englishman observed that in no country in the
world did people so commonly have recourse to law as in
America; and he linked its popularity to the traits of acute, inquisitive, and dexterous men, prompt in attack and ready in defense. Immersal in the law helped them augur misgovernment at
a distance and sniff the approach of tyranny in every tainted
breeze.

A few American lawyers, having studied in England at the
Inns of Court or in Scotland, enjoyed the advantages of a European education. Most, however, could only dream of completing
their preparation at the Temple and instead entered practice
through apprenticeship. Doing odd jobs in an established office,
they learned to fill out the necessary writs and read the standard
books. Of course, the auspices available made a difference. Gouverneur Morris could afford to pay a fee of £120 for a three-
year apprenticeship, which brought him useful contacts. He also
became a member of the Moot, an exclusive legal society that included many men of influence. William Livingston, a Yale
graduate, born to wealth, received his training under James
Alexander and William Smith, Sr., among the most prominent

attorneys in New York. Livingston began by drawing up wills,
indentures, and bonds for relatives and friends, receiving at first
low fees, for incompetent lawyers, he thought, kept attracting
away prospective clients. In time, ties of blood and marriage to
the Schuylers, Van Cortlandts, and Beekmans brought him
ample business involving real estate, probate, trade, contracts,
debts, and land disputes, which made his fortune. Few lads
could find sponsorship this favorable; most studied with relatives
or clerked for whatever attorney gave them access to his book-
shelves.

In a well-developed colony like Massachusetts, the profession
was far from homogeneous. The lawyers themselves tried to establish three levels of practice: barristers entitled to plead before
the Supreme Court; attorneys not yet fully qualified but nonetheless allowed to practice; and others, usually young men who
appeared before the county courts of common pleas. Yet most
places leveled such internal distinctions, and entry into the profession remained open. Virginia planters who read some law occasionally charged for casual advice; only a few, like George
Wythe, gave full time to the law. A slow or late start did not
burden with an insuperable disadvantage youths whose modest
parents had neither connections nor the means of paying great
fees.

Control of the courts remained fragile, and any step toward
exclusiveness stirred up latent popular antagonism to the lawyers, who seemed forever to be feeding off the miseries of the
common people. Merchants considered attorneys rivals for political power; tenants in New York regarded them as landlords'
agents; and landlords counted them agitators, stirring up trouble over old titles and claims. To the general population, lawyers made a living from other people's problems and turned
straightforward and commonsensical issues into mysteries only
the chosen few understood.

In the end, however imperious the judge, however self-
confident the pompous established practitioners, the power of
decision rested with the jurors; and everyone knew it. The rude
men who brought in the verdicts had their own opinions and
made their own law, whatever the rulings from the bench. Be-

lieving that a "multiplicity of perplexual Argument & Verbose harangs" confused the plain sense of matters, they relied upon native understanding tempered by their own prejudice and interest. Elegant complaints that "want of Learning, join'd with want of Sense," was "the most certain Source of Impudence" made no impression. Nor did barristers succeed in importing English restrictive technicalities. Lawyers could not risk alienating those who brought in the verdicts. Since power was local, the opinions of the neighborhood counted far more than statutes or precedents, and juries far more than judges.

Popular wariness of the wiles of lawyers expressed, not hostility to the rule of law, but an insistence that the law reflect local concepts of justice. Colonists on the frontiers welcomed the eastern court system and indeed often protested against the slowness of the authorities in extending its benefits to them. Justice, however, meant not the application of ancient dogmas but doing what was right according to a jury of good men and true; and jurors were perfectly ready to join in bands and enforce their wills. Consciousness of these facts tempered the control exercised over the bar.

Furthermore, official preference and privileges were not the only roads to advancement. A young Philadelphian contemplating a legal career noted that the best aid to success was a temperament for mingling in the world of business. Since many attorneys had difficulty collecting their compensation (testified to by a notice in the *Virginia Gazette: cash in advance*), it was only prudent to supplement incomes with mercantile activities. In the South, where lawyers often received their fees in tobacco, even those not themselves plantation owners had an interest in the price of crops. Practice in the towns opened opportunities for investment and chances for gain. Business expansion, especially in New England, New York, and Philadelphia, increased the volume of litigation and the scope of legal work. Joseph Hawley of Hampshire County, Massachusetts, collected the accounts of Boston merchants in Rhode Island, Connecticut, and New York. In the countryside, law accorded well with ownership of an estate or a plantation, with land speculation, and with politics. Samuel Chase of Maryland tried his hand at investment and made his reputation as a popular leader through the defense of debtors, thereby easing his entry into politics.

Crowding in the ranks stimulated the desire for professionalization. But efforts to introduce more selective qualifying tests, to recognize applicants of good family by way of character assessments, and to strengthen the distinction between barrister and attorney ran up against a political stone wall, as when the New York Supreme Court sought to favor college graduates. Local pressures resisted standards based either upon an imperfectly known English law or upon precedents vaguely recalled. New Jersey, in violation of accepted customs, even allowed lawyers to appear without wigs.

Appointments to the bench depended on factional alliances rather than on learning. When Massachusetts Governor Francis Bernard appointed a crown favorite, Thomas Hutchinson, Chief Justice of the Superior Court rather than James Otis, Sr., a respectable professional, he outraged the lawyers. Young John Adams insisted that mastery of so immense and involved a science as the law required not just a general education but extensive technical study that qualified only a few. But neither before nor after the Revolution did his view prevail.

Professional standards, difficult enough to sustain in Boston, where judges presided in robes of scarlet English cloth, broad bands, and immense judicial wigs, were altogether fanciful in the backwoods county seats of Pennsylvania or Virginia. There was no denying a license to Patrick Henry when he began to practice in Hanover Courthouse in 1760. At age twenty-four his experience was meager; he had clerked in a crossroads store, had twice failed in businesses of his own, and had lost his wife's dowry farm. What law he knew was self-taught. But the numerous acquaintanceships made in his father-in-law's popular tavern, and a mastery of the emotional New Light preaching style, endowed Henry with more persuasive power than that gained from English books. Five years later he sat in the House of Burgesses, well on his path to the Continental Congress and the governorship. Abraham Clark of New Jersey, Abraham Yates of New York, George Bryan of Philadelphia, and David McMechen of Balti-

more followed similar routes through law to politics without
benefit of formal education.

The events leading to independence tested the loyalties of all
lawyers. Some, trained to respect government and predisposed to
venerate the past, chose to support the cause of Great Britain. In
the last instance, they found it impossible to condone the settlement of disputes by other than legal means. Others became revolutionaries and felt no professional inhibitions in setting aside
their reverence for the common law and dissolving their allegiance to the mother country. A few, conscious of the need for
new laws to meet the exigencies of a new country, conceded that
application of the English common law would no longer suffice.
Law thereupon became simply the product of legislation; and
the ordinary people qualified to vote could also interpret and enforce it.

Least demanding of all the callings that in Europe required
some form of certification was that of the teacher. Ministers
without parishes staffed the colleges, and schools drew upon
whatever talent was available. The Reverend Jonathan Boucher
suppressed a profound distaste for teaching to earn extra income
and to scrape up friendships with parents of his aristocratic pupils. Now and again insolvent merchants, such as John Harrower, escaped the consequences of ruin by taking on children or
even adults for pay. Some instructors were self-taught; the Virginian Devereux Jarratt, later an Episcopal priest, considered
becoming a teacher as he studied arithmetic while the horse with
which he harrowed or plowed grazed an hour or two at noon.
For him and others the occupation was provisional, on the way
to becoming something else—which did not mean that they were
inferior, but which showed the complete absence of any pattern
of formal accreditation.

The casual quality of careers, although most extreme in teaching, asserted itself in other professions as well and prevented
their lines from hardening. Matthew Thornton moved from
Maine to Worcester, Massachusetts, and then to Londonderry,
New Hampshire, where he acted enough of the physician to earn
an appointment as under-surgeon in the expedition of 1745

against Fort Louisbourg, Cape Breton Island. He returned, immersed himself in politics, served in the provincial and continental congresses, and after 1776 held the position of justice in the state superior court. Clergymen dispensed drugs and medical advice as freely as moral guidance. They also resolved quarrels among neighbors in a quasi-judicial fashion. Joseph Hawley, who began as a preacher, went on to a career in law. Doctors furnished not only cures, but also advice on hazards to health, on cleanliness, and on the structure of houses and the number of windows necessary to ensure a salubrious atmosphere. Lawyers became businessmen. Since no group could validate the claim to exclusive knowledge, all made their voices heard on everything.

Insecurity in a fluid society forced professional people to defend their self-esteem and community standing. Doctors, lawyers, and ministers became politicians to make their influence felt. Through speeches, newspaper articles, pamphlets, and books they sought to eradicate ignorance and to wield power through knowledge.

The self-imposed obligations of public service loaded them with responsibilities related to their work. The doctors who returned from Edinburgh considered themselves the vanguard of their profession, with a duty to weed out quacks, interlopers, and incompetents. Benjamin Rush linked medicine with participation in the war and in politics, activities that permitted him to criticize military sanitary conditions, supervise hospital expansion, and improve the education of women. Lawyers, too, engaged in spirited political activity, their only available avenue to desired changes. And everywhere the clergy, guardians of public morals, tied the nation's fortunes to God's providence and sober living.

Ironically, some occupations without certification did acquire status, influence, and even power. London was home to a variety of people who were not professionals and fitted into no other socially recognized category. Actors, musicians, and writers, for instance, were persons of some prominence, yet of uncertain status.

Their counterparts were just beginning to appear in American cities. Most artists were transients who passed through communi-

ties without sinking roots or who remained strangers even when
they stayed. And the colonies supported few full-time writers,
even at the hack level. Nevertheless, the individuals best able to
communicate occupied key positions there.

Since verbal modes of communication still predominated, the
preacher's voice had obvious importance. So, too, did the informal eddies of opinion that formed about the keepers of numerous neighborhood taverns. But the printers, now becoming
journalists, supplied important new channels. They were artisans, yet somehow more than that. Benjamin Franklin, for instance, by the 1770s had acquired a status not dependent on
training, education, or certification but that nevertheless sustained his influence far beyond the borders of Pennsylvania. And
events after 1763 increased the value of the ability to set a newspaper, broadside, or poster into type.

Printing was an honorable, sometimes lucrative, and always
diversified business. In addition to their usual stock of contracts,
bonds, deeds, and other legal papers, these establishments sold
tracts, writing materials, coffee, chocolate, and patent medicines
and served as news centers, post offices, and advertising media.

The printer followed the practices of other eighteenth-century
businessmen. His shop was an extension of his household, and he
drew no distinction between one kind of expense and another.
Trade was good while there was cash in the till, bad when
nothing remained for barter. The premium upon ready money
influenced the choice of ventures; each transaction stood or fell
on its own merits, with every calculation of profit and loss
confined to the specific entry in the account.

The printer suffered from pressures familiar to other businessmen: uncertain supplies, and unpredictable sales. Paper was
always scarce (skilled papermakers were so much in demand as
to be relieved of military duties) and all newspapers carried periodic appeals for rags, the major raw material. The *North Carolina Gazette* (November 14, 1777) told young ladies that "an old
handkerchief, no longer fit to cover their snowy Breasts," sent to
the mill might return "in the more pleasing Form of a Billet
Deaux from their lovers."

But limited markets and exceptional skills also affected the nature of the printing enterprise. Since no town had the customers to support more than a few printers, apprentices, once trained, had to move on unless willing to serve indefinitely as subordinates. Jonas Green, a journeyman from Boston, still worked for others in Philadelphia, then set up for himself in Annapolis; his wife, Anne Catherine, took over when he died and carried on with the help of her sons. William Goddard, born in New London, where his father was a physician and postmaster, opened a shop in Providence with the help of his sister, Mary Katherine, then went on first to Philadelphia, then to Baltimore. All these entrepreneurs discovered that the heavy fixed capital investment for presses and type yielded no return unless sustained by adequate volume. Sales of books and sundries helped a little but were subject to the general uncertainty of commerce.

Privilege was the favorite source of security, and that meant government patronage. Jonas Green's income came from his role as chief printer to the province of Maryland—inherited in 1767 by his widow, who received 48,000 pounds of tobacco annually for the years the legislature was in session, 37,000 for others.

Lest the presses idle, the Greens were also publishers, as were other ambitious printers. But it was a hazardous venture; whoever issued a book without support from a subscription list risked competition from cheaper imports and the accumulation of stocks no one wanted. Newspapers were more dependent still. A weekly, Isaiah Thomas estimated in 1775, needed six hundred customers and a considerable number of advertisements to keep going.

The journalist simply had to hold the attention of subscribers; even the willingness to accept almost any form of payment—firewood, butter, cloth, eggs, chickens—did not forestall defaulters. The roads, weather, and suppliers all conspired against the printer. When in 1768 the northern post did not arrive and the southern brought no mail and frozen rivers stopped up the flow of intelligence from within the province, Anne Catherine Green, editor of the *Maryland Gazette,* could put out only a single half sheet for January. In the poorly heated shops the damp paper froze as it went to the press in the winter. Deliveries failed in that season, and subscriptions lapsed. In the absence of ships arriving from Europe, and therefore of foreign papers to plagiarize, these months always seemed dull, with nothing happening.

Other circumstances hampered the expansion of circulation necessary for survival. The printer had direct access only to buyers in the immediate environs. Newspapers carried elsewhere by postriders, or by ships stopping along the coast, might be lost, drowned, or snowed under. If delivered at all, they might well arrive when the contents were decidedly historical. William Goddard of Philadelphia and later of Baltimore learned to his dismay that carriers refused to distribute his sheet to subscribers because of rumors that he had been a radical sympathizer while they were under British orders not to disseminate such propaganda. He thereupon began to plan an impartial, thoroughly American "constitutional post office," to rescue the news from the "horrid fangs of Ministerial Dependants." Complaints about similarity of titles reflected the bitter competition. John Holt accused James Parker of New Jersey of preventing postriders from carrying the *New-York Journal* and substituting for it the *New Jersey Journal,* printed in a similar format and under a similar head.

The war revealed the extent of journalistic dependence on rumors and gossip. Military operations that interfered with postriders increased the significance of word of mouth. The *New-York Gazette and Mercury* on February 2, 1778, reprinted from a month-old Boston newspaper word received by the Hartford post of a gentleman in Springfield, who had seen in a letter from an officer in General Howe's army the information that France and Spain had declared war against Britain. The news would become true only a year later.

Publishers succeeded when in a position to glean bits of information scattered throughout the community, and when otherwise able to generate the reading matter to attract subscribers. Jonas Green of the *Maryland Gazette,* for instance, was alderman of Annapolis, vestryman of St. Anne's parish, postmaster, clerk of entries for Annapolis races, secretary of the local lodge of Masons, auctioneer, punster, punch maker, and all-around jolly good fellow. Benjamin Franklin busied himself in cultural and philanthropic societies not only out of concern with their activities, but also to pick up useful items for his paper and almanac.

Franklin possessed the additional wit and talent to give life to his stories and to sprinkle his publications with enough squibs, jokes, epigrams, and tales to keep the pages full. The daring printer also attracted attention by attacks on authority and exposure of corruption that made for lively reading, if not for reform. The *New-York Gazette* reported during the French and Indian War that guns purchased for the army were out of date, that graft was rampant, and that beef was the Americans' most lethal weapon (its odor enough to drive the enemy away). Repeatedly, therefore, printers devoted their attention to politics and converted columns into battlefields across which essayists fought over the proper theory and practice of government. Readers eagerly consumed the product.

Events both at home and abroad increased interest in political news after 1765. The Stamp Act controversy divided the press; patriot and loyalist groups alike sought outlets for their opinions. The circulation of the *Boston Gazette,* mouthpiece of the radicals, zoomed; Governor Bernard's effort to indict its editors for libel foundered when the grand jury refused to cooperate. Although the *Massachusetts Spy* tried to avoid partisanship for a while, its editor, young Isaiah Thomas, soon moved to the rebel side, while John Mein, editor of the *Boston Chronicle,* branded a Tory, had the dubious honor of watching his effigy carried through the streets, placarded "Mean is the man—Mein his name." The fearful editor of the *Boston Evening Post,* uncertain of which way the wind would blow, preferred not to print any accounts of Lexington and Concord.

Circulations and incomes rose during the war, when printers became openly partisan. In the absence of any restraint upon the freedom to publish, they wrote what they wished; and in the absence of support by privilege, they prospered to the extent that they attracted readers who agreed with them.

The journalists became part of a pivotal group that also included lawyers, physicians, and ministers. Similar social roles, common personality traits, and shared ideas and attitudes held them together. Since they stood outside the weak established social structure, their positions were vulnerable. Ever on the alert to fathom and adjust to public opinion, to guess at market trends and to guard against failure, they provided a good part of the revolutionary leadership and eagerly welcomed a new communal order more amenable to their own control.

The status of these professional people, like that of other Americans, depended less upon inherited position or wealth than upon achievement recognized by the community. To the *South Carolina Gazette* in 1775 their whole lives seemed "one continual Race in which everyone is endeavoring to distance all behind him; and to overtake or pass by, all before him; everyone is flying from his inferiors in Pursuit of his Superiors; who fly from him, with equal alacrity. Every Tradesman is a Merchant, every Merchant is a Gentleman and every Gentleman one of the Noblesse." The capacity for self-improvement permitted a man to master the world in any sphere of life by diligence, industry, and frugality. But since the display of selfless public virtue was the highest form of gratification, politics was the finest study and science in the world.

The events that led to Revolution drew such men together. The delegates to the Continental Congress in Philadelphia represented the Americans but were not a random sample of the population. They had earned their leadership by the ability to speak for those who followed. A restless people, constantly off balance, looked for the expression of their wills to spokesmen qualified not by status, titles, or licenses but by command of popular confidence.

4
The Family,
Refuge for the Restless

Americans—urban or rural—could not just be; they felt the unremitting pressure to become, to make of themselves something more than they had been at birth. From the anxiety that obligation engendered, a family was the only refuge. The ties of kinship established by blood and independent of merit or blame, of achievement or failure, endured through life and by the act of marriage extended into the next generation. Yet, all too often, social conditions threatened that source of security also.

The well-being of every individual hinged on the prosperity of the family—the household within which each member earned a livelihood, the elemental unit of every other association, the communion within which all worshiped, the orbit within which all intimate personal relationships revolved, the focus of every emotion. Men and women who passed from childhood to adulthood in the same place attached memories of the past to the parents who preceded them, expectations of the future to the children who would follow. Those who wandered away took their families with them. People who lived precariously had only one another to cling to, and knew the importance of kinship. Yet restlessness and the harsh New World environment repeatedly

wounded sensibilities, bruised feelings, and created family difficulties.

Home was a place—a physical setting for the life of parents
and children. Immense differences set apart the residence of the
wealthy merchant or planter from that of the yeoman or artisan.
Housing varied according to region and income. But general
traces of social instability exercised a subtle influence upon the
experience of all.

Necessity accustomed people at all economic levels to close
spaces within, in ironic contrast to the open spaces without.
Small structures conserved heat in the long chilly months; even
so, fires were necessary much of the year as far south as North
Carolina. Twenty-eight steady fires that consumed four loads of
wood a day warmed Nomini Hall in Virginia. Smaller homes
required less fuel, but their owners also had less means than the
Carters who owned that estate. Candles or whale oil lamps,
though expensive, provided the most effective illumination;
poorer people used pine knots. During the long winter hours everyone shared the kitchen hearth: father, mother, children, visitors, apprentices, servants, and slaves.

Travelers unfamiliar with the country learned with surprise
that they could find rest only by bedding down with strangers.
Americans, having grown up in tight quarters, took them for
granted and achieved privacy in their own way. The shared bed
was a fact of life and provided warmth and security. A married
couple set their couch off with curtains to leave the rest of the
chamber for others. Large families in small rooms learned, by a
variety of tactics, not to see, not to cross one another's path, to
make allowances, and to avoid collisions. Solitude was not
prized. Work in the fields was lonely enough to make the intimacy of a house full of adults and children, servants and lodgers
pleasurable.

A society short of labor welcomed increases, and the birth rate
was consistently high. Yet few fathers and mothers made any special provision for the newborn or for children in early infancy.
Outside the South, where female slaves played the role, only the
uppermost families employed nurses, and did so more for the

convenience of the mother than for the advantage of the infant. Mostly the very young took care of themselves or got by under the charge of an older sibling. As in other parts of the eighteenth-century world, high rates of infant mortality were commonplace; and the distinctions between lack of resources and neglect, neglect and infanticide, were tenuous indeed.

Childhood was not a separate world, with its own rules and requirements. Children shared family life to the fullest extent; regarded as miniature adults expected to exercise their own wills, they also bore the obligations of prescribed forms of behavior. Child-rearing manuals urged parents to thrust the boy or girl on to adulthood, instilling as early as possible character traits essential to a later orderly and useful life. John Locke's *Some Thoughts Concerning Education* (1693) still earned the flattery of frequent plagiarism. Plain food, dried fruit or apples instead of candy and sweets, plenty of sleep on a hard bed (feather beds led to indolence and laziness), early toilet training, fresh air, and cold baths laid a foundation for future health. Only in substituting rum and water for the small beer he recommended did well-read colonists deviate from the philosopher's advice. In accordance with Locke's suggestion, Josiah Quincy, born in Braintree in 1772, every morning as a child descended to the cellar and plunged into a tub of fresh spring water, New England winters notwithstanding. Sick children were often "dipped," and a cure for rickets advocated in 1769 included a daily head soaking in cold water, followed by a rest in the cradle dripping wet and a dose of water, rum, snakewood, and saffron.

John Witherspoon's widely read *Letters on Education* urged the overwhelming significance of parental authority, established as early as possible. Taking something away from the infant each day would train it to obedience by the age of one; a tardy start would in all likelihood render the case hopeless. Fathers and mothers had to be on guard against the craftiness of their offspring, who speedily learned how to get around their elders. The letters admonished adults not to go too far in small rewards; Roman emperors had discovered the evil consequences of bread and circuses.

Parents, unable to forget their own harsh upbringing, did not apply rigorous standards to their offspring, knowing the hopelessness of trying to keep high-spirited youngsters in line. Planters evaded the disciplinary obligation by ordering the tutor to do the whipping. Other fathers, however, lacking that resource, learned to ignore the rumbling in the boys' pews, and rarely invoked penalties when their offspring pulled girls' hair or tripped their sisters on the ice. On Long Island, pranksters casually profaned the Sabbath by racing and conversing of "vane things," while in Albany children often deserted their parents on the way to church and spent Sundays in rolling down the hills and other pastimes. Sober Philadelphians looked the other way when a band of boys dashed around the square in a footrace, stripped to their shirts, shoeless, knee bands loosened, and handkerchiefs knotted around their heads to keep sweat from their eyes. Not the most mannerly of practices, but then the competitiveness it expressed was a desirable trait. That attitude reflected the ambiguity of Americans, who wished their offspring to be free and venturesome and yet to conform to accepted standards.

The numerous flocks of children—perhaps half the total population—received a hasty rearing until they could fend for themselves. Neglect and permissiveness were aspects of the same basic judgment—it was never too soon to be on one's own. The child's role was transitional, in preparation for the inevitable point of departure from home. To that extent the family unit lacked cohesiveness. Its sons and daughters expected to go forth, some within the same community, others a greater or lesser distance away.

Girls, early on, saw the way before them: marriage and motherhood. However unstable it was, this society possessed an excess of men, and every woman could expect to be a wife. It made sense to prepare early for the role and, by usefulness in the household, to acquire skills and habits of frugality and economy. The proper maiden carded, spun, wove, and bleached, learned to cook, make cheese, dip candles, preserve fruit, and tend the vegetable garden. Abigail Foote, a young girl in Colchester, Connecticut, listed her activities on a bright day in 1775. In addition to reading a sermon, and carding two pounds of wool (which

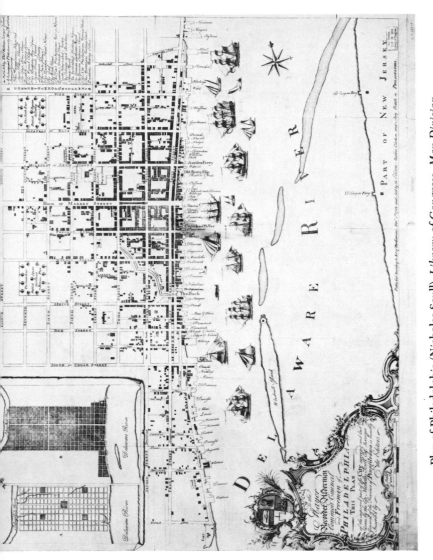

Plan of Philadelphia (Nicholas Scull). *Library of Congress, Map Division*

A view of part of the town of Boston, 1768 (engraved by Paul Revere). *Stokes Collection, New York Public Library*

A view of Boston Common, 1768 (watercolor by Christian Remick, engraved by Sidney Smith). *Stokes Collection, New York Public Library*

The great New York fire of 1776. *The Bettmann Archive, Inc.*

Governor
Benning Wentworth's House,
Portsmouth,
N.H.,
Peter Harrison, architect.
Courtesy Wayne Andrews

Paul Revere,
American artisan:
Portrait by
John Singleton Copley.
The Bettmann Archive

New Yorkers pull down
George III's statue
on Bowling Green.
The Bettmann Archive

The Dwarf that lately made
her Appearance in this Town,
from Nathaniel Ames,
*An Astronomical Diary;
or Almanack for . . . 1772.*
*Courtesy American
Antiquarian Society.*

An ASTRONOMICAL DIARY; or

ALMANACK

For the Year of our LORD CHRIST 1772 : Being Bissextile or Leap-Year.

Calculated for the Meridian of BOSTON, New-England, Lat. 42 25 North.

CONTAINING

Besides what is usual in Almanacks, a Description of the Dwarf that lately made
her Appearance in this Town ; as also a curious Method of taking Wax and
Honey without destroying Bees.

By NATHANIEL AMES.

Price 2s. 8d. per Dozen, and Six Coppers single.

Daniel Boone as an old man: Portrait by Chester Harding. *The Bettmann Archive, Inc.*

Boston Massacre, 1770 (engraved by Paul Revere). *The Bettmann Archive*

Battle of Concord, April 19, 1775. *The Bettmann Archive, Inc.*

made her feel "nationly"), Abigail milked the family's cows, worked on a cheese basket, mended her mother's riding hood, pleated and ironed, spun linen, constructed a broom of Guinea wheat straw, and scoured the pewter.

In these and other respects, the daughter was her mother in miniature. Together they picked geese and weeded; and as soon as her hands were steady enough, the girl learned to knit stockings and mittens for her family. She even tried to look like her mother. Anna Green Winslow, twelve years old in 1771, wore for a special party a "yellow coat, black bib and apron, back feathers . . . on the head . . . paste comb and . . . paste garnet marquasett and jet pins together with . . . a silver plume . . . locket, rings, black collar around . . . the neck, yards of blue ribbon (black and blue is high taste) striped tucker and ruffles and silk shoes." The daughters of other families, less elaborately clothed, also modeled themselves on their mothers. Though jewelry was expensive, anyone who could pick berries could tie "Job's tears" into a necklace.

A few young ladies in boarding school acquired the conventional female accomplishments such as shellwork and needlework. Mrs. Sarah Wilson, proprietor of a boarding school in Philadelphia, promised her charges an education in "a genteel manner," including waxwork, "embroidering curtains or chairs," and the usual "writing and cyphering." But education did not depend on formal courses of study; Abigail Smith Adams, at home, became as learned as any of her contemporaries of either sex.

Boys early on helped on the farm and in the workshop. As soon as they could walk, they followed their fathers, wearing a child's version of doublets, knee breeches, and knit caps. In town they commonly made the break from home through apprenticeship, accepting the discipline of a master in return for training in a skill. Occasional equivalents existed in agriculture. A lad with no prospect of inheritance found a place in a neighbor's family where he learned to work and waited for the chance to get land of his own. The best master was one unrelated by blood, the worst an elder brother, for distance preserved formality and respect in the connection, while fraternal intimacy became an excuse for exploitation of the weaker by the stronger. The discontented often ran away—out of loneliness, homesickness, disgust with strange surroundings, or cruel treatment. When the Trenton, New Jersey, blacksmith George Tucker offered a forty-shilling reward for the return of John Gorman, about nineteen years of age, who disappeared wearing a coat, a cape, a jacket, buckskin breeches, and two shirts, he publicly acknowledged his own and the boy's inability to work together.

Only a minority among the youngsters derived their education from formal instruction. In cities, children learned their letters first in a neighborhood dame school and then in a grammar school. In many towns, older youths and adults who had missed out early on could catch up in evening writing schools. Occasionally also various wanderers settled down to offer instruction, as when an Italian dancing master turned up in Providence in 1768. His counterparts, there and elsewhere, conveyed to students a range of skills from French to psalmody.

In rural regions the choices narrowed. Boys between the ages of eight and twelve intermittently attended a local school, so long as some struggling preceptor maintained it. Well-to-do farmers and planters bought or hired a Scottish indentured servant or some other tutor or sent their offspring to board with a minister willing to do some teaching. A few children went to England. But the family, the shop, the farm, and the church remained more important than the classroom, although the gradual attrition of the apprenticeship system, the inclination to let sons move off early, and the breakdown of other forms of training increased the load on the ill-prepared schools.

Youths who wished more advanced learning could reside with a bookish minister or attend Latin schools and academies. There was no fixed order or pattern to these institutions, and students entered at any age. In 1769 the Friends' Public Schoolhouse in Philadelphia offered pupils night courses in reading, writing, and arithmetic. In 1772 every Boston school made available a tutor in writing and arithmetic at 6:00 P.M. Young ladies shared the teaching available at home, and occasionally at schools, which, however, usually catered almost exclusively to males.

Colleges stood at the apex, but in practice often did mostly a grammar school business, so poorly prepared were the students. That in Pennsylvania grew out of an academy, and those in New York and Princeton both depended on elementary branches. Jefferson, when governor of Virginia, abolished the grammar school attached to William and Mary, hoping thus to elevate its dignity, but remained dissatisfied with the result.

The source of the trouble was the aimlessness of faculty and students. One planter complained that he could not send his children to William and Mary with propriety, for he had known the professors to play all night at cards in public houses and had often seen them drunk in the streets. But then the scholars were less often seekers for learning than unruly young men sent by their parents to disciplinary institutions that would teach them how to behave. The students, caught up by the spirit of the times, considered themselves the statesmen of the future and took up politics. Their forensic disputes revolved about liberty, but their studies suffered neglect.

A bookish lad destined for the ministry might seek out instruction at Harvard or Yale, or live in a minister's household preparatory to doing so; but few American youths looked forward to such careers. Some sent by their parents to acquire prestige or polish at college or academy whiled the time away in indecision. Alexander Graydon, scion of a good but not wealthy Philadelphia family, tried the academy until the age of fourteen, then spent a year and a half doing nothing until set reluctantly to study law. Meanwhile he fell in with a group of young men—mostly seamen and mechanics—whose rough independence attracted him. Through them he learned the excitement of the billiard table and met girls; and with them he climbed up and staggered down three flights of a narrow staircase in a Race Street inn, where a fiery beverage flowed in abundance, no questions asked.

How to manage such youths concerned the well-to-do, able to choose future careers among the desirable places as merchants, lawyers, or physicians. But most fathers and mothers contentedly watched their children go quickly out on their own; opportunity awaited those who seized it as soon as possible. Wise parents knew that however much they might desire a son to stick it out through Latin school, the likelihood was slim that a headstrong young American would do so against his own will.

Separation was therefore the norm, as it was not in Europe. Sarah Bache sent her son Benjamin off to live with his grandfather Benjamin Franklin in Paris and saw him again nine years later. George Washington insisted that his mother live in a house of her own at Fredericksburg rather than at Mount Vernon. The exigencies of war kept apart Abigail and John Adams and Esther De Berdt Reed and her husband, Joseph, prominent Philadelphians, without diminishing the fervor of conjugal affection. The strength of the family did not spring from proximity or from incorporation in a single household, but grew despite partings.

Young men and women often entered upon a period of bachelorhood after apprenticeship or schooling, full grown and independent yet not in a position to establish their own families. Neither sex could extend the interval indefinitely, girls for fear of losing out to fresher competitors, boys because society frowned on bachelorhood. Maryland taxed unmarried men above the age of twenty-five, and Americans everywhere held single men who evaded matrimony to be in violation of God's command to multiply.

Courtship and matrimonial practices differed according to region and status. Well-established urban families preserved the most formal procedures; churches and ministers, near at hand, provided communal sanctions for adherence to custom. Philadelphians believed that obstinacy doomed Elizabeth Graeme Ferguson. Parental opposition having dissolved an early engagement to William Franklin (Benjamin's son), she eloped secretly at night with a Scotsman ten years her junior. Her husband's loyalist sympathies led to estrangement and plunged her into poverty. Having disregarded the advice of her elders, she lived from one misfortune to another. Marriage was also subject to close social supervision among large landholding families, northern and southern, for every alliance affected the possession and transmission of estates and of political influence.

Elaborate procedures with well-defined rules governed courtship, although Benjamin Franklin believed lovers less bashful and modest in the 1770s than formerly, for they no longer limited themselves to sidelong glances when before their elders. Young women early learned to play the game as expected. Surprised by the attention of suitors, they turned down the first request and played hard to get—ladies who gave themselves with ease were not worth having. A proper girl, neither coquettish nor capricious, kept the young man dancing in attendance as long as decency allowed, but not overly long lest he give up altogether.

Fewer formalities ruled the unions of less privileged men and women, vulnerable therefore to unsettling shocks. In small communities the pool of eligible partners, limited to begin with and diminished by sectarianism, allowed the questing swain little choice. Ethnic and religious divisions also narrowed the range of permissible selections in the towns, although the opportunity for encounters among large heterogeneous populations offered a greater margin of selectivity. But in any setting only families of wealth and status wielded the sanctions to make approval—good dowry—or disapproval—disgrace—meaningful. Otherwise the decision was a product of the calculations and passions of individuals. On the frontier, casual unceremonious arrangements were common in the absence of ministers and the remoteness of courts. Often the formation of a family involved no more than the simple agreement to establish a new household.

Numerous violations of the seventh commandment, against adultery, compelled churches to soften punishment lest they deplete their congregations. Confession as an act of contrition replaced excommunication. In towns like Sharon, Danvers, and Groton, Massachusetts, several members every year admitted to fornication. One community printed a form that the transgressor completed, declaring that he or she had engaged "in scandalous offenses . . . being instrumental in weakening the bonds of society." The increase in the number of premarital pregnancies did not in itself mark a change in family patterns, since most women so involved married the father. But it signaled the inefficacy of conventional strictures.

Guidebooks rarely helped the susceptible avoid the dangerous trap of sex, for few of them discussed the subject openly. When describing delicate matters (such as menstruation and pregnancy), Mühlenberg lapsed into Latin, more scientific and there-

fore less tainted with worldly passions than the vulgar tongues.
The female center of mind, body, and soul rested in the uterus,
and when God in His infinite wisdom and mercy punished Mrs.
Setzler for consoling herself in adultery for her husband's impo-
tence, her "right spot"—the uterus—became inflamed, putrefied,
and was finally consumed.

Advice in *Aristotle's Master Piece*, a frequently reprinted and
widely read manual, was no more illuminating. That sex was altogether pleasant everyone knew, but, "Aristotle" cautioned, excess led to blindness, brain damage and shortened lives (witness
the sparrow, who copulated frequently and lived only three
years). The act itself was really disgusting and contemptible but
rendered pleasurable by God's wisdom. Although the male was
the more important sex (and wise parents of hermaphrodites so
classified their offspring), three quarters of the manual dealt
with the female, perhaps in the expectation that most readers
would be men. Virgins remained susceptible to hysteria until
marriage, when legitimate intercourse cured it. Well and often
never went together; infrequent but properly executed relations
were best. Conception was the ultimate goal, guaranteed to take
place when the couple were of different humors, one hot and
moist, the other cold and dry.

A high degree of individual choice elevated the position of single women. The female who chose not to marry enjoyed extensive rights; spinsters inherited and controlled their own property,
entered trades, and practiced crafts, including some outside the
law. Widows too, as often as not, carried on the affairs of their
deceased husbands, not only on the farms but in the workshops—
Betsy Ross as upholsterer, and Ann Rawlins as plasterer in Baltimore, for instance. Mary Katherine Goddard of the same city
took over her brother's press and established herself as a printer,
issuing the first published copy of the Declaration of Independence to include the names of the signers. Clementina Rind
became Virginia's public printer and Anne Franklin of Newport
published the *Mercury* until her son James took charge.

Ladies left with incomes too slender to support their families
often took in lodgers. Others operated retail shops as independent entrepreneurs. Elizabeth Murray left Scotland to visit

her brother in North Carolina in 1749. Prudently she brought along a stock of millinery and dry goods and, when her ship put in at Boston, decided to remain there and set up in business. She thrived and in 1755 married Thomas Campbell, a Scottish merchant, though still importing goods from London for sale in her store; and she continued to do so after her husband's death. In 1760 Elizabeth found consolation in union with James Smith, a wealthy sugar baker. When his turn came, the widow married Ralph Inman, whose estate in Cambridge she managed with competence.

Women entrepreneurs were familiar in many lines. In Philadelphia on the eve of the Revolution, some 20 percent of the taverns had female operators; and Widow Manking of Market Street advertised drugs. Mary Cahell, a milliner, specialized in "turbans for Negroes." Mary Salmon of Boston was a blacksmith, Margaret Pascal a cutler, Elizabeth Russell a coachmaker, and Sarah Jewell a rope maker. Lydia Darragh, of Philadelphia, an undertaker, by 1774 also announced herself a doctor, administering injections to purge the lower intestine.

Marriage made the difference in status, for women then entered households of which man was master. Certainly they did so voluntarily and not out of necessity or for want of an alternative, and the law honored prenuptial contracts and held husbands to obligations they therein assumed toward their wives. Nonetheless women fully expected to devote themselves to their homes, husbands, and children. Their upbringing conditioned them in that direction; and the toll of frequent childbirth explained the quip: like early fruit, soon ripe and soon rotten.

Death carried some away at an early age, not only those like Alice Needham, who did not survive her triplets, but also others like Nancy Worster, on whose cheeks the rose still bloomed "yet her dear babe became her death while she became the infant's tomb." Thomas Jefferson's wife, Martha, bore six children in ten years and died soon after. Married at nineteen, Eleanor, wife of Henry Laurens, President of the Continental Congress, bore twelve children in the twenty years of life that remained her. Seven of them predeceased her. Nevertheless, Mary Buel, who died in 1768 aged ninety, was proud of her 13 children, 101 grandchildren, 247 great-grandchildren, and 49 great-great-grandchildren, of whom 336 were still alive.

Female roles were not narrow. Although only the Quakers recognized them as ministers, women played an important part in religious affairs. They had their own meetings for business in that sect and enjoyed a full vote among the Baptists. Their opinions also counted among Congregationalists and Anglicans, and their influence, although not as open in those established churches, was often decisive.

Nor were wives the helpless creatures of their husbands. The grounds for divorce were the same for both parties to a marriage, with desertion the ultimate recourse for both. Massachusetts in 1763 permitted a woman living apart from her husband to convey real estate independently. Legislative action to dissolve a marriage became a political issue when Parliament attempted to halt what it considered colonial usurpation of its authority. In 1772 the Privy Council disallowed a private divorce bill enacted by the Pennsylvania assembly and also similar measures in New Jersey and New Hampshire. But the assertion of imperial power had little effect. Some Americans believed divorce a means of increasing contentment in marriage and of reducing fraud in courtships, thus prompting obdurate bachelors to find wives. After independence, statutes broadened the basis for separation and simplified the legal mechanism by transferring the decision to the courts in Pennsylvania and Massachusetts. Connecticut soon acquired such a liberal reputation that the legislature required a three-year residency of plaintiffs. More restrictive policies persisted primarily in the South.

Husbands rarely regarded their wives as inferior. Upper-class ladies were as literate as their spouses, and at all levels of society, women acquired the necessary skills to carry on the business in their men's illness, incapacity, or death. The wife, of course, also kept house, attending to every aspect of its internal economy, maintaining its cleanliness, conserving garments and linen, and preparing the food. The mistress of a plantation, in addition, provided nourishment and clothing for a large establishment and cared for the health of its dependents.

An advertisement in the *Pennsylvania Packet* of September 23,

1780, listed the requirements of a gentleman looking for a house-keeper. An "affable, cheerful and amiable Disposition" was essential, along with an unsullied reputation, cleanliness, and industriousness; her duties would include "raising small stock, dairying, marketing, combing, carding, spinning, knitting, sewing, pickling, preserving, etc." The "etc." usually referred to care of a vegetable garden and to the instruction of daughters. Through the winter the housewife stored refuse grease and wood ash for spring soapmaking, a laborious task of repeated pourings of barrels of water and boilings of the mixture. Late autumn was the time for candle dipping, which required foresight, preparation, and a strong back. Rods and wicks, dipped periodically in kettles of melted tallow until of proper size, had to cool slowly to prevent cracking. Molds—metal cylinders, usually made of pewter and provided by itinerant candlemakers—sometimes eased that work. These heavy jobs had counterparts in others left to the man of the house: repairing the furniture and the physical structure, care of the grounds, doctoring the family, and making most cash transactions. These were tasks shared in a common enterprise, not those assigned by a superior husband to a subordinate wife.

Statutes defined the obligations and protected the rights of both men and women. But to the extent that they still reflected the English common law, a wife shared her husband's identity. More important than occasional enactments to guard the weaker against the tyranny of the stronger was the awareness that the whole society depended upon its women. Abigail Adams' call to "remember the Ladies" was superfluous; none could forget them. The American woman made no fuss about political rights, willingly behaved politely, inoffensively, and agreeably, and allowed Dr. Rush to explain that she had "no will of her own." She knew whence her power sprang: from control of the home.

The American man's chances of prosperity depended upon "the acquisition of a good wife." Sober calculation (the need for a reliable helpmate) and sentiment (defense of the frailer sex) shaped his ideal of womanhood. The same elements defined the wife's image of the ideal man—a good provider and a gallant, chivalric defender. She, Crèvecoeur pointed out, contributed "her future economy, modesty and skillful management." He worked the fields a little harder than before because he toiled for her. Love, gratitude, and pride filled his bosom as he performed his role as husband and father while she did her duties with equal fidelity. Marriage was thus a partnership that served the joint interest of the participants.

But there was more to marriage than that, as John Witherspoon, Scottish-born president of the College of New Jersey (now Princeton) and signer of the Declaration of Independence, explained in three letters on the subject of love in 1775 and 1776. He sought to counter the dangerous expectations of young people, inflamed by novelists like Samuel Richardson who emphasized female beauty and the spirituality of marriage. Wedlock was a necessity ordained by God, for the good of society and the individual. Sex in the course of matrimony gave human relations their special quality. But young dreamers were to guard against disappointments sure to overwhelm those who expected prolonged ecstasy, rapture, or unalloyed happiness in the married state.

Witherspoon objected to glowing definitions that ascribed to love supernatural powers and the ability to triumph over all difficulties. Romances distorted reality. The world did not stop or nature mourn the departure of a beloved. Few women were divinely fair, but many were amiable—vastly more important. After the early years of cohabitation, happiness depended on the quality of the meals and the state of the husband's purse, not on the wife's facial features.

Husbands were not henpecked when they followed their wives' advice. Equality in marriage benefited both partners. Poor marital relations were the man's fault: he should have made a wiser choice. The woman, however, shared the blame when her nature rendered the union miserable. But in either case, with the vows taken, there was nothing to do but make the best of them.

But there was more to love than Witherspoon's letters spelled out. Another Scottish immigrant in 1774 wrote home to the family he had not seen for a year, the first letter he had time to send in six months. It brought tears to the eyes of an "affectionate husband until death" to think of the wife and infants it was not in his power to help. Men and women who addressed each other in the most formal terms, not only before strangers but also on paper, now and again let slip phrases expressive of mutual need, understanding, and emotion.

A traditional rite sanctioned by religion and a contract approved by the state, wedlock legitimized personal passion and provided the generational continuity of procreation and child rearing. But it also guarded the individual against the contingencies of a hard life, furnished helpmates to those who knew the hazards of standing alone, knotting them together through myriad ties of affection, faith, and welfare. In unstable communities, these two knew they had to cling to each other.

The dangers of isolation deepened the sense of dependence. Whatever hardships a marriage entailed, the burdens of living alone were harsher. Hence the readiness of those left adrift by the death of a spouse to accept a replacement. Hence, too, the protection by law of the rights of widows as against those of children likely to move away or acquire new responsibilities. The painful circumstances of the relicts of clergymen, incapable of carrying on the work or extending the income of their late husbands, therefore called for particular solicitude.

The marriage that united two persons also formed a new family in a new household, all the members of which partook of the same experience, although in different ways. Sons and daughters, brothers and sisters, like husbands and wives, felt the pressures and attractions of moving away, of getting out on their own. Hence few individuals could relax, feel secure in a community. Even after several generations the people of the New World still remained sojourners in a strange land, struggling to preserve familiar forms of behavior. The ever-receding line of settlement carried hundreds of families to the interior, away from old homes, so that everything bore the appearance of newness. Even places long settled lacked monuments; those recently redeemed from the wilderness changed by the day. The conditions of existence spared none the risk of disaster, offered few the prospect of comfort.

Longing for order, Americans reached out toward one another, those most likely to strike out as individuals as much as any others. Having broken away, they learned the need for federation; able to exercise their wills, they chose for their own good to accept discipline; persistent separatists, they wished to be a part of a whole community. The contradictions generated by the hard life of a restless society raised the value of kinship. Those ties alone preserved elements of durability where all else changed.

5

Lives Roughly Passed

The uncertainties of a hard life threatened Americans with dependence and made them victims of anxiety. Few enjoyed safeguards against the bruises of a rough existence. Strangers noted superficial indices—the unkempt appearance of many people or the negligence of even gentlemen in sometimes going forth without wigs. A disposition toward nervousness and unexpected mental collapses such as ended the career of the patriot lawyer James Otis also measured the harshness of experience.

Anxieties of fashion and manner affected only a few colonists but were nonetheless real. Ladies slept sitting up to protect the locks curled the night before a party; and gentlemen held their long-skirted coats smooth by buckram linings and lead weights, but found no protection against the cold because the open sleeves that showed off fine linen and buttons also welcomed the wind. Advice spoiled many a digestion: bite not the bread but break it; take salt only with a clean knife; dip not the meat in the same.

Such worries were largely self-imposed; others mirrored the difficulty of establishing an orderly life in a raw society. The uneven pace of day-to-day work prevented the formation of a dependable routine. Long periods of leisure alternated with sudden, often unpredictable, spurts of frenetic activity. The merchant idled weeks away, while fortune or failure turned upon the caprice of distant winds; then a ship came in and calculation and negotiation crammed the waking hours. The artisan readied his tools, usually imported at some expense from Britain, but had nothing to do until a customer appeared, and then hastened through the task to be ready for another—if it came. Agriculture was seasonal and therefore more predictable, but no less discontinuous. Periods of frantic toil followed prolonged languid stretches.

Constant vigilance against sharp dealing raised the level of anxiety. If the butter for sale in the marketplace went putrid, the seller, as a matter of course, avoided loss by smearing a fresh layer across the top; the buyer incautious enough not to sample downward deserved the penalty of his negligence and would take greater care next time. Laws regulated the quality, price, and measure of many commodities, but flexible enforcement made shrewdness and watchfulness ever necessary. Outwit or be outwitted was the rule.

Debt, omnipresent, sprang from sources different from those in the Old World. The loan was not in America a transaction between wastrels and moneylenders. Members of every social class were borrowers and lenders, and it was not unusual for the same person to be both a creditor and debtor. Debt in the colonies was a necessity of life, a consequence either of the mode of investment or of the obligations of neighborliness. In the absence of banks and other mediating financial institutions, any unforeseen demand for scarce cash compelled people to turn to one another. And nerve-racking speculation was the only means of using any gain, great or small.

The inability to find out what was happening cast a shadow over every transaction and left everyone dependent on gossip. On a cold Friday in February 1777 the Virginia planter Landon Carter, bothered by colic (disposed of by means of "a friendly pillow to press the wind back from the stomach into the bowels"), welcomed neighbor Neal, who stopped for warmth and a chat. Neal had encountered Isaac Deggs, who had learned from a certain Jno. Heath that "Colo. Somebody" earlier in the month had seen letters with accounts of happenings in the North. New Englanders had destroyed at least seventy enemy ships, and General Heath had just burned New York to the ground. The skeptical Carter suggested that Jno. Heath had a poor reputation. The next day the rumor became a certainty when Carter learned that Captain George Turberville, crossing by Faunteleroy's ferry, heard from the ferry keeper that Heath had retaken New York (without burning it, however) and General Worster had possession of Long Island. Turberville had read letters from Baltimore confirming the story of the capture of the ships.

Encounters in homes, churches, or stores spread the news, true or false. But taverns were the focal points for these exchanges, places where courts and assemblies sometimes met, where mail and newspapers arrived, where notices appeared of auctions or runaways, and sometimes where the highest bidder bought pauper labor. Although opinions differed about their quality and cleanliness, the inns provided a setting for meetings with strangers and for important transactions. So inquisitive and news-hungry were the hangers-on that Benjamin Franklin made it standard practice, upon entrance, to state his name, profession, place of birth, and destination in a loud voice, adding that he had no news and wanted his dinner.

Precarious travel slowed the flow of information. Schemes for a post office dated back to the early eighteenth century, and a stage linked New York to Philadelphia in 1756. After 1772 another, once every two weeks, connected Boston and New York. By then Mercereau's Flying Machine had reduced travel time between New York and Philadelphia to a day and a half and prided itself on seats suspended on strings, a vast improvement over the usual fixtures, which jolted passengers whenever the carriage hit a rock. Few eighteenth-century coaches had any means of locking the wheels, so that drivers relied hazardously on great boulders, fallen trees, and holes in the road to slow their speed. Overturned and abandoned stages were a common sight along the wayside.

The arrival of news and of passengers therefore remained a source of anxiety. In the absence of a dependable postal system, colonists defied British law and set up private services. But the transport of mail was prey to the vagaries of the weather and of unreliable carriers. Postriders bided their time until enough letters accumulated to make the trip worthwhile; and carelessness or illness could delay delivery for weeks. In any case, the carriers, burdened with merchandise for sale along the route, took care of their own business before making deliveries. A Pennsylvania postrider, to no one's surprise, knitted socks as his nag ambled leisurely along the road.

Passenger travel was no more dependable. Josiah Quincy's trip from Boston to New York in 1784 took more than a week, with six people crowded into an old carriage, much of its harness made of ropes. Periodic stops for changes of horses or drivers were also occasions for drinking. At about 10:00 P.M. a halt for the night provided the rider a frugal supper and a bed shared with at least one companion, if not with bugs. Sleep did not last beyond 2:30 A.M. when the journey resumed. Since the drivers were often drunk by then, the stage might overturn or sink into a quagmire, leaving the passengers the task of lifting it out. Mishaps and the caprice of the weather also turned a voyage by coastal vessel into an adventure. A traveler from Norfolk, Virginia, got to within sight of Manhattan Island in four days but spent the next ten days at sea as unfavorable winds blew the ship away from shore.

Experience in a hard and uncertain life taught Americans to accept opportunity to dare. As youngsters they learned to compete. As adults they gambled. The boys in New Haven had played football with a blown-up bladder at least as far back as 1765 and, although forbidden to scrimmage, accumulated a goodly number of bruised shins. Later, Princeton sternly but ineffectually outlawed ballplaying as a menace to health, maiming some students and exposing all to deleterious alternations of heat and cold. The best sports, according to Franklin, prepared men for life with lessons about foresight, caution, patience, and circumspection. Competition, Dr. Rush believed, taught the value of labor, planning, and profit. His countrymen joyously took risks in the game of life.

Gambling was not unique to the New World. Visitors saw abundant evidence of the mania in eighteenth-century London. But Americans of all classes, indoors and out, in homes and taverns, bet on horse races, on the fall of a card or the roll of the dice, on the weather, or on the outcome of political contests; and public lotteries raised funds for charitable purposes. Greed and avarice were less responsible for the addiction than the thrill of uncertainty, a passion unrelated to gains or losses. The Virginia aristocrat Colonel William Byrd III was never as happy as when he held the dice box in his hands; and Jeffrey Grisley, of the same colony, who wasted his inheritance on games of chance, left a wife and three children to starve when he was jailed for failure to pay his debts.

The *Virginia Gazette* of October 7, 1773, explained the damaging effects of gambling. Players oblivious to the time of day, their countenances somber, yielded to the madness. In the ordinaries and taverns the dissatisfied carried anger to extremes, and the resulting brawls spilled out into the street. In the houses of the wealthy, where large sums passed across the table, few knew how to lose graciously and decorum vanished. The Virginia assembly passed rigorous antigaming laws, but in 1777 Ebenezer Hazard observed thirty dollars bet on an odd trick at whist and the legislators themselves addicted to gambling.

The clergy disapproved as well. To trust to luck rather than to God was impious, and easy winnings ran counter to injunctions to earn one's bread by the sweat of one's brow. Gambling was a form of cheating; although overt trickery was frowned upon, the skillful use of deceit separated serious players from amateurs. Hazardous games were especially dastardly among the poor, tempted to quick riches. The warnings had little effect upon Americans, all of whose lives involved risks and the calculation of odds. War and speculation had an advantage over other forms of gambling, one acknowledged by the clergy and recognized by law, for the whole society imputed communal purposes to these ways of taking chances.

No one escaped the anxiety that emanated from afflictions of the body as well as of the spirit. Discomfort, ever present, frequently turned into hazard. Ticks, flies, mosquitoes in their season were so familiar that only strangers commented upon their presence. Locusts swooped periodically across the land. The colonists stumbled through the mud and sand of unpaved lanes; they shivered under blasts of arctic wind and sweltered in the flow of heat from the Gulf. The blessed hyacinths of spring promised relief, only to yield quickly to gusts of frigid or humid air. Knowing no other use for the umbrella than to shade ladies from the sun, drenched by rain, blown by sand, buried in snow, Americans learned the meaning of a temperate climate: one subject to frequent drastic changes.

A short growing season imposed constraints upon diet and subjected Americans to additional strains. They had plenty to eat; never in this period, not even during the war, did they approach the famine or the deprivation that afflicted many Europeans in the eighteenth century. Townsfolk as well as farmers owned at least one cow, a source of milk, cheese, and butter. Meat, fish, grains, fruits, and vegetables were seasonal but abundant, pork more so than beef or mutton, wheat more than corn or rye. Salmon, sturgeon, and herring appeared regularly in the rivers, although in diminishing numbers, and oysters and clams lined the shores. A taste for horsemeat never developed; that animal had more value in transportation than on the table.

Not lack of quantity but mode of preparation accounted for the deficiencies of diet. Open fires served in the absence of ovens, so that bread in many regions was less common than hoecakes baked in the ashes. The provident consumed preserved, smoked, or dried foods, hung slightly salted in the kitchen, often to the point of monotony. Quantity—and alcohol—were the preferred remedies for tastelessness. Meals followed no set course. All the dishes appeared at once in wooden trenchers or on pewter platters, and everyone pitched in. The gentry took wine with their food; others gulped down goodly drams of cider, beer, whiskey, and rum. Sensibly, everyone stayed away from water, all too often drawn from wells polluted by nearby privies.

Many Americans began the day with an eye-opener. Already in 1743 the *Pennsylvania Gazette* berated Philadelphia women for mixing their toast with beer rather than milk; and a Georgian later plaintively asked, "If I take a settler after my coffee, a cooler at nine, a bracer at ten, a whetter at 11 and two or three stiffeners during the forenoon who has a right to complain?" An Englishman in 1779 noted that "the planter rises about eight o'clock, drinks what he calls a julep, which is a large glass of rum, sweetened with sugar, and then walks or more generally, rides around his plantation," returning about ten o'clock to breakfast on cold meat or ham, fried hominy, toast, and cider. About noon, "he drinks toddy, to create him an appetite for dinner which he sits down to at two o'clock. After he has dined he generally lays down on the bed, and rises about five, then perhaps sips some tea with his wife, but commonly drinks toddy until bed time, during all this he is neither drunk nor sober, but in a state of stupefaction." A few years later the town meeting in Worcester, Massachusetts, damned as an infringement on liberty a tax on liquors, considered the necessary refreshment of farmers.

Rum (once known as the kill-devil) was consumed pure, or mixed with sugarloaf and water, diluted with beer, or strengthened with molasses and herbs. A dash of rum added zest to the New England flip, a drink made in great pewter mugs with beer, molasses, and dried pumpkin as sweetener, to which a red-hot iron poker imparted a bitter, scorched taste. Americans brewed beer from spruce, birch, or sassafras bark. But New Englanders preferred cider, which, mulled, was particularly good for infants at bedtime; it guaranteed parents a restful night. John Adams began each day with a tankard full of hard cider, and those who liked it even harder made a "stone-wall" by adding rum.

The censorious claimed that such drinks thinned the blood so that it was "constantly on the fret," enfeebling the frame and stoking slow fevers. Nevertheless, the consumption of alcohol rose further during the war. Sixty distilleries operated in Massachusetts alone. Militiamen would not risk drill or combat in the heat without sustaining drafts of grog, and civilians sympathized. By 1777 both Massachusetts and Rhode Island forbade the distillation of spirits from grains, not out of concern for sobriety but to conserve scarce corn and rye for food. Patriots after the Revolution hoped that native beer and cider would supplant imported beverages, to help the balance of payments and reduce intoxication. Local drinks, displaying the virtue and simplicity that had won the war, would keep the nation free from vices calculated to dishonor and enslave the people.

The well-to-do drank Madeira, claret, and port. Jefferson, a connoisseur, once calculated that his cellar had to contain at least five hundred bottles of champagne to entertain his guests for a year. Since he considered whiskey vile and nothing more than poison, he sought to encourage wine drinking. However, no cookbook failed to include at least one article on distilling. Many gave directions on how to restore "sour" or "dead" beer, how to make the home brew taste like French burgundy or Jamaica rum, and how to use such ingredients as raspberries, oranges, cherries, horseradish, and turnips. In East Derry, Connecticut, James Ervins nonetheless had his tombstone carved in 1781: "My glass is Rum."

With or without an accompanying glass, the weed offered solace. Taking snuff was almost as popular as the pipe. In addition to a slight narcotic effect, a pinch induced a succession of sneezes, thought to clear the head of "superfluous humors" and brighten the eyes. Warnings of the evil effects of this pernicious habit informed "sniverlers and snorters" that their sense of smell would fade, their heads would fill with soot, and their brains would dry out. Charges that snuff increased the appetite and caused a variety of diseases provoked heated defenses—among them the claim that tobacco cured a long list of ailments.

A few Americans preferred the cigar, introduced to the colonies by sailors from South America. Israel Putnam returned to Connecticut from Cuba in 1762 with as many Havana cigars as three donkeys would carry. By 1765 New Yorkers could buy their own, while the Pennsylvania Dutch manufactured some for private use. And of course tobacco could also be chewed. Nicotine, like alcohol, offered solace to people who had to accept discomfort.

Americans learned to live with pain, for which alcohol and opium were the common nostrums. The clumsy surgeon pulled the wrong tooth when Baroness Riedesel complained of an ache, for dentistry was a sideline rather than a distinct skill. Isaac Greenwood, who served his clients as a tooth drawer, also sold umbrellas, cane for hoop petticoats, and dice. William Greenwood extracted teeth and sold pianos, and Dr. Flagg, surgeon dentist, advertised in 1797 that he could get good hand organs from Europe for church use. Those who could not afford such help depended on do-it-yourself "Teeth Pullers" (and often suffered broken jawbones as a result). Paul Revere, silversmith, promised relief for loose artificially inserted teeth, according to a method learned from the renowned Joseph Baker, surgeon dentist. Ingrafted teeth were best supplied direct from someone else's mouth; John Templeman (who was also a broker) advertised for live specimens, and Dr. Skinner promised "a generous price paid for Human Front Teeth perfectly sound." To improve vision, only bridge spectacles of uncertain stability and doubtful utility were available, on a trial and error basis.

No degree of preparation could mitigate the state of helpless dependence that followed with old age. Vain was the quest for security; mobility and change could erode alike children's love and gratitude and the worth of stored-up property. The dangers all foresaw none could forestall. Illness was frequent, and sometimes reverse of fortune led to poverty. Lacking the Old World's institutional safeguards, the individual could count on little support in moments of crisis.

In any case, concern about the grave, everyone's destination, was less pressing than worries about the dangers on the way—the strokes of bad luck and illness that deepened into poverty and disability. Travelers blamed ill health on the climate and on primitive medicine. Summer heat rose above one hundred degrees; winter cold fell below zero. Windows left open on a hot day admitted the piercing wind that shifted to the east—no wonder few escaped colds, the ague, flux. Vague calculations of the average life-span were less eloquent than the pervasive miseries all suffered.

Although itinerant healers guaranteed *no cure, no pay,* a doctor was usually the last resort. Every good housewife possessed a store of medical knowledge, often inherited, mingling common

sense, old wives' tales, and folk experience. Many Pennsylvania
Germans had themselves bled every year in May, as a precau-
tion. Numerous health manuals circulated in the colonies. One of
the most popular, John Wesley's *Primitive Physic*, intended for
the use of Methodists but useful to others as well, listed common
ailments, described symptoms, and prescribed remedies simple
enough to be mixed at home. Newspapers freely gave medical
advice, and many a printer stocked medicines along with other
wares. If these cures failed, the victim could always turn to the
almanac.

Widely used remedies varied in ingenuity as in effectiveness.
Turnip broth was good for coughs, cow dung poultice for
bruises, and rotten apples for sties. A mixture of garlic, pewter
scrapings, ale, and Venice treacle cured the bite of a mad dog—
nine tablespoons for humans, twelve for horses, four for hogs
and sheep. Dr. Walker's Jesuit Drops and Sheed's Specific Solu-
tion took care of the "unfriendly diseases" (syphilis and gonorrhea), as many testimonials could show but for the reluctance of
those made well to admit having suffered at all—so the advertisement went. Perkins' Metallic Tractors, long thin nails, promised relief from every pain when stroked over a sore spot. The
tractors sold for five guineas a pair and earned the inventor, a
native of Norwich, Connecticut, a small fortune. People in desperation turned to Turlington's Balsam of Life or to other herbs
and pills. When all else failed they prayed, sometimes ceaselessly
—visitors during the day, family members at night. God heals,
Franklin quipped, and the doctor takes the fees.

Well-informed invalids relied upon physicians, who usually
confined the patient to a tightly sealed room into which no fresh
air penetrated, hoping thereby to sweat out from the blood the
poisoned matter that was the cause of disease. In the sick chamber Dr. Rush treated nature as he "would a squalling cat—open
the door and drive it out." When necessary, bleeding, vomiting,
blistering, purging, and the use of saltpeter as a diuretic helped
nature on its way. If Benjamin Rowe died serene and calm, the
mind in peace, it was despite four years of illness with a dropsy
in the course of which he underwent sixty-seven times "the oper-

ation of Tapping" that drew from his body 2,385 pounds of water.

William Maclay of Pennsylvania suffered from the gout and also from the ministrations of two doctors. He learned immediately that the knee bothering him was the least of his problems; his entire body, indisposed, cried for attention. The blood needed alteration (with "antimonials"), the stomach wanted cleansing (by vomiting), and the knee required a poultice of Indian mush. With medications thrust at him from all sides, Maclay felt like a customer in a country store.

The unremitting concern with health expressed itself variously. Such a diarist as Landon Carter conscientiously noted the state of his bowels, its colic, motions, and commotions, and the effects of evacuants and astringents. In an attempt to rid himself of his "costive tendency," Carter kept track of his own daily functions ("three voluntary motions, the first really large . . . the others rapid and watery without any gryping"). At one point he discovered a cure that involved eating raw eggs, onions (to increase the motions), balsam, and a domestic elixir. By the twentieth day (when he was swallowing three egg yolks in addition to other medication), he informed his diary, "the wind run about my body like the rats behind a wainscot."

In addition to the colic and to a costive tendency (which called for purgings), Carter suffered from fevers (for which he took Elixir Vitriol), from a crick in the neck (treated with an "embrocation" made of ammoniac and olive oil), and from bad dreams (caused, he believed, by the colic). When not busy ministering to himself he oversaw the health of his slaves, assisted local doctors or quarreled with them about appropriate cures, performed operations on his dependents, supervised the pregnancies of his daughter-in-law, read numerous medical manuals, listened to his neighbors tell of their maladies, and speculated on bodily functions and the philosophy of medicine.

Concern with health dulled the emotions. Sensibilities toughened when tenderness became a source of infection. The deepest scars scabbed over with time, as parents learned to absorb the

loss of children, easy victims of disease and injury. Laconically
the gravestones explained:

> *grim death is come*
> *his life is called*
> *to take its flight*
> *the means—a scald.*

Or:

> *The oil of vitriol he did taste*
> *which caused his vitals for to waste*
> *And forced him to return again*
> *unto the earth from whence he came*

Infant mortality actually declined during the eighteenth century
and was lower in the colonies than in Europe, but the harrowing
experience of a child's death by infection, epidemic, exposure, or
accident spared few parents. Often mothers and fathers kept
vigil by a youngster's bedside for weeks or months, periods of
anticipatory mourning that eased the ultimate bereavement. Prolonged exposure to the unalleviated sufferings of a child sometimes made death a welcome relief and taught survivors how to
bear the stress.

Epidemics tore at the emotions. Smallpox made periodic fearsome appearances; in 1776 the commanders of the American expedition, reminded of the ravages it had made at home, re-
treated from Quebec at the first signs of an outbreak. When
yellow fever raged in the seaports, the survivors could not mourn
their losses in the haste to bury the dead.

The ordeal of inoculation against smallpox lost some of its terror when it became a social occasion. Whole families or groups
joined "to take the smallpox" either at hospitals like that at Point
Shirley near Salem, Massachusetts, or in private homes. The procedure, which infected patients with a touch of disease in order
to build immunity against a full attack, became, dangerous
though it was, an occasion for a prolonged vacation. A hierarchy
of retreats developed in which the rich got the operation "with-

out Mercury," and with food, lodging, medicine, and care, while more modest places offered only one sheet and a pillow case to a customer. Dr. Uriah Rogers of Fairfield, Connecticut, announced in 1767 that his establishment, not far from the harbor, took all care to make the process enjoyable for the price of Four Pounds Lawful Money. In 1772 Ibrahim Mustapha arrived in Boston calling himself former Inoculator to His Sublime Highness and the Janissaries. With his Circassian Needle, he claimed, he had treated 50,000 patients in Constantinople (without losing one). Mustapha allowed customers to choose for themselves how many pimples to have. He had eradicated smallpox throughout the Turkish Empire, he boasted, and wished to extend the benefit to the colonies.

Fear lest inoculation spread the disease acquired a political overtone. When a group of Norfolk, Virginia, gentlemen decided to immunize their families in 1768, they proposed to retire to a country house to undergo the ordeal together. An anti-inoculation group, led by patriots experienced in riots, identified the practice with loyalty to the Crown, and their attacks led to prolonged litigation and, in 1769, to the sacking of some homes.

Illnesses less precisely defined simply remained beyond comprehension. In Wethersfield, Connecticut, on the morning of December 11, 1782, William Beadle, an infatuated man, knocked his sleeping wife and two children in the heads with an ax, then cut their throats, went back to the kitchen, and, placing a pistol at each ear, pulled both triggers at once. The community could not understand the horrid sacrifice but firmly believed that the secret grave twice refused to welcome the madman's body. People cold-bloodedly accepted occasional suicides and gave little thought to moral or therapeutic treatment of the insane, who were confined to cellars and disciplined by whippings or purgings. Persons considered simple or idiotic wandered about, the subjects of rude jests, casual employment, charity, or mistreatment, alike thoughtless.

Callousness, on the surface at least, was the only defense against ill-defined maladies that swept through panicky settlements. The onset of any sickness in an isolated frontier cottage was a calamity so total that those who recovered could only shrug off the deaths of those who did not. Though the mortality rate was not high by the standards of Europe at the time, every loss threatened a thinly settled continent.

In former generations, death had been the threshold that opened into life eternal. Now it was a more casual acquaintance. Once a baby's death had exposed the devout to troubling issues of infant damnation, hell, and God's benevolence. Children, no longer incarnations of sin, now passed away in the certainty of salvation.

> *Christ took Small Infants in his Arms*
> *Such infants He will save,*

a rustic tomb proclaimed. The occasion for mourning, shrouded by custom, allayed the sense of permanent loss. Funerals had always been family gatherings, to which relatives traveled for miles to feast on lavish dinners at which liquor flowed freely, in accordance with the biblical injunction to give wine to those of heavy heart. Children, very much a part of these affairs, at an early age learned something about dying. Young Harry Carter wished that his turn might be next, so that he could be the center of attraction. For one nine-year-old boy the death of his father in 1770 came as a shock rather than as a source of poignant grief. The distress of the family and the dismal apparatus of coffins and hearses spread gloom. But the funeral honors, dispensed with an unsparing hand and with much pomp and expense, even though contrary to the will of the deceased, gave the occasion a festive tone.

During the war ostentatious gifts to participants in funerals went out of fashion. Occasional wills limited the sums to be spent for mourning rings, gloves, and scarves, and patriotic citizens agreed to use only locally manufactured products. Practical problems then seemed more important—how to preserve corpses on ice until the spring thaw permitted proper interment, how to prevent wolves and bears from digging them up through the use of a stone slab. All expressions of sentiment were rather detached, not far different from those with which a Pennsylvanian buried his poor cat that had been sick for some time past, by whom he had set store.

The casual acceptance of death owed something to the frequency with which it was incidental to the pervasive violence never far beneath life's surface. Rum and whiskey heated tempers, but even sober young Virginia gentlemen in a fistfight resorted to bruising, kicking, scratching, pinching, biting, butting, tripping, throttling, and gouging, egged on by the spectators.

People who defined justice by communal consensus rather than by code kept its administration in their own hands rather than delegating it to officials. Frontier districts therefore had no monopoly on vigilante action. The establishment of a private smallpox hospital on Cat Island in 1774 infuriated the people of Marblehead, Massachusetts. A mob tarred and feathered four men caught stealing from the hospital clothing that might spread the disease, then paraded the culprits through town to the accompaniment of fife and drums. Threats of violence forced the owners to close down the contagion center, and a convenient fire burned the structure to the ground after a rumor of its reopening. The arsonists, captured and jailed in Salem, found freedom when a crowd of Marbleheaders interceded and the sheriff thought it wisest not to pursue lest blood be spilled. The accused never came to trial.

The duel, the extreme form of personal and violent justice, remained a fashionable folly. Though the New England colonies legislated against it and Franklin, Jefferson, and Paine decried the absurd, gothic practice, Americans continued to respond to the demands of the code of honor. The shock that followed when Lachlan McIntosh in 1777 killed Button Gwinnett, patriots both, did not abate the calls to the gun and sword, any more than had earlier instances of mortal encounters of explosive consequence. In many parts of the country, honor, respect, reputation, and standing in the community still hinged upon acceptance of this convention.

Armed men threatened travelers everywhere (taking cash, silver buckles, surtouts, and coats). One gang operated in New Jersey, with connections to Philadelphia and New York, until broken up by the local citizenry. Another gang in Williamsburg in 1771 hid from pursuers among local householders and Negroes and concealed loot that included brass kettles, silver spoons, mugs, coins, and bills of credit. Horse and cattle stealing occurred everywhere.

The preservation of peace and order often required of the populace familiarity with the gun and the sword. The hue and cry of the posse, the town watch, and the county militia were the primary agents of law enforcement. The result dispersed the use of force in many hands rather than concentrating it in a few.

Punishment was retribution, cruelty commonplace. Pennsylvania, not the harshest of provinces, whipped, pilloried, and cropped the ears of horse thieves and cast into irons persons taken for passing counterfeit money. Elsewhere fines, duckings, lashings, mutilations, and hangings penalized cohabitation, fornication, quarreling, blasphemy, Sabbath breaking, and numerous felonies. Gashed flesh and spurts of blood aroused no qualms in people who gouged each other's eyes out in a fair fight or made a sport of baiting animals or watched spurred cocks tear at one another.

Fear restrained few from the resort to violence, for risk was an accepted condition of life. Daniel Morgan, who had left New Jersey at the age of eighteen to settle alone in the Shenandoah Valley, joined Edward Braddock's army as a wagoner and in 1756 thrashed a British lieutenant. In return Morgan received five hundred lashes applied to his back so vigorously that chunks of flesh the size of his thumb hung down in ribbons. He did not, because of that, shy away from a military career twenty years later.

Real war in 1775 came as no surprise to people inured by a hard life to the use of force. The conflict appalled only the Quakers; other men heeded the summons to battle out of patriotism, out of hope of glory, or out of boredom—the danger of loss of life was not a deterrent. By the same token they shipped out on privateers for a share of the prizes and embarked on long whaling voyages in the expectation of profit. Sailors had shunned service in the Royal Navy not out of concern with safety but because there was no gain in it for victims of the press gangs. Piracy declined after the middle of the eighteenth century less on account of its hazards or out of delicacy in the use of force than because substantial mercantile communities, dependent on respect for law, no longer tolerated it.

Anxieties fed from many sources in colonial experience added to the strain of rough American lives. Pervasive worries beset people whom neither secure families nor dependable standards of behavior guarded against shocking spurts of violence, against disease, against early death. Pressed at the same time to achieve, to make of themselves more than they were, they fell victims to a nagging discontent that only thought of a new start could relieve. Hence imaginations turned to the opportunities the West of a whole continent offered.

6

The Frontier

For generations, the mountains stood in the way. Indian captives, fur traders, and hunters brought back from the forests stories of the untracked slopes and rearing peaks, of a wild, weird land that seemed to lie sublime—out of space, out of time. Until the middle of the eighteenth century, however, ignorance shrouded the barriers and what lay beyond them. For the moment, the continent's vast interior was a concern for the future; there seemed room enough on the hither side of them.

Then this West had become the battle area in the clash of European empires. From Montreal the French had moved down the chain of rivers and lakes to establish a link with their base in New Orleans. In Florida the Spanish struggled to strengthen their hold on the southern flank of the colonies. And the British, hemmed in along the coast, had thrust outward, penetrating the mountains on their way to the great valley of the Ohio and its tributaries. The outcome of the contest, after 1763, gave Britain control of a vast inland domain. The Revolution transferred much of it to the American republic, exposing long-awaited opportunities to the grasp of restlessly daring invaders.

Before the intrusion of the Europeans this had been the home of scattered Indian tribes. Perhaps thirty thousand people occupied the whole area, about half of them south of the Ohio River. No tribe numbered more than five thousand, and some had only a few hundred members. None could muster the resources to resist the new occupants of the land. The culture of the aboriginal inhabitants had been traditional and static; when it changed, it did so through external pressure and in ways beyond their control. The economy, largely self-sufficient, rarely left surpluses capable of carrying these people from bad years to good and forced them into frequent migrations. Few as their numbers were, the tribes often impinged upon one another's space and drifted into intermittent warfare.

Indian life had always attracted some Europeans by its laxity, apparent ease, opportunity for adventure, and release from the cares and solicitudes of home; even transient travelers picked up squaws who fetched and saddled the horses, made the fires, cooked the food, and did other pleasing things. Nineteenth- and twentieth-century sentimentalists glowingly described tribal existence as a happy adjustment to the environment. That adjustment meant, in fact, inability to overcome the limits of surface resources. Rude agriculture supplemented by hunting and fishing neither permitted the number of "Redmen" to grow nor equipped them to cope with the harsh climate. Available clothing and shelter were sadly inadequate to guard against the frost and rain, the wind and storms that buffeted the region.

A handful of people in a vast space had only a vague sense of territorial boundaries, a fact that would cost them dear in the future. Each tribe had a feeling for the place to which it belonged, but that area faded off indecisively into grounds controlled by others; and from time to time, shifts in location obscured even that limited awareness of geography. Ownership had little significance in so empty an area, and there were no recognized means of making either individual or tribal decisions about the precise character of possessions. A sparse population, lacking any concept of trespass, welcomed transient strangers and readily adopted those who wished to stay. This culture, which measured distance in terms of time rather than of space, so that the number of acres was meaningless, equipped few members mentally for the bargaining problems when dealing with advancing European settlers and speculators. The Indians learned too late.

Nor had the scattered warriors developed political organizations for successful self-defense. Tribal units were small, guided by the aged, and bound by tradition. The most advanced group, the Iroquois, had worked out a larger structure which, however, left a good deal of discretion to the constituent subgroups; and powerful though the confederation was, it was slow to make and execute decisions. Internecine conflicts, though common, did not involve space; the ample land permitted compromise in boundary disputes. War was rather a kind of game that established the warriors' images of themselves, and fighting tended to extend beyond the bounds dictated by rational considerations. Long-range goals rarely shaped general tribal policy.

Danger from the encroaching whites spurred on attempts to develop a larger sense of confederation. The spread of British control beyond the mountains awakened the Ottawa chief Pontiac to the need. A skilled orator and a warrior of repute, he traveled through the interior in 1763, appealing to the Indians' sense of common identity and purpose or at least of common grievances. His exhortations persuaded the tribesmen to launch a coordinated attack against the settlements along a thousand-mile front from the Great Lakes to Virginia; some two thousand white intruders fell victims to these assaults. But the ultimate defeat of the confederation and, in 1769, the death of its leader ended effective, large-scale resistance.

Little local alliances appeared from time to time, but from the point of view of the individual tribe it made as much sense to enter upon treaties with the Europeans as with other Indians. Until 1763 the French actively sought allies from their base in Canada, as did Spanish agents in the South. After mid-century the British did the same through two organized districts, each with a competent superintendent of Indian affairs: in the North Sir William Johnson, and in the South John Stuart. Molly Brant, Mohawk-born mistress of Sir William's mansion and mother of his eight natural children, was living evidence of the bond between reds and whites.

European missionary activities also created ties between the two peoples. Catholic priests had carried the gospel into the wilderness from French and Spanish bases since the seventeenth century; in the British areas the task of converting the savages remained a challenge. Representatives of the Crown and occasional devoted settlers labored to spread Christianity and Western civilization to the Indians. The vision of conversion also brought to America the United Brethren, German Moravians, who more easily won over the Indians than did the hostile white settlers, who wished only to be rid of the native possessors of the soil. The missionaries succeeded in building posts at Gnadenhutten and elsewhere on the western Pennsylvania frontier. One European visitor found greater regularity, order, and decorum in the churches there than in any other place of worship he had ever seen.

Some whites arrived for commercial motives, for the moment, at least, more welcome. These strangers came on errands of peace and brought with them goods that the tribespeople had not even known they wanted but that, once glimpsed, became objects of their avid desire—cloth to wear, alcohol to drink, knives of steel, and guns and powder. In return the traders asked only for fur, available in the thick woods for the taking.

For more than a century the fur trade had moved west as the forest receded and with it the beaver and the deer. The hunters and the trappers led a life apart. With the first signs of fall they loaded packsaddles with flour, Indian meal, and blankets and began the chase, searching out their prey in the sheltered places of the forest. The woodsmen earned a reputation for savagery. Benjamin Franklin expressed the common view that they were greater barbarians than the Indians. A buckskin was a combination "betwixt a man and a beast."

A motley group of dealers followed close by, men of every ethnic antecedent, working out of the seaboard colonies and Canada. In the 1740s the Scotch-Irish George Croghan made long circuits deep into the Ohio country from Pennsylvania, bringing back bundles of pelts for export to England. Among the important middlemen were the German-born Conrad Weiser and Jews such as Chapman Abram and the Gratz brothers. After 1763 Pensacola and Mobile joined Augusta, Georgia, as starting points for southwestern fur operations. Experienced traders like Croghan and such large Philadelphia houses as Baynton, Wharton & Morgan wanted government control of traffic into the interior to preserve peaceful relationships with their Indian suppliers. The idea also pleased the British agents Johnson and Stuart. But no system of regulation developed; entry into the business was too easy to yield to rules. Anyone with a bit of capital could get in, and every frontier farmer, in the nature of the case, was a potential sutler, swapping for furs with the nearby Indians. Temptation often drew "cracking traders" over the line between sharp dealing and fraud. Integrity seemed wasted on savages not recognized as neighbors, whose lands were the object of envious attention. Bitter disputes followed.

Colonists already in the West or eager to get there would not allow the remote imperial government to determine the fate of these domains. The royal ministers wanted peace, which would spare them the expense of maintaining garrisons in the interior. Recognition of Indian territorial rights seemed a modest price for calm and had the support of powerful fur-trading interests anxious to preserve the wilderness intact as a source of the flow of skins. Then, too, London officials doubted that they could control large numbers of settlers far from the centers of power and regarded with concern the prospect of any precipitate westward rush by Europeans. More than a century of experience had demonstrated the difficulties of ruling a remote population; people out of reach of the law slipped into a disorderly way of life, while the structure of authority crumbled. Much better, once the French threat disappeared, to confine settlements to the east of the mountains—for some generations at least. Several statesmen and merchants in the mother country argued that the empire would gain more by opening the area than by keeping it closed. Expansion might increase colonial population and thereby create a great future market for goods manufactured in Britain. But at the moment the odds favored restraint. Impatient Americans saw the issue more simply: they resented any obstacle to satisfaction of their land hunger. The makers of western policy thus felt the pressure of complex forces—from settlers, Indians, merchants, and officials, but also from subgroups within each category on both sides of the Atlantic.

Caught between conflicting demands, the imperial government procrastinated. It intended as provisional the proclamation line of 1763 that held settlement back east of the Alleghenies. Later it would decide on some firmer, more durable policy. But the interval of postponement stretched out for more than a decade. Then, to the dismay of Americans impatient with delays, the Quebec Act of 1774 threw the whole area north of the Ohio River into the province of Quebec and made it forever Canadian, foreclosing the possibility of farther advance from the east. The British handed a vast domain to a traditional foe, intending it to remain thinly settled, French, and Catholic.

Let the government in London plan what it would; other forces decided the outcome. Yankee farmers cramped within their rocky hills; Virginia planters wearied of tobacco, which exhausted their fields and drew them into debt; Europeans dazzled by New World visions; merchants who imagined the advance of armies of buyers and sellers into the unpopulated distance; lawyers eager to be judges; clergymen persuaded of the need to diffuse their faith—all turned their eyes to the mountains. In vain Virginia governors thundered against "this enthusiasm of running backwards" to hunt for fresh lands. Restlessness engrafted in their nature convinced Americans of the superiority of the places farther off over those they occupied. No document from the pen of an alien minister could deny them hope—not though it issue with the approval of King and Parliament.

In 1763 the expulsion of the French from the Northwest and the Spaniards from Florida had suddenly revealed space in all its amplitude. Like a discovery afresh of the continent, it set people free from their surroundings, giving them a sense of primitive, unattached being, all potentiality, no limits. From Robert Rogers, whom he met at Mackinac deep in the interior, the Yankee explorer Jonathan Carver glimpsed the possibility of further discoveries; renewed visions of a Northwest Passage opening upon trade for the riches of China gleamed in the book he published in 1778.

A nagging prospect of opportunity put families on edge. Those near the wilderness began to spin plans for its conquest; those farther off dreamed of the possibilities. For years impatient settlers waited to move into an area they considered vacant, away from the disadvantages of their own places. The imagined virtues of the West goaded the colonists on; and removal of the French obstacle allowed them to enter, or seemed to do so. Moreover, ignorance of geography was no longer an impediment; travelers by then had located the mountain gaps and had revealed how the Ohio and its tributaries provided entry to the region.

The possibilities turned many into speculators. In this time for dreams in vast dimensions, impatience mounted with every new thought of what might be. Companies formed to get into the area, some with charters from the royal or provincial governments, some without; the rival claims soon covered hundreds of thousands of acres. The Ohio, the Loyal, and the Grand Ohio, the Vandalia, the Illinois, the Transylvania, the Susquehanna, and the Delaware drew together motley groups of royal favorites, parliamentary maneuverers, friends of the governors, big men in the colonial assemblies, partners in fur-trading enterprises, and influential local worthies, united in various combinations by the exhilarating expectation of great gains. Schemes multiplied after the Revolution, although with a different cast of characters; and the promoters both stimulated and directed the flow of settlers.

The land was there, empty; thousands of families waited to use it. They regarded concern for the interests of a few savages and fur traders as but the excuse of dilatory, corrupt officials. Impatient settlers poured in, despite proclamations, disregarding inconvenient rules made in London and the titles of speculators who held tracts simply for future gain.

For a time the migrants pushed south and north as well as west. Florida, ceded by Spain in 1763, boomed. Andrew Turnbull, a Scottish physician inspired by imperial visions, led hundreds of Greeks, Italians, Corsicans, and Minorcans to a death trap in New Smyrna, East Florida, where starvation, heat, cruel overseers, mosquitoes, malaria, and Indians plunged all into ruin.

Nevertheless, some four hundred families left Connecticut for other parts of Florida in 1773 and 1774. Meanwhile the spread of settlers away from the coast of Georgia swiftly expanded the population of that province, which attracted hundreds of Irish as well as thousands of people from bordering colonies.

Yankees also moved eastward along the coast into Maine, many holding land grants for military service; ninety-four new towns appeared in the district between 1759 and 1776. In time, New Englanders also pushed farther east to pitch on the improbable soil of Nova Scotia. Still others made their way up the Connecticut and Housatonic valleys into the region then in dispute between New Hampshire and New York that would later become Vermont. By 1776 that area held some 20,000 people in seventy-four towns.

But always, in actuality as in imagination, the West exercised the most powerful attraction, as if to provide evidence for the savant's theory that the earth's eastward rotation drew man ever westward like a squirrel in a cage. The movement involved at first a trickle, then larger numbers. Gaps in the mountains directed the flow across the frontier; and the military roads cut by the army during the war against the French eased travel after 1763.

In the North, the settlers had already come up the Hudson and had inched along the Mohawk River, thus discovering the sea-level route to the Great Lakes. From Philadelphia the advance had gone by way of Harrisburg and York toward the Ohio country and down toward western Virginia. Connecticut people, mobilized by the Susquehanna and Delaware companies, laid out scores of farms in Pennsylvania's Wyoming Valley. Within a very short time they engaged in the timber trade, erected sawmills, and began to float black walnut and other logs down the river in rafts. Nearby, they also found sea coal near the surface, which they hauled in boats brought alongside or close to the deposits.

Meanwhile English, Welsh, German, Scottish, and Scotch-Irish settlers had come down the Great Valley of the Shenandoah; and Virginians had moved up the James, the Potomac, and the Roanoke and were in process of discovering the way in which the tributaries of the Tennessee and Cumberland also poured via these rivers into the Ohio. In 1769 a party of Marylanders followed Evan Shelby to settle on the south fork of the Holston, in what became eastern Tennessee, and Carolina people dribbled over into the same area. By 1772 the nearby settlements along the Watauga River were strong enough to form an association for self-government under the leadership of James Robertson, an early settler of Nashville, experienced in the defiance of authority as a North Carolina Regulator.

Every manner of person joined Yankees and southerners in the migration. One group of fourteen that entered the Ohio country in 1775 consisted of two Englishmen, two Irishmen, one Welshman, two Dutchmen, two Virginians, two Marylanders, one Swede, one African Negro, and one mulatto. Since early in the eighteenth century the American wilderness had provided homes to thousands of immigrants who had clung to their Scottish Presbyterianism after generations of residence in northern Ireland. The Scotch-Irish, dissatisfied with the Anglicanism of Virginia and the quitrents paid the Pennsylvania proprietor, drifted down the Great Valley to the North Carolina backcountry. Their paths crossed those of natives of Ireland, Germany, and the Scottish Highlands.

Migration to the frontier expanded patterns of movement already familiar in the East. Every town and every county was both a loser and a gainer of population: departures left space and opportunity for new arrivals. Massachusetts families entered Connecticut, the residents of which spread to Pennsylvania and Florida. Pennsylvanians came down to the western Carolinas, while people from those colonies moved to regions later to become Kentucky and Tennessee. And adding everywhere to the unsettling pressure were boatload after boatload of Europeans in quest of a promised land.

Travel remained hazardous, whether by land or water, whether by wagon, with packhorse, on foot, by canoe, or by raft. On hilly terrain, even paths wide enough to accommodate a wagon concealed perilous spots. The only means of braking a vehicle on the downhill stretches was to trail logs behind in the hope of slowing the descent. On sharp turns the passengers, if forewarned, got out to pull on side stay ropes to keep the vehicle from tumbling over. The more prudent voyagers used packhorses.

The undaunted pressed on. In 1784 the Wilkeson family headed west from Carlisle, Pennsylvania. The parents, three children, and a fourteen-year-old bound boy made up the party. Mother and infant perched on one horse, surrounded by the table and cooking equipment. A second bore all the food and agricultural tools. A third carried two creels, woven of hickory withes, loaded with bedding and clothing, out of each of which projected the head of a laced-in child. A cow meandered along as the party moved up and over passes and across running streams to its new home.

Colonel John Donelson, one of the founders of Nashville, came with his daughter, Rachel, on a flatboat down the Tennessee along with a group of other families. Indians plagued them most of the way and massacred the occupants of one craft, entangled in weeds along the riverbank. The others, floating by, observed the dread warriors moving along the shore, waiting for an opportunity to attack. Before the journey ended, jagged rocks had sunk several boats, and with provisions exhausted and crews worn out by hunger and fatigue, many yielded their lives to snow and frost. Rachel later communicated the horrors of the voyage to her husband, Andrew Jackson.

Some wanderers, at one remove or several, approached the Edenic refuge they had long sought. An observer noted in the Shenandoah Valley able, active, and handsome young men and women, such as he had seen no place before, products of abundant food and milk and of a healthy situation among the mountains and pure waters. When all went well, the new arrivals found tracts laid out, drew lots for particular plots, and proceeded to build shelters and plant crops. The population of Virginia's Great Valley more than doubled between 1763 and 1776. Crops of wheat, subsidized hemp, and ginseng provided a nice return, supplemented by animal husbandry, while an iron mill supplied the area with plows and other utensils. Isaac Zane, proprietor of the mill, built a mansion surrounded by fountains, orchards, gardens, fishpond, bath, icehouses, still, smithy, sawmill, stores, and stables.

Trails broadened into roads, not by planned construction but by the passage of travelers. From Philadelphia a way led through Lancaster, York, Hagerstown, Winchester, and Staunton more than four hundred miles to the Yadkin River, in North Carolina, and thence by Boone's Wilderness Road on into Kentucky. Soon wagons carried thriving crops to markets and returned with unfamiliar or forgotten luxuries. At the first encounter with tea, one wife drank the liquid as a broth while the husband ate the leaves as a green; in time both learned the uses of a nonalcoholic substitute for grog.

Roads that formerly led to remote places now passed through nearby towns. The fortified post, the trader's store, the county courthouse attracted a cluster of buildings—a tavern for the passersby, a church or chapel, an occasional craftsman's shop. Slowly cities took form. Ten years after its transfer to the British, Fort Pitt boasted thirty houses, and Harrodsburg, Kentucky, and Wilkes-Barre, Pennsylvania, were not far behind. Now and then a minister arrived, and a physician, to help save souls and bodies, and occasionally a schoolmaster, while the presence of judges attracted lawyers. Stable communities appeared. The little cities drew their residents into nascent societies. The presence of a garrison, as at Fort Pitt, sparked efforts to organize dances and other entertainments; and with time landowners, traders, and lawyers—and their wives—began to form a local gentry.

The process was swift in those Yankee settlements which came intact from New England. Former neighbors, moving together, carried with them family ties, common habits and attitudes, and memories of shared worship. They supported one another in times of need, and the power of approval and disapproval established a consensus of desirable modes of behavior; fixed the responsibilities of parents, children, husbands, and wives; and made some provision for appropriate schooling and religious services. The German sects that migrated as groups, as did the Salzburgers to Ebenezer (Effingham County), Georgia, also held together in the process of resettlement.

Elsewhere, frontier communities gained cohesion and established discipline among their members more slowly. In the South, movement was by individuals, drawn to a future less of towns than of landed estates. Joseph Kershaw, an immigrant from Yorkshire, left Charleston, South Carolina, in 1758 to establish Camden in the west. But his earnings went into the twenty thousand acres and seventy slaves he owned by the time of the Revolution. John Chestnut, a Virginian who got his start in Kershaw's store, came to possess ten thousand acres and twenty-six slaves. Here in the upcountry, clannishness was often the only stabilizing force. As some British administrators had feared, many settlements fell into rough, disorderly, and brutal ways. They varied greatly, according to the circumstances of their establishment and the character of their founders. But all shared the general traits of societies formed in defiance of authority: an unwillingness to accept orders from outside, a disposition to improvise, and a stubborn insistence on autonomy.

Weakened by distance and by the uncongenial environment, eastern restraints fell away everywhere along the frontier. In a home only eighteen miles north of Albany, Ann Eliza Bleecker recalled the horrors of the dark forest, infested by wolves and bears that growled at her very dooryard. Affliction broke her spirit. She suffered a nervous collapse, grew daily weaker, more emaciated, depressed, then died at the age of thirty-one.

To survive, people learned to tread alertly where copperheads might be, to disregard July mosquitoes, and, undismayed by fleas, to rise in the morning spotted and bepurpled like a person with measles. Families made themselves comfortable in cabins built of felled logs, with bare earth for floors. Two young trees, cut down entire and set up at the end walls, supported the ridgepole. Bark laid out like shingles formed the roof. Windows made of paper coated with hog's lard let in the light. Clay chinking between the logs to keep away the winter was knocked out in the summer for ventilation and light. One long room in the interior served all purposes, equipped as it was with a bed, split-bottomed chairs, and a large puncheon on four legs that could be either bench or table. The fastidious could sweep the cabin with a turkey-wing brush. But Delftware or other crockery pieces soon crumbled and in any case were too small to satisfy hearty appetites. More often, clam shells set in split sticks served as spoons and gourds as bowls. The Zanes were well off. But most of their neighbors in the Shenandoah Valley lacked any kitchen utensils, few had chairs or tables, and not many had beds, having learned to cook Indian fashion, to sit on stools sawed from logs, and to sleep in bunks nailed up in the corners. Clothing was equally simple: leather hunting shirts, leggings, and moccasins for men, homespun jean trousers, cotton stripes, and linsey-woolsey for women. Imported calico for a dress was a rare luxury.

Food at first was what the wilderness supplied: lean venison, wild turkey, some bear, fish, and later pork. Potatoes, pumpkins, squash, and corn—grated on a perforated tin when dry and baked into johnnycakes—filled out the larder. Treasured salt arrived on packhorses from as far away as Augusta, Richmond, or Lancaster, at great expense. Families that got only a pound a year or less invented other methods to preserve food. Meat packed in wood ashes, then washed in boiling water and smoked over a fire, survived almost as well as when salted. Roots gathered in the forests, dried, and browned over heat supplied the essence for ordinary nonalcoholic drinks. Adults treated themselves to coffee or tea and to sugar, drawn from the maple, on Sundays or such special occasions as weddings or christenings.

Outside the Yankee areas, few churches rose in the wilderness. In the southern backcountry, Presbyterians such as James Waddell preached under the trees; and Baptist enthusiasts held forth against gambling, dancing, and Sunday diversions. But the established clergymen, though few in number, all too frequently brought with them or earned unsavory reputations. Gatherings were less often the occasion for worship than for heavy drinking, racing, cockfighting, and shooting.

Charles Woodmason, a priest who came to the wild Carolina backcountry to advance the interests of the Church of England, left a bitter description of the conditions he found. "Herds of Sectaries" from New England and Pennsylvania, bad weather, and irreligion defeated his efforts. The people living in the Back Parts frequently interrupted his discourses against vice and immorality and threatened him with physical abuse, once obliging him to cut his way through a swamp and pass through some woods, so that he tore his clothes to pieces. Hunger and cold were his lot. Unable to eat local cookery, "being exceedingly filthy and most execrable," Woodmason developed a paranoid streak. The Presbyterians, he believed, hired ruffians to insult him, calling him a D——d Black Gown Son of a Bitch. They intercepted letters announcing the time of his arrival, and when he appeared no congregation was there. They also arranged the robbery of his home. Presbyterian guides gave him wrong directions, while others carried away the meetinghouse keys and once set fifty-seven dogs loose among the congregation.

Overdrawn as it was, Woodmason's choleric account reflected reality. In the absence of guidelines, confused people floundered and, in their ignorance, behaved in fashions that shocked transient visitors. A bewildered Englishman considered the alternate weeping and drinking by mourners at an infant's funeral on the Monongahela as bizarre as the woman who served three brothers and a nephew as mistress. Here as in many other places, there was no one to preside over marriages, births, or deaths, or even to record those occurrences. The minister, passing through a settlement and administering marriage vows to brides who seemed extraordinarily large, judged them all "Rogues and Whores." The fact that they bothered to come before him at all revealed a flickering spark of respectability.

Lack of a blessing in church further unsettled family life, none too stable in the East. On the frontier some men chose to lay down the burden of parenthood and skip out for the woods—as did the father who left behind Big Harpe and Little Harpe, who grew up bandits, the scourges of Tennessee. Accidents and illness left widows in desperate search of any helpmate, and offspring in the casual charge of relatives, neighbors, or no one at all. In the absence of communal controls, children, as naked and fully as nasty as the local pigs, educated themselves, learning the lessons of the forest rather than those of the book. Woodmason, ever sanguine, planned a school but could not prevent the local tavern keeper from turning the building into a stable; and in any case, only three of two hundred boys appeared, while the rest ran wild like Indians.

Frontier life forged courageous and resourceful women, as

self-reliant, if they survived, as the men. Harsh conditions, primitive hazards, the lack of goods, great empty distances, and poor roads forced them to do everything themselves. Man and wife shared duties; the old divisions of labor did not hold. Women who learned to handle guns, to trap and hunt, and to defend the homestead against marauders had no time for the fashionable "vapours and hysterick Fits" of ladies in the East. Nevertheless, the absence both of close family to whom to turn for help and of restraints that protected females in more stable communities often, on the frontier, increased their dependence on men. Feelings of helplessness and power, of resentment and gratitude, of hatred and love, and above all of common needs infused conjugal relationships under these conditions.

Hardship bred superstition and fostered strange customs. A sick woman ought not to get out of bed on Sunday, or she would never get well. A calamity would befall the family that failed to complete its household tasks before certain dates. And no housewife on the Pennsylvania frontier cleaned her cabin on Ascension Day lest it become infested with fleas. On St. Andrew's Night, young women might glimpse the faces of their future husbands; and eating a salt cake, then going to bed backwards without drinking or speaking, guaranteed them rosy dreams.

The habits of home dropped away. In the Ohio country, men's garments—breechcloths, leggings, and hunting shirts—got a washing when rain caught their owners without shelter; otherwise, the same grime spread across the skin worn and that of the wearer. Farther south, men could not keep their eyes on the preacher, for the women, "many very pretty," came to church "barefoot and Bare legged—without Caps or Handkerchiefs," literally "in a State of Nature for nakedness counted as Nothing" in a society where everyone slept in the same room and dressed openly in front of others.

Trained physicians appeared but rarely on the frontier, unless in disgrace in the East or drawn by some wild speculative impulse. With reason, sufferers from pervasive maladies preferred to rely on folk remedies or on the counsel of their own trusted quacks.

Miseries yielded most readily to doses of alcohol. Seasons of high emotion—days, festive or sad, of worship or reflection, of birth or death—reminded men and women of past partings, of places left behind and others not yet reached, of the transience of all things, including themselves, and kindled a pain that only the fiery draft would quench. Whiskey from the stills or brandy from the fruit trees offered a kind of communion incomprehensible to the minister who perceived the congregation hollering and yelling in the street, reveling, drinking, dancing, and whoring in the fields. The Presbyterian preacher, ranting under the trees about hell and salvation, had more to say to people such as these than any doctor of divinity.

In the absence of firm, proximate authority, the settlements lacked dependable means of coping with crime. Horse and cattle thieves swept by, and banditti robbed all the houses while people attended church. The only reliable defense against robbery was a paucity of possessions. Ominous events shocked a whole region. It might have been one of his parishioners, angered at the effort to introduce a new psalm book, who lashed the bridle around the neck of the murdered Waxhaw, South Carolina, minister, or it might have been his widow, who married a nearby landowner in indecent haste. No one ever knew, for the woman's hand had failed to bleed when placed upon the dead man's decaying skull.

Easily triggered violence flared out at the least provocation and all too often rewarded those who first unleashed it. People who amused themselves in sport by tearing off a gander's greased neck and expressed hostility to neighbors by eye-gouging, Pennamites (Pennsylvanians) who made war with Yankees in bloody battle at Muncy and Rampart Rocks, in Pennsylvania's Wyoming Valley, felt no restraint whatever in dealing with the Indians. At best, innocent misunderstanding and divergent modes of behavior plagued the relations of white and red men and women. The tribesmen could not make head or tail of the English common law or of the concepts of contract or family. And local juries rarely convicted settlers of offenses, even murders, when Indians were the victims. The intent of the government counted for nothing in the face of the frontiersmen's wishes.

Greed gathered up the stray wisps of violence into storms of war. Down in Georgia and the Carolinas, vivid memories smoldered for decades of the two-year conflict with the Cherokees that had erupted in 1759. In 1774 Dr. John Connolly, a wild Irishman, commander of Fort Pitt under Virginia authority, rebuffed the Kentucky Shawnees who asked protection against attacks by settlers. The Indians—their lands, their very lives at stake—fought back but, isolated, could not win and in the end gave up Kentucky, which, all along, had been the object of their antagonists' lust.

Well before 1776 Americans had shown the disposition to take the law into their own hands and to deny the legitimacy of any power other than that to which they themselves had consented. Distance generally enabled them to make their will felt. Up in the New Hampshire grants, determined bands of Yankees calling themselves the Green Mountain Boys ousted the New York landlords, laid out their own towns, and defied the sheriff and the Crown. They followed the example of the Massachusetts men who had intruded upon the claims of the lords of Philipse and Livingston manors and refused to pay rent as tenants. In Pennsylvania the Paxton Boys, angered at their underrepresentation and at the softness of the province toward the Indians, wiped out a village of "Redmen" and had started to march on Philadelphia when Franklin's diplomacy headed them off.

Regulators attempting to root out corruption controlled the west of North Carolina between 1768 and 1771, closing down the courts they believed easterners dominated. Although the province finally crushed the uprising at the battle of the Alamance, a new royal governor in 1772 conceded that the insolence and cruel advantage taken of people's ignorance by mercenary, tricking attorneys, clerks, and other little officers who practiced every sort of extortion had provoked resistance. Many Regulators came out in support of the royal government during the Revolution. Others subscribed to the principles of the Mecklenburg Resolves (May 1775), which pointed toward independence.

In South Carolina, on the other hand, the Regulators resented the government's slowness in creating a court system and administered justice on their own. There the more prosperous inhabitants used force to reproduce patterns of obedience and respect familiar from the East in order to control outlaw bands, horse thieves, counterfeiting drifters, miscellaneous bruisers, and runaway slaves.

Before 1774, and after, some personality types, passing through the filter of the frontier experience, thrived; others either never got through or perished in the hostile environment. Those who moved were the most restless at home, the least like contented yeomen, the most eager for newness—of opportunity, of space, of perspective; also the most willing to take the risk of setting forth. The same attributes furthered success after arrival. The frontier people were the extreme cases of the character the New World fostered and, in that sense, the most similar to Americans of the future.

Before its people gave a name to the United States they had already developed a new society indigenous to the soil. Here emerged a fresh breed of humans, self-reliant, rationalistic, disdainful of established ideas and authorities, vain, provincial, sometimes violent, often reckless. Buoyed by a sense of unlimited power, they boasted as glibly of the ability to throttle a bear bare-handed as to subdue a royal regiment single-handed. Such people appeared almost everywhere, but more particularly on the frontier.

Ethan Allen was the model of a Yankee frontiersman. Born in 1738 in Connecticut, he and his two brothers in the 1760s had secured title from New Hampshire to a large holding in an area also claimed by New York, which set its eastern boundary at the Connecticut River. For years the Green Mountain Boys, led by the Allens, carried on an intermittent border war with that colony. They turned unhesitatingly against the Crown, out of sympathy with other Yankees, out of native suspicion of remote authority, and out of calculation that they could thus best make good their claims against the Yorkers. Their blustering, self-confident leader Ethan in May 1775 led an expedition that captured Fort Ticonderoga. His later military career was not as auspicious. Nor did he make as much of his speculative holdings as he had wished; Vermont was on the way to establishing its independence when he died in 1789, but his hopes of riches had by then dissolved. Meanwhile he had drifted into deism, although the book he claimed he wrote, *Reason, the Only Oracle of Man*, was largely the work of his friend Dr. Thomas Young Prentiss. Self-assertive, calculating, rational, but rarely successful: these traits of Ethan Allen matched features of the emerging popular image of the frontiersman.

Daniel Boone shared some of those traits and to them added a preference for isolation and detachment. For years he roamed the wilderness, hunting and trapping. Such wandering had been no novelty to him, for his family had earlier moved from Pennsylvania to the North Carolina frontier. In 1755, when Boone was about twenty years old, he had joined Braddock's unfortunate campaign and had learned something of the Ohio country. In the decades after the defeat he remained restless until the Transylvania Company in 1775 asked him to lead a group of settlers westward to Kentucky, where he established Boonesboro. Captured by Indians, who held him for five months, Boone returned to help beat off a new attack by the tribesmen. He gained little by the whole endeavor and continued to drift ever farther west, until he died in Missouri. But Boone had opened up the region and popularized it with the stories of his dramatic escape.

George Rogers Clark, another personal failure, nevertheless contributed substantially to expansion. He would die in 1818, a lonely alcoholic whose speculative ventures had come to naught. Almost a half century earlier, in 1772, at the age of twenty, Clark had entered the old northwest as a surveyor for the Ohio Company. The vision of that region stayed in his mind after the outbreak of the Revolution, and he resolved to dislodge the British troops and their Indian allies then in control. In 1777 he led a small force of militiamen into the Illinois country, captured the British posts at Kaskaskia and Vincennes, and by years of fighting made the area safe for settlement.

The interplay of personality and environment fitted Allen, Boone, and Clark for encounters with the frontier but not for the settled life that followed. So, too, frontier communities produced no political novelties; except for Vermont no new state appeared during the Revolution despite many futile plans for their formation. That evolution would come later in the years of peace. The turbulent, restless types who cleared the way rarely enjoyed the fruits of their striving; the discontent that drew them on prevented them from settling down.

The grasping yet sentimental people reared in precarious frontier communities plagued by difficulties about family, church, law, power, and authority long remained an unstable factor in American life. Young Andrew Jackson grew up in one such region, a place of violence, the force of which mounted during the war and remained after the peace, offspring of folk many times transplanted—from Scotland to Ulster to Pennsylvania, thence by the great wagon road to the North Carolina backcountry. His parents had settled in the Waxhaws, a river valley devastated by the Cherokee War a few years earlier and still unstable.

Germans, Swiss, Scotch-Irish, and Virginians in the Waxhaws fell into frequent quarrels the courts could not handle, and bloodshed became an accepted way to resolve conflicts. Those realities drove people's thoughts inward. Safety lay in clannishness, though many a man discovered that he had misplaced even the trust placed in his own kin.

Andrew's birth in 1767, two months after the death of his father, led into a turbulent youth, commonplace in violence, deficient in discipline or guidance. Victim of a skin disorder known only as the "big itch," he also slobbered, and a quick temper plunged him into frequent fights. Jackson learned little more than to read and write and spent his time in horse racing.

The Revolutionary War was even more vicious in the Waxhaws than elsewhere on the frontier, implicating the Indians and dividing neighbors. Imprisoned at the age of fourteen, Andrew earned a deep scar from a British officer's sword for refusing to play the servant and lost a brother and his mother to smallpox that he ascribed to the war. An unhappy youth spent in this environment left its mark on the future President, as it did on his countrypeople.

Looking back, after 1783, Americans would subtly change their perception of the frontier experience. The frontiersmen in retrospect would become native heroes, uniquely American and representative of the best for which the nation stood. Selective memory would transform them from fugitives from civilization— vile rascals, drunkards, and wretches—into its cultural vanguard —pathfinders and pioneers, the advance men of the conquest of the West.

Crèvecoeur had a more balanced view. He still saw the frontiersman living in a condition of nature "a perfect state of war, that of man against man," molding a type that was "ferocious, gloomy, lawless, and vicious." But people of that type were also pathetically eager to bring to the backwoods inherited notions of family life and property. The redeeming tension between wildness and order created a truly new civilized world, Crèvecoeur believed. Analogous tensions turned the battlefields of the revolutionary decade into another test of national character.

7
War

Imperceptibly, violence passed into war. Resistance deepened into habit. Unruly men and women formerly swept along in mobs became formal fighting units incorporated in the militia or enrolled in the continental line. The sporadic acts of individuals fell into a larger pattern when commands issued from governments that claimed legitimacy—towns, assemblies, congresses. Well before the decision for independence, Americans fired the shots heard round the world at Lexington and Concord in April 1775. Much changed in the years that followed, not from planning, but from the unforeseen consequences of little steps taken to meet the necessities of the moment.

The little steps were such as restless men and women took whose inner eyes fixed upon dreams of achievement and whose hearts dared risk movement toward the unknown. America slipped toward chaos after the unpremeditated break with the mother country. Suffering spread. Illusions collapsed. Unanticipated costs mounted. Yet the rebels survived the effects of deprivation and muddled through the economic and social disorder. The habit of taking chances, the incessant gamble of everyday life, had taught them to shrug off the odds and to dare reach for the distant prize.

After 1775 force became paramount even in areas remote from the fields of battle. Power, now exercised in the name of the King or of the People, legitimized the extraordinary use of violence. Unintimidated, Jonathan Boucher preached in 1775 with a brace of loaded pistols on the cushioned seat beside him. New York City lost half of its population between the firing at Lexington and the conclusion of peace, and other cities suffered almost as badly. The proximity of the enemy plunged York, Virginia, for example, into confusing bustle: sailors, soldiers, marines, boatmen, British merchants, American speculators, Jews, infidels, Negroes rushed about—so bemixed, behurried, befrightened, and bedeviled that nothing short of Hogarth's pencil could do justice to the scene.

The rhetoric of the day relied heavily on images of horror and terror. With relish, Joseph Warren's oration after the Boston Massacre portrayed the melancholy walk of death, summoned gay companions to drop farewell tears upon a body recently vigorous and warm, asked tender mother and widowed mourner to weep over beloved son and husband gasping on the ground, and, to complete the display of wretchedness, besought tiny infant children to bewail their father's fate, cautioning the babes lest, while their streaming eyes were fixed upon the ghastly corpse, their feet slide on the stones bespattered with their parent's brains. A fast-day sermon warned Americans that after a British victory they would be drawn on hurdles to the place of execution, hanged awhile by the neck, then taken down and their bowels removed to be burned before their eyes, then beheaded and quartered, with the limbs disposed of at the King's pleasure.

The shuddery thrill of the words edged often to the verge of reality. The Massachusetts woman left alone in charge of the farm could not tell whether the intruder who threatened to blow her brains out unless she supplied dinner and a horse was a soldier or a bandit. She fled his dreadful language and frightful looks, but thereafter the sound of a drum or the sight of a gun still put her in such a tremor that she could not command herself. Where armies frequently passed, panic became more familiar. Until caught and hanged, the robber Joseph Mulliner of Egg Harbor thus terrorized the New Jersey countryside.

The fighting men left, conscious that they might lose their lives—but wives and children were hardly less victims when husbands or fathers did not return. The long coastline exposed civilians to attack from an enemy who generally commanded the sea. And when British troops occupied cities, they did so as conquerors rather than as fellow subjects of the Crown. The pounding guns destroyed the little villages across which the battles passed, and such big places as Newport also suffered from shelling. Indirectly, too, the colonists paid the costs of war, as the conflict displaced all normal economic relationships and accelerated the steeply rising inflation.

For six years the fighting spread, not continuously but persistently. In eighteenth-century style, the clash of arms concentrated in a few moments of a few days. Through much of the rest of the year, maneuvering armies attempted to gain or preserve strength, so that battle, while in itself limited and contained, was always an impending possibility.

People learned to live with the possibility, got used to it, hardened. A young lady in Pennsylvania toward the end of 1777 went cheerfully about her business and conversed calmly about the two hostile forces six miles away. A few months before, she noted, the very idea would have distracted her. When the troops left Reading, Pennsylvania, in 1781, the town looked distressed, no drums beating, no men parading up and down the streets, no jolly officers gallanting the women. Now and again, a farmer's daughter, attracted by the young officers, confessed, 'twas impossible not to feel regret at their departure, which would leave her again immured in solitude. Her father felt only relief, for the sight of uniformed men usually meant trouble, whether they were British or American, foraging or seeking to buy food or horses, or just passing through. Too many soldiers wandered the countryside for comfort.

There was more to the war, however, than girlish hearts or cattle stolen. Brief as they were, the battles took a heavy toll. Of the total population of 2.5 million, almost 400,000 men at one time or another served in the Continental Army and the state militias, quite apart from irregulars and privateers at sea. War thus exposed a very high percentage of males of fighting age to some danger. Contemporaries thought casualties heavy and believed disease killed ten for every one who fell to the sword or bullet. Soldiers suffered from various fevers, diagnosed at the time as putrid, hectic, bilious, slow, nervous, remitting, and inflammatory. As among civilians, treatment consisted of "good purgings," administered whenever possible and prescribed also for diarrhea, dysentery, measles, mumps, and consumption. Dr. Benjamin Rush introduced some sanitary practices at the opening of the war, based on the observation that men were more often sick in their tents than out in fresh air, and in better condition on the march than while in camp. He also believed southern troops more sickly than northern and knew that a flannel shirt next to the skin fended off diseases and that drunkards and convalescents attracted fever.

The British prison ships were worst of all, for the same reason that greater dangers lurked in hospitals than on battlefields: confinement concentrated and multiplied the hazards. Army physicians ran more risk than line officers, and a soldier had a 98 percent chance of escaping death in combat, but only a 75 percent chance of leaving the sickbed alive. Crowded shelters, inadequate ventilation, and primitive sanitation increased fatalities; typhus fever and smallpox reduced the size of the eastern and northern armies. But only in February 1777 did Congress and General Washington decide on a general inoculation program.

On the frontier, as in the East, death was less common in battle than by disease. Conditions in the forts and blockhouses where the troops and their hangers-on spent long periods bred typhoid and dysentery. An observer in 1779 noticed that the whole dirt and filth of Harrodsburg (in what became Kentucky), as well as the putrefied flesh of dead dogs and horse, cow, and hog excrement, festered in ponds that poisoned the spring upon which the station depended for water.

Death had never been far out of mind in the settlements. Now battle made it a familiar presence. In the early days the hobbling wounded and the coffin-laden carts made a shocking sight; in January 1777 Deborah Norris noted with dismay that the poor creatures died without number and were buried forty or fifty in the same hole. Soon, however, conventional sentiment encased

the very idea of death and sugarcoated its reality. In 1780 Sally
Wister learned that two young friends were "no longer inhabitants of this terrestial world. Snatch'd in the bloom of youth by
unrelenting death from all earthly connexions." She did not allow
herself to sorrow. "Why lament a fate by heaven approved, to
die esteemed, admired, beloved." In *An Eulogium of the Brave
Men* (1779) the jurist and novelist Hugh H. Brackenridge assured the virgin "whom in a few revolving moons the Hymeneal
chain was to bind" that her fallen swain lived in yonder heavens
and that his fame would honor her.

The war diffused among women habits of violence conven-
tionally confined to men. Frontier fighting, of course, had been
no respecter of sex. Two generations earlier the Reverend Ebenezer Gay had explained that no one enjoyed immunity from military service, not the righteous, nor the wicked; not the high, nor
the low; not the rich, nor the poor; not the old, nor the young;
not men, nor women. But in the eighteenth century, once Indian
attacks receded, fighting had occurred on remote battlefields, for
short periods. Now it moved across the settled areas of the colonies, extended over long periods, and compelled females as
well as males to participate.

Deborah Sampson, for instance, was about twenty years of age
in 1780 when she learned that her foster brothers had lost their
lives in battle. She had been the one girl reared with ten boys in
a farm family near Middleboro, Massachusetts, after her own
parents abandoned her. Deborah hungered for glory and re-
venge and had not the least difficulty playing a man's part once
she had cut her hair, wrapped her breasts in a linen binding, and
appropriated a set of male garments. She enlisted in an infantry
company, served more than two years, and was twice wounded.
Years later, the Massachusetts General Court, in hailing "this extraordinary instance of female heroism," noted that Deborah had
faithfully discharged the duties of a soldier, "at the same time
preserving her virtue, and the chastity of her sex." Six feet tall,
big-boned, cross-eyed, rude in speech, and a deadly shot, Nancy
Hart, terror of the Georgia Tories, easily took care of herself and
of her enemies. She liquored up the five loyalists who demanded

dinner after having shot a patriot and her turkey, then captured them ready for the gallows.

But more important than an occasional Molly Pitcher (Mary McCauley), who may or may not have fired the cannon at the Battle of Monmouth when her husband fell at his battery, were hundreds of women who accompanied the army, some of them wives, some of them prostitutes, some of them housekeepers and homemakers. A horde of camp followers went with the troops, and if some among them tended the passions of men, others took care of more prosaic domestic needs as nurses, laundresses, or cooks. A similar train attended the enemy forces. Hordes of women, barefoot and clothed in dirty rags, marched like beasts of burden with the Hessians, bent double by bushel baskets on their backs, laden with children and kitchen utensils.

The Revolution also altered conventional female roles. Patriotic girls resolved to be mighty industrious at stitching uniforms, knitting stockings, and making caps, which brought extra income and the satisfaction of aiding the fighters. In the little domestic industries that produced saltpeter and cartridges, women worked by the side of their men. The departure of the husband-father elevated the wife-mother to a position of authority within the family; she now made the decisions, looked after the farm, tended the shop, or practiced the trade of the absent bread-winner. She was on her mettle, managing affairs with frugality and economy, finding time somehow to ready a suit of homespun against the day of his return. We must study to make the most of husbandry or we must starve, explained a lady who wished to know how to whiten cloth and raise flax. Sarah Bache and Esther Reed organized committees to raise money and sew shirts for the army.

Women before had been diffident and unwilling to enter upon political discussions, which were not their province and only created disagreeable sensations. Now wives of fugitive loyalists, remaining to safeguard property, shifted allegiance. Others urged husbands in the patriot armies to desert and come home. Responsibility compelled them to speak out, think out—even begin to wonder why they should not have an education equal to that of men. Need and a willingness to try the unknown impelled these tentative and hesitant departures from custom and habit.

In the West, where need and venturesomeness had long since shattered custom and habit, the Revolution simply legitimized violence already endemic. The frontiersmen were ready to fight, some willing to resist the Crown, others to defend it—in either case in their own interests and not on behalf of some abstract loyalty, idea, or principle. Good fighters but poor soldiers, they went their own way and deserted or mutinied with distressing promptness. Ready to protect their own homes, they could not be counted on to leave the neighborhood on command, and no external orders could force them to mobilize. Whether they chose the King's side or that of Congress depended largely upon local and personal considerations.

War along the frontier rarely set armies against one another in formal battle; more often it involved sporadic raids by irregulars or militia bands. Atrocities, common on both sides, further brutalized a society already brutal, and bitterness grew in areas where the conflict took on the qualities of a civil war. Loyalists gave their enemies rough treatment and received the like in return, for in the West the conflict arrayed not merely American against Englishman and patriot against Tory but red against white, poor against rich, tenant against landlord. Here Sir Banastre Tarleton, intimate of the reigning beauties of the London stage, abandoned chivalry and became the fearsome Green Dragoon when he killed helpless Americans even as they surrendered their arms and hoisted a white flag. Here furious yeomen after the battle at King's Mountain butchered their defeated enemies, and Daniel Morgan's horsemen carried the sword of the Lord to the foe, decimating the British at Cowpens. Savage fighting spurted forth from the South Carolina backcountry to the Wyoming Valley of Pennsylvania and New York. Pillage and indiscriminate slaughter in pitched battle or in the secret forest vented pent-up hatreds remote from the eastern drawing rooms in which brushed and polished British prisoners played the gracious guest.

Some Indians, such as those at Stockbridge, fought with the patriots. Most tribes, knowing where their interests lay, favored the British as a result both of attachment to Stuart and Johnson and of inveterate hostility to the settlers. However, the warriors, helpful in small forays, proved unreliable in extended campaigns, and intertribal wars at critical moments diverted attention from the common enemy. The Creeks, Choctaws, and Cherokees turned upon each other so frequently that they could not effectively launch a sustained drive even where the colonists were vulnerable. In June and July 1776, when a series of desperate Cherokee attacks rocked the southern frontier, John Stuart failed to mobilize the aid of the Creeks. Troops from the Carolinas and Virginia then came down to lay waste the Indian villages in retaliation; and all the tribes lost ground they could never make up in the years that followed. John McDonald, a Scottish trader, helped the Cherokees establish themselves on the Tennessee River, but no one interceded in 1782, when the Americans wiped out their town at Tuskegee. The revolutionaries also ravaged the Iroquois country, burning villages and dispersing the population so that the Six Nations never again threatened settlement.

Since the war just happened, with no specific decision that it should, Americans never reflected on the implausibility that they would win it. Against them stood the great empire whose redcoated troops had long protected the provinces. Its generals and admirals had campaigned successfully in many parts of the world; and abundant fiscal resources, sustained by the spoils of a thousand victories, enabled it to draw manpower from Europe as well as from the home islands. Among the rebellious colonists, by contrast, none had held rank higher than that of militia colonel; no army existed, or navy, nor yet a government to bring them into being.

Furthermore, military operations of long duration and intensity, conducted on the colonists' own soil, posed novel problems. Previously the Americans had depended upon local militias, drawn into service as a civic duty and expected to operate in their own neighborhoods. Efforts to move such troops long distances created serious difficulties, particularly during the long intervals between pitched battles. Many a soldier wondered, why rot in camp when work at home remained undone? Desertions mounted spasmodically.

No one paused to calculate the chance of victory, however. Had any taken stock, they might not have dared.

They dared. It was not their way in these matters to calculate chances.

Many factors contributed to the war's successful outcome: in Britain, political dissent, disappointment with the loyalists, and weariness with the struggle; in the colonies, European aid including an army and navy from France, and the slowly acquired skills of American military commanders and diplomats. Together these elements yielded a treaty of peace in 1783 that outdid the wildest expectations of the people of 1774.

But beyond these contributory factors lay the one impelling force of a people recklessly determined not to yield. In dark days as well as bright, when the enemy, united, held major colonial cities, when France and the Netherlands played neutral roles or pursued selfish diplomatic objectives, when their own blundering officers and bickering statesmen put victory beyond reason, most Americans left no doubt that they would somehow continue the fight. Daring to persevere, they would simply outlast everyone else.

Daring was akin to necessity. Major General Charles Lee, always proud of his career in the British Army, gloomily surveyed the patriot troops at Bunker Hill, "composed in part of raw lads, and old men, half armed, with no practice or discipline, commanded without order and God knows by whom." Washington took charge of a force of "exceedingly dirty and nasty people," a motley crowd with little uniformity of men or material. The soldiers neither marched properly nor held their heads erect, they did not turn out their toes as they should have, and hardly a man wore his cocked hat correctly. When the Prussian volunteer Baron von Steuben arrived, wearing fur robes and a scarlet and blue uniform and attended by a retinue of servants (at John Hancock's expense), he found the army literally naked, its muskets covered with rust and its bayonets used for roasting meat when available. The camp at Valley Forge was extreme: men sick with dysentery, unattended, never left the huts. General Anthony Wayne declared that he would rather go into battle than make an inspection tour, so awful was the stench.

Earlier, at Cambridge, people wandered in and out of camp, among them backwoodsmen in moccasins, perpetual trouble-makers addicted to fistfights, cider, and nude swimming in the Charles River, which Washington tried to outlaw. To the general's horror, officers performed menial chores, one stooping to shave a private. Theft, violence, brawls, drink, and corruption compounded the effects of ignorance. No one even knew the exact number of soldiers. Rivalries between northerners and southerners, between New Englanders and Pennsylvanians, engendered discord, and camp followers, prostitutes, wives, and children added to the disarray. The exhortations of clergymen and officers could not halt gambling and other vices. Soldiers got drunk when money and rum were available and wandered away in search of girls when the camp was short of willing women. In New York the troops discovered the hags and whores of Holy Ground and participated with delight in frequent riots. Prostitutes murdered two clients in bed, castrated another, and bestowed syphilis and gonorrhea upon countless others.

Yet motley assemblies such as these won the decisive battles—not because Congress in 1775 or later provided effective organization, or because the states learned to cooperate, but because these men proved effective fighters when needed. Fortunately Washington understood that a people unused to restraint had to be led: they would not be driven. Even those committed to the war would accept discipline only by degrees. However regiments varied in size and organization, troops routinely refused to accept officers other than by election, and had their way despite doubts whether a poor man could make the proper appearance or muster the qualifications to keep company with gentlemen. Baron von Steuben expressed to a European friend the difficulties of defending a country where Caesar and Hannibal would have lost their reputations, and where every farmer was a general but nobody wished to be a private. "You say to your soldier 'Do this' and he doeth it; but I am obliged to say, 'This is the reason you ought to do that:' and he does it."

The best-disposed troops still required ammunition, food, clothing, shelter, and a little pay to spend or send home. When those necessities did not appear, the men in the ranks responded less often by such mutinies as stirred the Connecticut regiments and the Pennsylvania line in 1780–81 than by simply going home. The army on the verge of disappearance while encamped around Boston disintegrated in New York. The Connecticut militia shrank from 8,000 to 2,000 when harvesting time approached. Surgeons sold certificates of disability, and forged passes made departure easy. Almost half the New England troops disappeared by the end of 1777, and at Morristown, New Jersey, in January 1778 soldiers could not sleep for the racket of those packing to go home. It was a miracle, Von Steuben said, that an army existed at all.

Most Americans had no desire for the white coats, long waistcoats, and spectacular fur hats the French wore. The immediate problems were bare feet in the snow and bodies unprotected against the wind. In this respect, too, Valley Forge was extreme. Men roasted and ate old shoes, killed and consumed a small pet dog, and confiscated the corn used to feed the horses. With no meat, no clothing, and no shoes in sub-zero temperatures, Washington informed Congress that the army would have to "starve, dissolve or disperse."

On the morning of a crucial battle, Washington sometimes lacked powder and guns. Notwithstanding the requests that civilians cease firing aimlessly at birds or animals, and despite the saving when drums replaced cannon fire to awaken the camps, there was never enough ammunition. Franklin's suggestion, the use of bow and arrows, proved unpersuasive.

Lafayette, leading a force of New Englanders south, stopped in Baltimore and borrowed enough from local merchants to buy shoes, hats, and cloth for uniforms. Rarely could a commander arrange matters that simply. Soldiers resorted to theft, raiding the markets, orchards, and fields they passed.

Supplies often ran short, not because of the penury of the Congress or of the state governments, but because consumers, military and civilian alike, had to improvise everything. The lack of facilities for internal trade and, paradoxically, removal of the connection with the former mother country prevented the population in uniform or at home from getting needed goods. After 1774 the colonists discovered the extent of their dependence on overseas trade for many commodities, and the difficulty also of finding alternatives and moving them long distances either along the coast or overland to the site of the battles and the army. All this apart from the fact that the British occupied Boston, Philadelphia, New York City, and Newport for greater or lesser periods. Supplies from European allies helped after 1778 but still left the problem of distribution within the country.

The war destroyed property and sometimes whole cities. Newport, besieged and then occupied, suffered irreparable damage, its fine houses and gardens gutted for fuel. Foragers raked through the countryside. The British left desolation behind when they passed through New Jersey in the fall of 1776, there and elsewhere turning churches into barracks for soldiers and mangers for horses. Bombardment by the Americans reduced Savannah to ruins. And though the Moravian towns escaped destruction, the army turned Bethlehem and Lititz, Pennsylvania, into hospitals.

Revolution interrupted all usual pursuits. Men drawn off into uniform could not tend their farms, and the scarcity of rural labor posed difficulties for families left behind. Shortage hit the cities, then extended to the country. Suddenly there was a lack of paper—even writing paper—or of sugar, coffee, or tea; and craftsmen could not lay their hands on essential materials. Costs rose so that the Philadelphian who for twenty years had relied upon the same barber took to shaving himself; and gentlewomen, resigning themselves to broken chairs and teacups, dipped the water out of an iron skillet into the pot as cheerfully as if they were using a silver urn. In Massachusetts, as elsewhere, the assembly fixed wages and prices to halt the pernicious consequences of inflation. But government intervention in the interest of equitable distribution of goods and services botched the flow of supplies, in any case uncertain. Philadelphia merchants complained that overly zealous regulatory activities frightened away prospective buyers and sellers. Flour became unavailable when the government held down its price, but customers willing to pay enough could always get some. The black market flourished when traders learned that they could increase profits tenfold by breaking the law or held back goods in the expectation of future increases.

The aggrieved by then knew how to take matters into their own hands; anti-tea-drinking ladies, nonimportation merchants, and boycotting artisans had a decade of experience with direct action by 1776. Frustrated consumers turned in anger on the grasping middleman whom they blamed for high prices. In the fall of 1776 salt riots erupted in Maryland. In 1777, when Thomas Boylston of Boston refused to sell at reasonable rates, a crowd of North End women took what they needed by force while a concourse of men stood amazed, silent spectators of the whole transaction, for these were not "your Maggys but reputable Clean drest Women." But then, too, many dealers suffered from the interruption in the usual course of trade.

Inflation deepened the impact of shortages. The states and the Congress, pressed by the necessities of war, could not halt the printing presses. To the $450 million they issued, counterfeiters added an unknown but unsettling quantity. There was no alternative. Goods moved along channels of money and paper alone was available.

From the start the want of credibility hampered Congress and the states in raising revenue. People willing to lend funds or pay taxes to local governments for purposes close at hand regarded requests from a remote, untried authority with considerable skepticism. It was simple prudence to hold back, in the absence of assurance that others everywhere would contribute proportionately. Ignorance on the part of the money managers deepened the consequences of these doubts. Eighteenth-century accounting methods were in any case sloppy. Few Americans had experience in public finance, and only merchants knew how to handle large sums of any sort. Not until 1781 did Robert Morris propose a "Plan for Arranging the Treasury Department," and it took another four years before Congress accepted the decimal system based on the dollar. Trial and error proved an expensive way of learning. Swamped by trivial details, Morris lacked time to attend to those general arrangements appropriate to his position as Superintendent of Finance.

Only about 9 percent of expenditures during the war derived from tax revenues, about 12 percent from foreign borrowings (mostly Dutch), and about 19 percent from domestic loans. Fully 60 percent came from the issue of paper money, since there was no federal mint, and precious little gold or silver. The currency printed during 1775 and 1776 created little difficulty, provided the fluidity the economy had long lacked, and stimulated enterprises. A gradual rise in prices made those years prosperous.

Then inflation got out of hand. British obstinacy had prevented development of an indigenous American money supply, denying the colonists the right to print their own circulating medium. The war gave Americans the opportunity to remedy the lack. Once the presses moved into action—in each colony, and on behalf of the Continental Congress—a flood of paper poured forth. Then the value of the notes declined, steadily and precipitously. People consulted published scales of depreciation to judge the worth of money in any transaction. In 1779 the continental collapsed, to be revalued a year later at a ratio of forty to one. Throughout the war, there was no staying the falling currency; and even victory after Yorktown did not prop values up. The unending flow of paper further raised prices and forced a reversion to barter.

Inflation followed inexorably, whether reckoned in paper or in specie, for genuine shortages of goods added to the effects of the increased quantity of money. Common soldiers wondered about how their resourceless families fared, while some officers left for home when their wives' nagging letters complained that dependents of men in the ranks received help at public expense, but not they. However the draft operated, it left suspicions among the unlucky about favoritism or crookedness. At times everything seemed wrong, the whole country full of designing Tories and ignorant avaricious Whigs, while greed, contempt of authority, and inordinate love of gain prevailed everywhere. Those who risked their lives on the battlefield earned nothing but poverty and contempt, while those who attended to their own interests became men of mark. Men who lived at home in luxury and ease, quietly possessing their habitations, enjoying their wives and families in peace, had but a very faint idea of the continual anxiety endured in a camp, complained one husband and father. Pelf seemed a better goal than liberty.

Some people did indeed profit from the turbulence of the times. Enlistment opened opportunities to sons of poor farmers, to indentured servants, and to transported convicts. Going away was no hardship for them and offered unexpected chances of improvement. Election to office in the militia moved them up in society. Many farmers suffered few adverse effects, and those close to market enjoyed rises in the price of their products. Furthermore, since they raised much of what they consumed, they could refrain from unessential purchases and thus escaped the hardships of inflation.

Speculators flourished, especially those whose political connections rewarded them with juicy contracts for provisions and other supplies. Samuel Chase of Maryland made more from deals in flour than from his law practice. Fortunes rewarded the shift of produce to places with the laxest regulations. New York farmers, compelled to sell wheat at home for $20 a bushel, could get $75 by transporting it to Pennsylvania; and Connecticut beef was available everywhere but within that state, which enforced price-fixing after others gave up.

Aggressive newcomers, vigilant in spotting fresh opportunities, also did well. Inflation and changes in the tax laws operated to the advantage of borrowers and tenants able to pay off fixed loans and rents in depreciated currency. A few gobbled up the confiscated estates of loyalists. The dynamic elements in the population gained—merchants, the value of whose stocks mounted by the day; debtors, who repaid their borrowings in worthless money.

The rise in costs, however, pressed people on fixed incomes to the wall; the salaries of ministers, the established fees of doctors and attorneys, and small incomes derived from money on loan did not keep up with increased costs. "Living is double what it was one year ago," complained a lawyer's desperate wife in 1776. Her husband, who saw no sense in price-fixing laws that would lead to civil war, dealt with the overcharging rascally upstarts in trade by boycotting their goods. The wealthiest and genteelest families breakfasted on milk and discovered the virtue of home-made cider. All these inert though worthy elements in the population suffered.

Townspeople had a rough time of it, particularly those without a garden, a cow, or an apple tree. Bostonians complained that farmers from the surrounding countryside were starving them out in order to lower prices for trade goods. Artisans were in a bind; carpenters, tailors, printers, and cordwainers could not readily pass on to customers the higher costs of nails, cloth, paper, and leather. Workers demanded higher wages and, when refused, went on strike. Day laborers and seamen, thrown out of work by stoppages in trade, drifted sullenly about unless they enlisted. Even some merchants suffered. The break with England disrupted the normal course of commerce to the injury of the large established firms, and some small shopkeepers were hard put to keep their shelves stocked.

The altered circumstances of trade thus brought down the formerly great and raised up the formerly small. Newport merchants never recovered; those of Providence launched upon a sustained boom. The cattle market established at Brighton, outside Boston, to supply the revolutionary army endured after the troops departed and through the nineteenth century controlled the city's meat supply. Samuel Blodget left Boston during the war, set up a manufactory of linen, duck, and sailcloth in nearby Haverhill, and prospered. The demand for saltpeter, iron, gunpower, and muskets sustained other industrial ventures. Debtors escaped the burden of past obligations and staggered to their feet with energy renewed for a fresh climb, while once wealthy creditors sank into ruin beneath the avalanche of worthless paper. Instability encouraged movement, from east to west, from country to town. Stylish homes showed off the gains of the fortunate; the failures sought opportunities in new places. Inflation penalized the conventional and rewarded the daring, and the experience, though often painful for the moment, revitalized the whole American economy.

Nothing ventured, nothing gained: the old saw acquired new meaning. Where prudence was a liability, those who ventured nothing lost all.

People willing to chance trade found opportunity at every turn. War, which set the stable fortunes at risk, created new prospects of wealth for people of vision. Eighteenth-century convention recognized the respectability of the privateer. It took only a letter of marque to legitimatize armed vessels that searched out enemy prey and earned crews and backers the value of the prizes seized. Investments in these raiders became more attractive once France and the Netherlands entered the war; their European navies then occupied the attention of the British fleet and expanded possibilities for raiding profit. Samuel Tucker of Marblehead, Massachusetts, thus sailed forth as a privateer's captain, took more than thirty prizes in 1776, and returned with the foundation of a fortune.

Thoughts of trade turned first to ports previously forbidden. The West Indies remained the hub of transatlantic commerce. Poking into the harbors of the poorly guarded islands, American vessels needed only the clearance of local officials and found numerous ways of gaining entrance—some legal, some not. St. Eustatius bustled with traffic as long as the Dutch held it. When the British captured it, the business moved to French, Spanish, and British Caribbean ports until peace all but closed them off.

The allies also opened up new lines of advantageous commerce across the Atlantic. American ships entered the Spanish ports of Bilbao and Barcelona and became familiar throughout the Mediterranean. The French trade gained in volume, owing to the desire to bypass the former mother country and to gain from carrying supplies Louis XVI granted the colonists. Dutch ports were equally receptive, so that a great stream of shipping moved in and out of those harbors free of British control. Despite the value set in Europe on Chesapeake tobacco, a permanent French connection failed to develop because of Bourbon monopolistic practices and differences in taste; but for the moment, business boomed and nurtured extravagant expectations for the future.

Here and there chances appeared for exchange with the enemy. Along the Canadian border, and elsewhere, traders found opportunities to deal with the British. The cities held by royal troops also put suppliers in a position to profit. Enterprising Yankees known as cowboys thus kept New York provisioned with cattle under the occupation, and ingenious modes of mutual accommodation swapped Connecticut agricultural products for English manufactures to the advantage of the King's forces on Long Island.

Along the grand lines of commerce poured funds that swelled into great fortunes. In lesser tributary streams, retail traders in the cities and towns and peddlers moving along the roads carried on their business under the unusual hazards but also the unusual possibilities for gains created by war, inflation, and disrupted communications. And farmers, as in Pennsylvania, spurred to calculation by demand, improved the yield of their upland fields by using clover and lime.

The times encouraged spacious speculative plans, audacious in their scope. Sudden strokes of fortune made ready riches available, and people thrust into new and unfamiliar positions by the total shakeup of society had to innovate to survive. For want of alternatives they compounded their risks. Every successful venture left the problem of disposing of gains; inflation drained value away from money hoarded or loaned; and only the renewed hazard of reinvestment offered the chance of safety. Many thus driven met disaster, ended in poverty, like Haym Solomon, merchant banker, whose efforts did much to sustain the government's shaky credit, and who died penniless in 1785. Robert Morris, financier of the Revolution, became one of the richest merchants in North America only to end his career in a debtors' jail when his wealth ebbed away in the failure of a land speculation scheme. But the clever or the lucky, piling gamble upon gamble, reached the century's end with great wealth and in the process also stoked the nation's economy.

The gleam of overseas trade glittered most brightly, although sometimes deceptively. James Madison dreamed of diverting the business of Philadelphia and Baltimore to Alexandria and Norfolk, tried to strengthen Virginia's commerce in the Port Bill of 1784, and planned a canal to unite the Chesapeake and the Delaware. The lure of a Northwest Passage to the Orient that had always tempted Americans now took a new form. In 1784 the *Empress of China*, dispatched by New York merchants to Canton, traced a route others soon followed—around Cape Horn. Its safe and profitable return drew rivals from Providence, Boston, and Salem. In 1789, when Robert Gray took command of the *Columbia*, he learned how to carry furs to China from the Pacific Northwest, in a business that thrived well into the nineteenth century.

Other channels of investment appeared within the country. Speculation in land continued to further development of the West, and also of eastern cities. Sale of the unoccupied Liberty Lands by Philadelphia in 1781 and 1782 thus totally altered the pattern of that city's real estate. The desire to ease communications spurred impressive improvements. The Charles River Bridge, built by Lemuel Cox and a joint stock company in 1786, spanned the 1,500 feet between Boston and Charlestown. At about the same time, Levi Pease, a Massachusetts blacksmith, put his stages from Boston to Hartford on a regular schedule and later sent them on to New York. George Washington in 1785 accepted the presidency of the Potomac Company, to which Virginians and Marylanders subscribed £40,000 for improving navigation on that river.

The aftereffects of war provided an impetus to industrial development, as when John Fitch went on from managing a gun factory to tinkering with the steamboat. Having acquired the patriotic and profitable duty of providing the country's guns, the primitive ironworks long established in Salisbury, Connecticut, recruited ore diggers and pounders, colliers, carpenters, founders, and dressers of cannon. Its woodchoppers and charcoal burners ranged in search of oak and walnut through Litchfield County as well as north into Massachusetts and west into New York. When peace came, the shops adjusted to making scythes, hoes, shears, bell clappers, and plows. Other establishments, often financed by townsmen though located in the country, did well in Massachusetts, Pennsylvania, and Virginia. And persistent demand enabled even the failures to make fresh starts. Matthew Lyon, a restless Irishman who had worked off his service in Connecticut, remained dissatisfied with his Vermont iron furnace and ultimately made his way to Kentucky, where he shifted from one enterprise to another, ever discontent. Many other artisans, the element in society most resistant to change, learned to accommodate themselves to new conditions.

The temper of the times encouraged mobility, in status as well as in space. People who were pressed on to discovery in order to survive welcomed the challenge. Although immigration from overseas all but came to a halt, the United States remained attractive, precisely because its fluid social structure made opportunity a reality. A significant number of German auxiliaries, known as Hessians, chose not to return to Europe, especially those who had the chance, as prisoners of war, to observe the life of their captors.

The experience of war profoundly affected Americans. Years of fighting and of inflation further unsettled people already restless. The deprivations suffered by some, the fortunes gained by others, kept everyone on edge. Society, always unstable, now quivered incessantly to the shock of recurrent unexpected changes.

Yet their past had taught Americans to live with chance. No certainties had ever marked off the daily round of their lives. In no corner of the continent did the planter or the yeoman, the merchant or the artisan, enjoy a situation proof against the unforeseeable stroke of hard luck that might wipe away a lifetime's efforts. No townsman could put out of mind the visitations of fire and plague that indiscriminately claimed victims among the buildings and their residents. Every frontiersman knew the isolation that arrayed against him the hostility of the elements and of strangers and that often reduced self to savagery in fighting off others.

Risk, everywhere familiar, ceased to impede action. Indeed,

challenges attracted people and spurred them on in the courses they wished to take.

That mode of behavior bore a relationship to distinctive patterns of thought, which the colonists pondered. When she reflected upon the various passions and appetites to which human nature was subject, Abigail Adams wrote her husband in August 1776, she was ready to cry out with the Psalmist, *Lord what is Man?*

She and other Americans had an answer that quieted anxiety and encouraged them resolutely to go on. They knew the nature of the Lord, of His universe, and of the humans who resided in it.

8

Faith and Reason

The ability to wage war against Britain successfully, surprising though it was to contemporaries, sprang from sources already at work before 1775. The determination and the strength to win owed much to the attitudes of Americans toward themselves as human beings, toward the world they inhabited, and toward their society. For a long time, religion in the colonies had evolved in a fashion that made revolution and independence seem expected outcomes. No similar preparation had readied the ground for the cultural renaissance many desired.

May 1775, when the Green Mountain Boys stole across the border into New York and, in a surprise attack, seized the British post at Fort Ticonderoga, marked no abrupt change in matters of faith. "By whose authority do you act?" the astonished commandant had asked. "In the name of the great Jehovah, and the Continental Congress!" was Ethan Allen's reply. True, the characteristic conjunction of Jehovah and the Continental Congress, of God and the Republic, made this account attractive to Americans. But by then the distinctive way of thinking about religion that associated it intimately with the state had long been taking form. The war only stimulated a development that would continue for decades. Thereafter, Americans would regard the Revo-

lution and the Republic it created as providential, a fit object for
reverence that united them as a people.

Before 1775 new tendencies appeared most visibly when individuals rebelled against orthodox faith. Allen himself was presumed author of a tract that stated the radical case; like other
Deists, he rejected all supernatural beliefs but ackowledged the
existence of a divine creator of the universe, a supreme legislator
who established its governing rules. Deists abjured institutional
churches and traditional worship, which they regarded as out-
moded superstition far less important than ethical behavior.

The question of independence tested religious attitudes toward
tyranny. Ministers, like laymen, had to decide which obligation
was more binding: obedience to the Crown or defense of freedom. John Peter Gabriel Muhlenberg told his Virginia congregation, in the language of Holy Writ, that there was a time for
all things: "There is a time to preach and a time to fight, and
now is the time to fight." He went off to become a brigadier general in the Continental Army, although his venerable father
worried about the validity of an old loyalty oath to the King.
John Cleaveland, Joseph Willard, and David Avery led their
Yankee parishioners into battle. George Duffield, a Presbyterian
minister, rebuked his flock because there were too many men in
the church and promised "there would be one less tomorrow and
no lecture on Wednesday." Patriotic tasks also involved clergymen who stayed home. One of them provoked a loyalist critic
to spiteful rhyme:

> *I've known him seek the dungeon dark as night,*
> *Imprisoned Tories to convert, to fright*
> *Whilst to myself I've hummed, in dismal tune,*
> *I'd rather be a dog than Witherspoon.*

Other Americans did not go so far as to make patriotism the
only required creedal affirmation, but nevertheless drifted in that
direction. Reluctant to abandon altogether the ways of worship
of their families and friends, they made little mental adjustments
and alterations of practice that cumulatively left them a distance

from the old forms and beliefs, although without a formal act of separation. Americans who joined Masonic lodges marched in occasional parades, participated in intimate rituals, attended balls, and in some places built halls with the proceeds of lotteries, all without surrendering their church membership. Yet the oath that admitted them to the order expressed views more tinged with Deism than with orthodoxy. Hannah Mather Crocker, whose middle name reveals her impeccable lineage, in 1778 organized a women's lodge in Boston with no sense of radical break with the past.

So, too, some ministers and many laymen and -women remained within the Church of England and within the Congregational churches, yet shrugged off orthodox doctrines, silently setting aside faith in the Trinity along with predestination, while responding to revivalist enthusiasm and acquiescing in deviations that would have shocked an earlier generation. Later such people would identify themselves as Unitarians or Methodists by breaking away in separate sects, as the Baptists already had. A new understanding of God, humanity, and society reverberated in their thoughts as in Ethan Allen's shouts.

In religion, as in everything else, the condition of the colonists varied from place to place and group to group—from such learned and urbane clergymen as Ezra Stiles and such widely read laymen as Thomas Jefferson to backcountry preachers and worshipers who remained ignorant of God and partook of the sport and diversion of the wicked then much in vogue, unless some spiritual crisis revealed the way to redemption. Nevertheless, common intellectual adjustments at all levels and in all groups moved emphasis away from dogmatic peculiarities toward the unity in pluralism, toward the sense of *e pluribus unum* —out of many, one. Clearly Jews differed from Catholics and Quakers from Baptists, yet all agreed on definitions of good and bad, or right and wrong. In a continent of differences, recognized and accepted by all, shared moral commitments bound people together. Those who divided on theological doctrines joined in support of the same ethical precepts. People of every creed agreed on such matters because they increasingly identified religious faith with nature and reason.

Although Americans often used a vocabulary drawn from Europe, their religious understanding sprang from indigenous sources. Toleration had long since become a practical necessity. Great distances and poor communications, intense localism, and historical differences that reached back to the era of first settlement generated internal pressure toward fragmentation, so that each group of worshipers ruled itself. Ecclesiastical forms varied, but nowhere did effective authority emanate from beyond the parish boundaries, and almost everywhere laymen held the power of ultimate decision. All the offshoots of Congregationalism had arrived at that position by 1775, despite efforts to draw the churches together in consociations; and the absence of a bishop and remoteness from London in effect left vestrymen in undisputed control of the Church of England. No rabbi, properly speaking, served Jews in the colonies; and the few Jesuits who tended to Catholic needs lacked contact with superiors and improvised as best they could. Appropriately enough, a sympathetic Englishman in 1775 described colonial religion as a refinement on the principles of resistance, the dissidence of dissent, and the protestantism of protestantism. Only such sects as the Moravians could discipline their members, and in the absence of any means of bringing the existing churches of Virginia and Massachusetts, of Quakers and Baptists, under a single form of governance, it was also difficult to assert control over, or deny legitimacy to, newer groups.

Since no mode of worship held the devotion of the whole population, political support could not lift one faith over another. Live and let live was the only acceptable principle. The very concept of orthodoxy became anachronistic because no group could impose its views upon others. The Philadelphians went to an extreme. They had built a nonsectarian hall to accommodate itinerant preachers so that even an emissary of the Mufti of Constantinople, come to preach Mohammedanism, "would find a pulpit at his service." Happily, no prophet out of the East arrived to test the sincerity of such affirmations.

Elsewhere, too, control was out of reach, even of the Church of England, despite the fact that statutes established it in some provinces. Its clergymen were in low repute; the choice between patriotism and loyalty to the Crown tried their consciences. Too many were self-seeking; Jonathan Boucher confessed when he prepared for ordination that he felt no sense of calling to the ministry, nor had he any interest in theology, but only in the opportunity to become a landowner and planter through acquisition of the parish glebe. Such men, sensitive to status, did not command authority. A New Englander in Virginia noted scornfully the perfunctory Christmas sermon—fifteen minutes, very fashionable!

In New England the descendants of the Puritans had accepted the presence of the Church of England and then of various deviant groups. Congregationalists and Anglicans dominated Bristol, Rhode Island; across the bay in East Greenwich most families were Baptists and Quakers. The Reverend Jacob Duché, an Anglican in full pontificals whose prayers opened the first session of the Continental Congress, won over the suspicious Yankee John Adams. Conversely, in Virginia and the Carolinas, where the established Church of England held a majority of the communicants, on paper at least, not many dared to consider proscription of the Presbyterians or even of the separate Baptists with their ties to New England.

In some places limited resources forced churches to cooperate. In Freehold, Shrewsbury, and Middletown, New Jersey, Congregationalists, Presbyterians, Baptists, Dutch Reformed, and Scottish Presbyterians worked out arrangements to share meetinghouses. Diversity bred acceptance, then tolerance, and finally equality. Interdenominational attacks from pulpits and press persisted. But having learned that invoking the aid of royal governors could result in the loss of liberty, Americans by 1775 were content to divorce doctrinal issues from politics.

Jews, Moravians, and Catholics, groups hardly tolerated in Britain, found security and equality in America. In this regard, practice was far in advance of theory. By 1775 Jews had lived in the New World for more than a century and had practiced their faith without interference. Indeed, Moses Michael Hays, a Newport merchant, rose to prominence in New England Masonic circles. British officials, however, were dubious. Sir James Wright, governor of Georgia, in 1781 asked the Secretary of State for

America to prevent the return of the Jews to Savannah, "for these people, my Lord, were found to a man to have been violent rebels and persecutors of the King's loyal subjects." But a young American visiting York, Pennsylvania, saw all about him unfriendly faces suspicious of a stranger. Then he stopped in at the house of a Jew who ran a small store. The traveler wasted no time on abstract speculation about religion, politics, and society; he warmed to a kindly reception. The political attitudes that enraged Crown servants encouraged Hays to refuse to sign a test oath and to demand "the rights and priviledges due other free citizens."

Other unconventional groups fared equally well. In 1777 a Yankee visitor to Bethlehem, Pennsylvania, noted critically that the Moravians loved money, that 120 girls slept in a single garret, and that the elders arranged all marriages. But he also noted approvingly that the Sectarians avoided lawsuits and had carried the mechanical arts to perfection; in particular he admired the hydraulic pumps that distributed water through lead pipes from the river to every part of town. The grist, bolting, fulling, tanning, and dyeing mills, as well as the machines for shearing cloth, were also good and eased the stranger's disapproval of other aspects of the community's life.

New groups repeatedly tested the breadth of American toleration. In 1776 Jemima Wilkinson, a twenty-three-year-old Rhode Island Quaker, claimed that a spirit had raised her from the dead; and thereafter called herself the Publick Universal Friend. Later her numerous followers established a Jerusalem in western New York. In 1774 Ann Lee arrived from England with a handful of followers after a revelation had directed her to establish a millennial church in America. The illiterate daughter of a blacksmith, employed in a cotton factory, she had fallen into an unhappy marriage and had borne four children who all died. Persuaded that she herself was the female element in God, Ann converted thousands and imposed strict celibacy upon her Shaker community. But her views were only a shade different from those of the Moravians, who also segregated the sexes and subjected marriage to strict control by the elders. Americans who had learned to value the virtues of one sect were ready to accept another.

The war created serious problems of conscience for Quakers and Mennonites. Pacifists by conviction, they dragged their feet as war approached and their refusal to fight or to pay a war tax inflamed their neighbors. Almost in self-defense, the Quakers expanded their concept of charity to include outsiders. As a result of their involvement in good works on behalf of the whole community, the crisis never deepened enough to undermine their neighbors' tolerance.

Almost overnight earlier fears of Papism and episcopacy disappeared. The roots of hostility to the Church of Rome reached into the colonial past. Fear of its influence sprang not from its foreign connections: Americans expressed no concern about the dependence of the Dutch Reformed congregations on the classis (the governing body) of Amsterdam, of American Friends on the London yearly meetings, or of Moravians on a German governing board. But the Pope was a bishop, and episcopacy was the heart of the problem, as it was for Anglicans. Jonathan Mayhew's warning of 1763 remained valid down to the Revolution: people could protect their liberty only "by keeping all imperious bishops and other clergymen who love to lord it over God's heritage from getting their foot into the stirrup at all." Popery, Samuel Cooper, the Boston minister, said ten years later, was "the everlasting enemy to freedom."

Anthony Gavin's *A Master Key to Popery* (1724) appeared in an American edition in 1773 and remained available in reprints for years thereafter. This lurid exposé of life behind monastic and convent walls described young girls seduced by friars, a nun who kept her lover by her for twenty-two days, and wives who yielded to inquisitors to save their husbands from torture. Gavin claimed himself to have been a priest and ended his days as a parson of the Church of England in Virginia.

Popular prejudices of this sort remained deeply embedded in the consciousness of Protestants and created an ambiguous situation for colonial Catholics—tolerated as persons, yet feared as foreign agents. Charles Carroll grew wealthy as both merchant and planter and exercised political influence commensurate with his status, yet, like other Maryland Catholics, paid double taxes and held no public posts. In the 1760s new church buildings and the acceptance of the Jesuits were evidences of equality; but Catholics resolutely opposed the appointment of a bishop for America, fearing the hostility such a move would arouse.

The Church of Rome emerged into the open during the Revolution and, in time, developed a hierarchy of precisely the sort the colonists had once feared. Catholics proved firm patriots: Carroll signed the Declaration of Independence, and Stephen Moylan, brother of the Bishop of Cork, attained the rank of brigadier general in the Continental Army. Encounters with the French allies eased the adjustment; and already in 1779 John Carroll, later the first American Roman Catholic bishop, found the "fullest and largest system of toleration" in almost all the states. As a matter of course the statute establishing religious freedom in Virginia ended discrimination there. The Church of England suffered some disabilities after 1775 largely because of its connection with loyalism and the Tories. But Americans casually accepted under the Republic the Anglican bishops they had feared under the Crown.

An analogous development helped define the Methodist Episcopal Church. John Wesley opposed the Revolution, and most of the clergy who followed him returned to England. Those who stayed behind severed their ties with the Church of England and developed their own institutions, emphasizing ideas shared with the patriots.

One Methodist joined two Quakers, two Roman Catholics, one Dutch Reformed, one Deist, seven Presbyterians, eight Congregationalists, and nineteen Anglicans to help in framing the Constitution of 1787—a fair measure of the spread of affiliations and of the triumph of tolerance. At about the same time, Pennsylvania abandoned the requirement of a test oath for voting or holding office, while New York's constitution ten years earlier had assured to all mankind "the free exercise and enjoyment of religious profession and worship, without discrimination or preference," as a safeguard against the bigotry of weak and wicked priests and princes.

Toleration led to practical, if not at once to full legal, equality and laid a basis for pluralistic assumptions about the whole society as a union within which Moravians, Jews, Catholics, Baptists, and Anglicans could cooperate. An observer noted that people of differing persuasions, living "together in the greatest harmony," proved "the candor and liberality of the age." A few ministers feared the spread of indifference and apathy; most recognized that no relationship of Church and state could rest upon a position that favored one group against others.

People unwilling to cut loose casually held on to creedal affirmations. A woman alone during the war, almost destitute, noted with resignation, "I have nothing to fear from the malevolence of man, and Physical evils must be patiently submitted to." Traditional ways of explaining the universe satisfied her and others like her. Other men and women performed religious duties in a cold formal manner. Family prayer in a North Carolina home in 1782 seemed to a visitor a burlesque of worship—mechanical, routine.

More characteristically, occasional noncompliance shaded into persistent unconcern. Molly Tilgham of Maryland, forced to travel six miles to the Bay Side church "in such a sun, it was enough to coddle common flesh," broiled all the way. Then the Reverend John Gordon's "slow croaking" put her to sleep. On the way back a perpetual cloud of dust prevented her from seeing the horses' heads or from speaking, lest she choke. After the trying trip she vowed to say her prayers at home till the rains came.

Yet neither the attitudes of acceptance of inherited doctrines nor the posture of apathy satisfied Americans. Instability and pluralism, restlessness of temperament and desire for improvement blocked the retreat to tradition. People eager to rise above their heritage regarded products of the past with skepticism; and the close proximity of equal but different modes of worship precluded the insistence that any one of them monopolized the keys to knowledge, behavior, understanding of the universe, or salvation.

More congenial to the actual situation in the United States was the belief that an element of truth resided in all faiths, so that each individual had a right to choose among them. A free republic accepted differences between Yankees and Virginians, Baptists and Catholics, not only as tolerable but as complimentary, ever revitalizing community cohesion.

In the near future as in the recent past, New Lights and Old Lights, Unitarians and Trinitarians, Antinomians and Calvinists did doctrinal battle. But they conceded to one another a degree of civility, recognizing that disagreement did not lead to damnation. Society held together less by participation in a common communion than by shared impulses that directed behavior along a moral course. Day-to-day life confirmed what people in more reflective moments understood. An Anglican did business with a Baptist and behaved as a good neighbor to a Presbyterian because an ethical sense, inherent in human nature, governed the actions of all and in much the same way. The Congregationalist minister Samuel Hopkins had derived from Jonathan Edwards the belief that virtue consisted of universal disinterested benevolence, the opposite of selfishness, thus giving appropriate orthodox theological validation to a proposition that made sense to men and women who led hard lives.

Sermons about neighborliness, mutual aid, and benevolence created no illusions about human nature in actuality. It surprised no one to learn of places in the United States where "every vice not only dishonorable to Christianity but shocking to humanity" prevailed "under the cloak of religion." A signed contract provided sanctions for an agreement as faith in unselfishness did not. That was reality: willful and ignorant men and women strayed all too readily from the paths of rectitude and required correction.

Any person could distinguish right from wrong, for the differences between them were neither hidden nor random but essential elements of an orderly universe, within which men and women could operate confidently because every fragment had meaning in relation to the whole. The common analogy was a wondrous machine, creation of a master clockmaker; infinitely intricate, its various parts meshed together in a pattern of relationships governed by the very rules of their being—precise, unalterable, but comprehensible. Americans termed the clockmaker

God, his handiwork nature, and its rules laws. Whoever understood the laws of the mechanism could take measurable risks and plan toward fulfillable goals.

The natural was therefore superior to the artificial as a guide in art and war and personal life. The composer William Billings considered "a few wild uncultivated sounds from a Natural Singer" vastly more agreeable "than a concert of music performed by the most refined artificial singers upon earth," and he rejected all rules of composition. The painter Benjamin West, growing up in America without assistance other than from Nature, learned more, he thought, than he could in Europe where he would "have known nothing but the Receipts of Masters." John Leacock's *Fall of British Tyranny* (1776) extolled the prowess of the natural Americans, their only perfume bear grease, contemptuous of British "slip slops and tea" and aware that "Liberty's the right of each creature." People who thought, felt, behaved without artifice, naturally, attuned themselves most sensitively to the rules by which the universe operated.

They could therefore take confidence in the regularity and the order of creation. The young tutor in the household of a Virginia planter noted with awe that the whole world was only a point, almost unnoticeable, when compared with the numerous systems that composed the universe. And yet all were under the particular direction and government of God. How insignificant, indeed how foolish, it was, therefore, to be uneasy and solicitous about whether to live in Cohansie or Princeton or Virginia, in America or Europe, so long as the divine agency was still in support. Earthly creatures were like the nails in a turning wheel, today up, tomorrow down. God would do as seemed good in His eyes. But the universe made His benevolence plain. "The heavens and the earth are continually employed in producing all things needful for man," a Delaware almanac for 1771 spread the word. People needed only conform to the laws to prosper.

Hence the genuine horror of atheism, which denied the existence of a Creator, therefore of natural law, therefore of the validity of ethical impulses. It was "the right as well as the duty of all men in society, publicly and at stated seasons, to worship the

Supreme Being," proclaimed the Massachusetts constitution of
1780.

People gave their consent to government to secure their rights
and to advance their security and happiness. The people could
also alter or abolish any form destructive of those ends and institute a new one protective, as "Philo Patriae" rhymed, of

> *Those rights, which God and Nature mean,*
> *RIGHTS, which, when truly understood,*
> *Are Cause of universal Good.*
> *Rights which declare "that all are free,*
> *In Persons and in Property . . ."*
> *No Laws should bind, without Consent,*
> *And that, when other Laws take Place,*
> *Not to resist would be Disgrace.*

The orderliness of the natural universe precluded any intervention in its processes. Divine interference with the mechanism
was inconceivable, for it would imply some initial imperfection
in the work of creation. Magic, witchcraft, spells, and impreca-
tions—even prayer—could not alter the course of events.

Men and women could act only within the rules and therefore
had first to learn to know them. Study and observation brought
the information within reach, and nature provided the instrument for comprehending its laws. Either the almanac or the
movement of the heavenly bodies informed the farmer of the
changing seasons, the fisher of the ebb and flow of tides. Reason
enabled humans to grasp the rules that governed the universe, to
understand their own beings, and to put knowledge to use. People had to free themselves from anachronistic beliefs and out-
moded habits that interfered with the exercise of reason. Thus
Timothy Pickering of Salem, who published an easy plan of discipline for the militia in 1775, warned against the reliance on
custom and prejudice in military thinking as in other fields.
Thus, too, Dr. Edward A. Holyoke insisted on performing autop-
sies on the bodies of his own children to learn the causes of their
deaths, and Dr. William Shippen, Jr., taught anatomy by dissect-
ing cadavers, whatever objections local prejudice interposed.

The test of utility measured reasonableness well. Benjamin Franklin's treatise on the art of swimming and its good results drew upon his own experience as a teacher. The beneficial exercise cleansed the pores, cooled off the body during the summer, and stopped diarrhea. To acquire the skill, the pupil walked slowly into the water, then turned to face the shore and dove after an egg thrown by the instructor as it sank to the bottom. The effort at retrieval would make students understand the supportive power of the water while all the time bringing them closer to shore.

Reason operated in great as in humble matters, since the Creator and sustainer of the physical universe was the first and necessary cause of all. Every visible effect had its own cause, linked to others more general and simple, "advancing by slow and sure steps toward the Great First Cause of all things." Nothing occurred in vain, and all was open and clear to those who rightly employed the divine gift of reason. For the Pennsylvania botanist John Bartram the telescope was but one means of seeing "God in all his Glory."

Astronomers used the telescope's lens to amplify and supplement by perception the inferences drawn from unaided reason. So, too, knowledge was useful—in teaching people to swim, in promoting common practical purposes, in stimulating agriculture, increasing trade, and refining daily life. The dignity of human beings derived from their capacity to learn, improve, and advance.

In addition, another type of aid helped them avoid both the trap of skepticism and the vanity of certitude, for alone among the animals they were both reasonable and accountable. That last term required no explanation in the 1770s. The Virginia Declaration of Rights (1776) made explicit the meaning of "accountable" by associating it with the words "conviction" and "conscience." Only reason and conviction, that document explained, could direct the practice of religion, the duty owed the Creator, which all men were equally entitled to do "according to the dictates of conscience." Conviction and conscience, in the Declaration of Rights, stood not in contradiction to reason but apart from it. Although God was one, the Creator and disposer of all, He made Himself known in two ways—through nature, perceived by the senses and apprehended by the mind, and through conscience, operating directly upon the heart.

Men and women exposed to a raw, hard life, deprived of tradition and of the consolation of ritual, could not in the end, however doughty they were, rely upon bare reason when they met the cruel contingencies of life and death. The loss of her brother brought an ordinary woman, Mary Hatheway, to some serious concern about her own soul and its salvation. Joseph Terry, an ordinary man, "awakened to sober Consideration by the sickness that prevailed & the Deaths that were multiplyed amonge us," began to "put more or less attention to Reading & Hearing the work of God, and to Meditation & Prayer." He acknowledged "with Shame and Humiliation that thro the Depravity & Corruption of" his nature he had spent his childhood and youth in sin and vanity. But now, if his heart did not deceive him, he (like Mary Hatheway) had seen the absolute necessity of Christ as prophet, priest, and king to help in hating sin, through obedience to His ordinances and commandments.

The ability to sound the call to conscience on the farms and in the workshops depended upon no previous course of education and ordination, only upon sensitivity to the precepts of nature and common sense. The harnessmaker came to do some work in the household, stayed some time, and spoke feelingly of the inward work of Christ in the soul. Departing, he left the family in a sweet frame of spirit. The Methodists, a peculiar people in their solemn dress, and the Baptists, insistent on the inner source of all true authority, numbered among their preachers men like John Gibbins, who painfully remedied the defects of his early schooling, yet always wistfully longed to "read the gospel in the language of Christ," to probe the real meaning of those "little particles, viz.: prepositions, adverbs, conjunctions, etc.," upon which so much depended. Shubal Stearns, Daniel Marshall, and other evangelists—shouting, falling, and losing physical control—carried the message from New England into Virginia and North Carolina. Even in Boston's restrained setting a foreigner noted the minister who frisked about in the pulpit like the devil in a fount of holy water.

By the 1770s decades of revivalism had made Americans well aware of the ways in which currents of enthusiasm overpoured the banks of reason, swept popular emotions, and carried passions along unpredictable courses. Benjamin Franklin, skeptic, never forgot that he had gone resolved to give nothing, then had emptied his pockets under the force of George Whitefield's oratory. Fiery preachers and turbulent awakenings had left vivid memories; and reconciliation of reason and faith remained a recurrent problem. Yet the assurance prevailed that the two forces were compatible as they had been in those sacred oracles the Scriptures. "O Lord, thou givest and at thy pleasure takest away. Blessed be thy name." The Pennsylvanian uttered the words knowing full well they would not help his marred apples. The devout of the revolutionary decade prayed not for intervention in the course of nature but for consolation and for the understanding and will to govern their own actions.

Eighteenth-century European intellectuals wrote extensively about nature, reason, and sentiment, and Americans readily borrowed from across the Atlantic words, phrases, and ideas that conformed to the teachings of experience. There was, however, no need, the minister Samuel Cooper, of Boston, stated, to delve into the writings of Locke, Algernon Sidney, and other glorious defenders of the liberties of human nature. Their plain and simple truths, level to every understanding, went home to every bosom because the acts and deeds of America also enunciated them.

Reason and revelation alike thrust the colonists into war. Intensely political, they respected power and knew its meaning. Wherever they lived, riots, Indian troubles, and domestic strife reminded them of the persuasiveness of the gun. But politics meant more than the application of power. In 1775 George III mobilized such resources as were beyond the Americans' imagining, yet they rose in rebellion because faith and reason required them to resist an oppressive and tyrannical government as much as to honor a just and beneficent one. Corruption, the ultimate charge against the Crown, against Parliament, and against British society, imposed the duty of resistance upon a virtuous people. In England in 1775 Benjamin Franklin noted how needless places, enormous salaries, pensions, perquisites, and bribes devoured all revenue and produced continual necessity in the midst of natural plenty. When he compared the extreme corruption prevalent among all orders in the rotten old state with the glorious public virtues so predominant in the rising New World, he concluded that any closer union would corrupt and poison his countrymen also and thus do more mischief than good.

Americans knew the face of corruption, on their own side of the ocean as on the other; but they also knew what to do about it. The misbehavior of men and women arose not from faults in their essential natures but from inadequate training. When they fell into error in personal behavior and in the use of power entrusted them, they required correction by the community. It was dismay at the card-playing habits of her friends and relatives that moved Barbara Heck to organize the Methodist Society in New York in 1766. Even in the midst of war, earnest people launched corrective efforts, as in 1780, when the General Conference of the Methodist Church adopted a statement against the use of distilled spirits. Corruptible man responded to moral appeals and stern measures by government. But popular control and constitutional limits had to keep government, itself corruptible, within bounds. In both respects, the Revolution created the liberty or the capacity to act.

Hence the war was a liberating force. At first people noticed the material losses. Some buildings suffered damage and endowment income shriveled in the inflation. But soon spiritual gains far outweighed the costs. More than a year after the fighting started, Americans recognized that independence was the means of establishing a state in accord with nature's laws. Freed from Britain, from the artificial restraints of an unnatural connection inherited from the past, people could now purify themselves and society. In primitive churches, often mere shells with the earth for floor and straw thatch for roof, worshipers who brought their own seats heard of the "necessity of religious violence to durable happiness." Ministers from various congregations banded together to stamp out vice and immorality, while congregations disciplined their members for eating stolen watermelons, gambling, dancing, and precipitating quarrels. Fine theological points lost importance as Luther and Calvin became rebels against unjust authority and John Knox became the fiery prophet who impudently informed Mary, Queen of Scots, of the circumstances under which subjects owed no duties to their princes.

Politics was the means of improvement, for, as election sermons, public prayers, and special days of thanksgiving made clear, the obligations imposed on individuals rested even more heavily on communities: the former received their rewards and punishments in an afterlife, the latter immediately, during their temporal existence. An appropriate government would root out corruption and in the process act as a moral agency. The true link between state and religion was not the support one rendered the other but the association of both in making human beings good.

Americans, pressed into an unavoidable conflict by tyranny, could win by uniting in a just political order. "The whole body of the people in these colonies," a minister said, had greeted royal oppression with "universal indignation and abhorrence." The solidarity among "so many distant colonies" under circumstances calculated to divide them expressed a clear sense "that the measures of the British government had infringed their most important rights and struck at the foundations of civil liberty and happiness."

It remained now to complete the tasks begun on the battlefields, to exploit unity for constructive purposes. "May we be purified in the flame," asked a prayer, "and made as a distinct nation a vessel of peculiar honor," capable of executing the wise and benevolent intentions of the Supreme Ruler of the universe. Success was certain. Sometimes—as had the Puritans—Americans saw a striking resemblance between their own condition and that of the ancient Israelites, who had also fled from civil and religious persecution to a wilderness and ultimately to a promised land. As often, the rebels saw themselves as many Europeans did, in the vanguard of the inevitable progress of humanity, unhampered by ancient institutions and superstitions, able to lead mankind to improvement. Faith in a particular providence and the reasoned logic of progress united in certainty about the special mission of the Republic, born in war. Bostonians in 1780 heard the message: "We are engaged in the common cause of mankind in defense of the inalienable rights of mankind—rights which once established and properly improved will make us a name and a praise through the whole earth."

With peace, the rebel clergy lost influence as articulators of public opinion, interpreters of events, and guardians of social stability. The "Psalm singing Myrmidons" returned to the plow and the counter, and a younger generation took their place, less interested in the old issues, more concerned with problems of general morality. At the Constitutional Convention in 1787 it was not Jacob Duché, a man of the cloth, but the Deist Benjamin Franklin, who invoked the aid of God to still incessant wranglings, disagreements, and differences of opinion. He reminded his colleagues "that God governs in the affairs of men" and no "empire can rise without His aid." All human understanding was imperfect, but prayers imploring the assistance of heaven would evoke sentiments all shared and would in the end produce the more perfect union all desired.

Society remained stable, coherent, united, and moral because civic piety supplied an alternative to creedal affirmation. The Republic had come into being under the will of God, who granted each person a moral sense to distinguish between right and wrong. Church membership declined, but constant references to God's will and wisdom in speeches, articles, legal briefs, and popular discourse revealed religious overtones in politics and law. Americans readily accepted the usage, for nothing more seemed involved than the restatement of old truths. Franklin spoke to people conscious that the Constitution, like the Declaration of Independence and the war, was the work of flesh-and-blood creatures prone to error. But suspicion and fear subsided with the suggestion that these efforts harmonized with the laws governing the progress of the human race, retarded in the past through corruption and despotism. In 1774 the purifiers had begun their task, not of their own volition but in response to urgings from on high. The fortunate generation of the Revolution could demonstrate in cultural and social achievements its worthiness for the mission.

9

Republican Culture

Surveying a world in which tyrant princes drenched distant lands in human gore to prove their right divine to wealth and power, while spaniel courtiers licked their masters' feet, an almanac for 1775 nevertheless reassured Americans:

> *While art and science fix their standards here,*
> *All hell combin'd no longer need we fear.*

The nation's providential mission required the shield of appropriate modes of expression.

Everything about this society was fresh; art would also manifest a republican character. In the Old World, under European and Asian despots, culture was a possession of monarchs and aristocrats. In the New World, freed from stifling vestiges of the past and nurtured by the moral character of a healthy citizenry, it would flower and safeguard virtue.

The results did not match expectations. Culture was a hardy growth, not easily altered by changes in government or nationalistic rhetoric. Where its roots reached deep into the past it flowered in its own way; and only where it gave form to the restlessness of the people did the Revolution mark a genuine break.

Cautious John Adams was among the skeptics about high American art. He had confidence in the future of his country but expected three generations to pass before it possessed adequate leisure and resources for the more elevated aspects of life. In any case, a time of war was not the moment in which to dissipate energies on such matters. Other New Englanders agreed. According to one critic, painters, hairdressers, tavern keepers, musicians, stage-players, buffoons, and exhibitors of birds and puppets fell into a single unproductive category; their labor existed no longer than the sound they made was heard or the sight of them was present. Connecticut was not Athens, Governor Trumbull explained to the son he sought to dissuade from becoming an artist. Besides, insofar as the arts appealed to the senses they diverted attention from conscience and reason, the safe guides for virtuous citizens.

The dominant tone, however, was one of exuberant confidence. Political moralists before 1775 had warned, "Freedom and Arts together Fall." It followed that elevation of the arts during and after the conflict would measure the rise of liberty. The rivalry between the Old World and the New in literature, painting, and music, as in other fields, would justify defiance of the Crown. Indeed, the very emergency to which Adams referred would have a positive effect. "The war not only required, but created talents," wrote the South Carolina historian David Ramsay a few years afterward. Men whose minds were warmed by the love of liberty and whose abilities were improved by daily exercise spoke, wrote, and acted with an energy far surpassing all expectations. Nationalizing tendencies expanded horizons to a continental scale and nurtured optimism. Americans no longer thought in terms of a county or of a province but of a whole country, larger than most in Europe. Furthermore, exposure to people recently strangers, now fellow citizens, brought a heady surge of confidence, as in the Pennsylvanian who learned from Virginian officers the excellence of turkey hash and fried hominy, and learned therefore the excellence of ways not his own.

In the effort to join battle in the arts, however, Americans, carried along by rhetoric, all too often stumbled over necessity

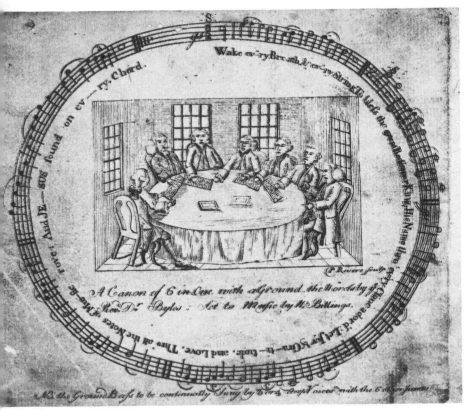

William Billings, *The New-England Psalm-Singer,* frontispiece (engraved by Paul Revere). The caption reads: A Canon of 6 in One with a Ground. The words by the Rev. Dr. Byles, Set to Music by W. Billings. The words that border the music are:

> Wake ev'-ry Breath, & ev'-ry String,
> To Bless the great Redeemer King;
> His Name thro' ev'ry Clime ador'd:
> Let Joy & Gra—ti—tude, and Love,
> Thro' all the Notes of Mu-sic rove;
> And JE—SUS sound on ev—ry, Chord.

Courtesy American Antiquarian Society

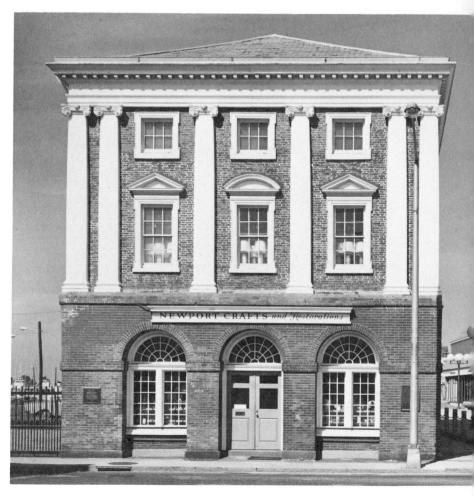

The Brick Market, Newport, R.I., 1761, Peter Harrison, architect. *Courtesy Wayne Andrews*

Touro Synagogue, Newport, R.I., 1763, Peter Harrison, architect. *Courtesy Wayne Andrews*

Miles Brewton House, Charleston, S.C. *Courtesy Wayne Andrews*

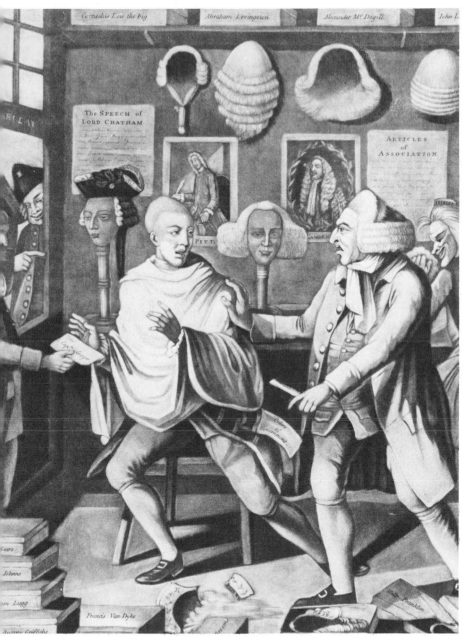

A patriotic New York barber sends off a half-shaved British officer, 1774 (mezzotint, London, February 14, 1774). *Stokes Collection, New York Public Library*

The Maſſachuſetts CALENDAR;

OR AN
ALMANACK
FOR THE
Year of our Lord Chriſt 1774;

Being the ſecond after Biſſextile or Leap Year.

By EZRA GLEASON.

A LIST OF CRIMES

1560

The wicked Stateſman, or the Traitor to his Country, at the Hour of DEATH

BOSTON: Printed by ISAIAH THOMAS: Sold at his Printing Office near the Market, and at his ſhop near the Mill Bridge

[Thomas Hutchinson], "The Wicked Statesman, or the Traitor to his Country, at the Hour of DEATH," title page of Ezra Gleason, *The Massachusetts Calendar; or an Almanack for...1774.* Printed by Isaiah Thomas. *Courtesy American Antiquarian Society*

An ASTRONOMICAL DIARY: Or,
ALMANACK
For the Year of Christian Æra, 1775.
By NATHANAEL LOW.

The VIRTUOUS PATRIOT at the Hour of Death.

IF Prayers and Tears th' PATRIOT's Life could save,
None but usurping Villains Death would have.

BOSTON: Printed and Sold by JOHN KNEELAND, in
Milk-Street. Price 2*s*5*d*. per Doz. 6 Coppers single.

"The virtuous PATRIOT at the Hour of Death," from Nathanael Low, *An Astronomical Diary: Or, Almanack for ... 1775.* Printed by John Kneeland. *Courtesy American Antiquarian Society*

APICTURESQUE VIEW of the State of GREAT BRITAIN for 178

EXPLANATION

I The Commerce of Great Britain represented in the figure of a Milch Cow.

II The American Congress fawing of her horns which are her natural strength and defence: the one being already gone, the other just a going.

III The jolly plump Dutchman milking the poor tame Cow with great glee.

IV & V The French and Spaniard each catching at their respective shares of the produce, and running away with bowls brimming full, laughing to one another at their success.

VI A distant view of Clinton and Arnold; in New York concerting measures for the fruitless scheme of enslaving America.—Arnold sensible of his guilt

drops his head and weeps.

VII The British Lion lying on the ground fast asleep so that a pug-dog tramples upon him; as on a feeless log; he seems to see nothing hear nothing and feel nothing.

VIII A free Englishman in mourning standing by him, wringing his hands, casting up his Eyes in despondency and despair, but unable to rouse the Lion to correct all these invaders of his Royal Prerogative and his subjects property

"A PICTURESQUE VIEW of the State of GREAT BRITAIN for 1780" from *Weatherwise's New England Town & Countryman's Almanack for 1781*. The caption explains the cow represents the commerce of Great Britain; the American Congress saws off her horns, her natural defense—one already gone, the other just going; a jolly Dutchman milks the cow with glee; a Frenchman and Spaniard, bowls brimming with their shares, laugh at their success; in the distance Clinton and Arnold plan fruitlessly to enslave America; the British lion sleeps while a pug dog tramples on him; and a free Englishman, in mourning, wrings his hands in despair. *Courtesy, American Antiquarian Society* and frequently overlooked achievements that satisfied humbler needs. As in other aspects of life, so in prose, poetry, and music the impulse to achievement accorded with neither the needs and abilities of contented yeomen nor with the interests of restless achievers.

In the Republic, as earlier in the colonies, words were the basic units of expression, heard in sermons or stories or gossip, read in books or journals. No American doubted the importance of equipping all with these keys to salvation and enlightenment, yet few were willing to do much about it—certainly not to meet the costs.

The inadequacies of their schools did not, however, deprive Americans of all opportunities for learning. The desire to know forged its own means of satisfaction. Many a young man did his studying not in the classroom but in the debating society or the library, and young women were not condemned to ignorance because no college admitted them.

Publications were everywhere at hand, either for sale or available on loan. Numerous booksellers in the larger towns (fifty in Philadelphia and sixteen in New York before 1775) stocked local as well as European materials. Newspapers carried long lists of newly arrived titles, and the business of publishers, who distributed their own catalogs, thrived. George Washington, worried in 1771 about the training of his ward, doubted that becoming a mere scholar was the education desirable for a gentleman but was certain that familiarity with books was the basis upon which to build all knowledge.

Schemes for borrowing by subscription went back to 1731, when Benjamin Franklin helped found the Library Company of Philadelphia. Similar organizations, on a cost-sharing basis, spread even to smaller communities, such as Lancaster, Pennsylvania. William Rind of Annapolis, who allowed neighbors to borrow books from his collection for one guinea a year, tried to develop an intercolonial network, but inadequate transportation forced him to restrict circulation to local people.

The war damaged some establishments. Newport's Redwood Library was in a wretched state, its books scattered, its members disbanded, until it was revived when the legislature reconstituted it as a corporation. New York by 1789 had three lending collections; the largest, the New York Society Library, boasted 3,500 volumes, with membership open to those who could spare five pounds for the initial fee and annual dues of ten shillings. The 4 percent of the city's total number of households that availed themselves of the society's services set the cultural tone of the community.

No gentleman's home was complete without a well-stocked private library, some of which ran to a thousand volumes or more. True, content was not always of prime interest—books sold at auctions according to size. And voracious readers who lacked the means either for fees or for private purchase usually found neighbors willing to lend. Many books thus borrowed, alas, never returned. A notice in the Annapolis *Maryland Gazette* appealed to one ingrate either to return the second volume he had taken or to come get the first one as well. *The Art of Cooking* came back to another lender in "such a pickle that one would imagine it had been several times in the pot."

American reading tastes, before and after the Revolution, reflected those of England. Fiction, travel accounts, and histories were the staples of borrowers and buyers; and Pope and Swift, Voltaire, Richardson, Gibbon, and Johnson were among the preferred authors. Best-seller lists, had they existed, would certainly have included Captain Cook's *Voyage Round the World,* Gibbon's *Decline and Fall,* and Johnson's *Lives of the Poets,* while Sterne's *Tristram Shandy* found an appreciative reader in George Croghan, the fur trader. Charlotte Perkins' five-volume novel *Female Stability* attracted numerous readers by the tale of a woman's loyalty to her dead lover. The virtuous heroine, an orphan who shed light and beauty wherever she went but also accumulated property en route, in Volume I gave her heart to the hero, who, however, died before openly expressing his affection for her. In hundreds of edifying pages she repulsed suitor after suitor, preserved her chastity, withstood temptation, grew wealthy, and sustained her constant devotion. Readers paid little heed to carping critics such as Dr. Benjamin Rush who argued

that the abortive sympathy that novels aroused only hardened
the heart in cases of real distress.

American printers stood ready to publish the products of native genius but, of course, on terms competitive with cheap imports, a constraint that excluded the payment of royalties and,
indeed, often required subsidies from budding authors. As a result, the books issued in the colonies and later in the Republic
were as likely to contain theological or political arguments as
imaginative literature. The pamphlets most widely sold in the
revolutionary period treated subjects of topical interest. Passed
around to be read and reread, even the most patriotic of these
works imitated such British models as the *Letters of Junius,* anonymous attacks upon George III in 1769.

Popular literature made no room for American themes by
American writers other than the always popular Indian captivity
narratives. Paper-covered books sold by itinerant peddlers (once
called chapmen, from the word "cheap," meaning "trade"),
found their way into the poorer houses. Most chapbooks were
anonymous and contained stories based on traditional belief and
customs, the heroic prototypes being characters from English
folklore such as Tom Thumb, Simple Simon, and Robin Hood.
But buyers could catch up on *The Whole Pleasures of Matrimony . . . , The Sweets of Wooing and Wedlock,* or other tracts
printed by Andrew Steuart in Philadelphia between 1763 and
1765. And among the "Little Books for the Instruction and
Amusement of all Good Boys and Girls" advertised in the *Boston
Gazette* of January 20, 1772, were abridged versions of *The History of Tom Jones, The History of Pamela,* and *The History of
Clarissa.*

Ambitious authors, actual or prospective, often longed for pe-
riodicals, analogous to those of Britain, that would expose their
efforts to the light of day and reward them with appreciation
and fame. Yet occasional faltering steps to establish magazines
aimed at a literary audience bore no durable results. Most staggered through a few issues and then failed.

On the other hand, newspapers did well, despite the high cost
of distribution. Delivered by postriders in some places, they
found eager readers; there were even some in the German lan-

guage in Pennsylvania. Political agitation in the decade before
the war had increased the number and the circulation of the
weeklies. The twenty-three published in 1764 had grown to
thirty-seven in 1775; and although some loyalist sheets then went
out of business, a total of thirty-five newspapers still appeared in
1783. During the war a paper shortage forced publishers to
scurry about for rags and the quality of printing deteriorated.
But the circulation and the influence of the press remained high
—the *Connecticut Courant* in 1778 had fully eight thousand
readers.

Almanacs remained popular, as in the past, some illustrated by
curious engravings, others laden with practical advice. Recipes
with political overtones directed patriots to do without imports
by making substitutes for molasses and sugar, by laying down
local wines and distilling corn liquor to take the place of rum,
and by turning their own wool into cloth. The approach of war
added urgency to instructions on the manufacture of saltpeter
and gunpowder. All along, too, the almanacs found space for
politics—not for the reasoned essays or learned legal arguments
printed in newspapers, pamphlets, or books, but for repeatable
lines that filled out blank space in aphorisms or squibs of verse
the readers recognized as truth.

Print remained but a supplement to oral communication. The
carrying power of journal, tract, or tome depended upon repetition, in the household, the tavern, the market, the church, and
private letters. And as they broadcast the messages read, so, too,
Americans amplified by word of mouth opinions heard in sermons and orations. The attention span, while not as long as in
Puritan meetinghouses, was still long enough to permit attentive
perusal of, and careful listening to, paragraphs densely packed
with ideas. In these matters, war and independence made
scarcely a difference.

An influential handful of young men and women wanted
more; they sought to express the surge of emotion that welled up
as they thought of their country's destiny, of the New World
they inhabited, and of their own powers now on the verge of

release. The will to create found outlets in drama, poetry, and prose.

In the decade before 1774 the theater had spread through the colonies; even smaller cities such as Providence, Rhode Island, heard readings from John Gay's *Beggar's Opera* without scandal. And during the war the garrisons in town sought this form of diversion, as did idle college students. In 1778 the *Connecticut Journal* acidly pointed out, people paid one dollar each to see a dialogue and a farce at Yale, oblivious "to the serious state of our public affairs." President Ezra Stiles worried lest dramatic exhibitions turn the institution into Drury Lane. The next year, Stiles forbade other students to commemorate the Battle of Lexington with a play; he would "not preside at the head of a society of stage players."

The theater banned in Boston was nowhere in good repute. New Yorkers had rioted in 1766 when a traveling company tried to open a playhouse, and preachers persistently branded acting a violation of God's commandments, the theater a den of depravity, and the dramas promoters of vice and of the dissipation of time that could be more usefully spent. Royall Tyler's *The Contrast* mocked Jonathan, the Yankee servant, who could not understand why people paid good money to attend "the devil's drawing room." Players and writers remained on the defensive despite dogged presentations of moral dramas—*George Barnwell*, revealing the machinations of unscrupulous women; or *The Devil to Pay*, explaining marital responsibility by transposing poor Nell and Lady Loverule. Filled out with afterpiece and vocal or musical interludes, performances lasted five to six hours, often punctuated with thrown eggs and unruly incursions onto the stage by patrons overly attentive to the charms of the actresses.

The most popular plays were English: Shakespeare's *Romeo and Juliet* and George Farquhar's *Beaux' Stratagem*, all love and blood. Acting methods were English, too: the stiff, prim, and unnatural style and the vocabulary of gestures derived from the popular *Thespian Preceptor*. That handbook gave common definitions of moods and emotions along with instructions on how to express such states as vexation or admiration. Wonder, for instance, required the actor to stand still, eyes open and fixed as in fear on one object while raised hands dropped whatever they held, the body contracted, and the mouth opened.

Young Americans gaining familiarity with a medium that bridged the gap between the spoken and written word insisted that the time was ripe for a native drama to rival the best of Europe. One thing led to another. Alexander Graydon's school books were collections of chores; he read little until the visit of a company of players from the West Indies introduced him to Shakespeare, whose works he then ardently devoured. Why, he complained, had school not imbued him with the same relish? His countrymen ought to be able to do as well. The technique came easily; and if no producer would stage a play, surely a newspaper or printer would publish it. All the themes were at hand. As an ambitious playwright put it,

> *Why should our thoughts to distant countries roam,*
> *When each refinement may be found at home?*

The same question spurred on prospective poets and novelists.

Early efforts had not been propitious. Philadelphians in 1767 had refused *The Disappointment* permission to open. Loaded with bawdy puns, the play included the declaration by a prostitute, Moll Placket, that she had "raised and laid 500" and her "cock-a-dandy" lover was an elderly black man. Political innuendo saved *The Prince of Parthia*, by Thomas Godfrey, who borrowed heavily from *Othello, Macbeth,* and *King Lear* but assigned the classical dialogue to a haughty, antidemocractic, villainous king who despised his subjects and to an archetypical Whig hero. Neither the play's authentic origins nor its relevance forestalled a debate over virtue and the stage. An agitated populace demanded that money and time go for more serious matters.

Patriotism made a difference. The prolific Mercy Otis Warren (sister of James Otis) started her activities as a dramatist in 1772 with *The Adulateur,* an attack on Massachusetts Governor Thomas Hutchinson (Rapatio in the play), which appeared in the *Massachusetts Spy.* The next year she published *The Defeat,* in the *Boston Gazette*. Prompted by the success of General Burgoyne's *Blockade of Boston, The Blockheads* set British officers and American traitors, swaggering, swearing, and kowtowing to their superiors, against virtuous Yankees living close to the soil and tilling the land. Jonathan Sewall's *The Cure* (Boston, 1775) which few read and no one ever saw performed, stated the loyalist case. Puff, representative to the Continental Congress and determined to behave as a gentleman should, knew no Latin and mixed up French and Greek while Fillpot the innkeeper and Trim the barber stuffed their pockets. The Tory Sharp, by contrast, represented true reason, true religion, and true education.

Revolutionary drama also took the form of dialogues read before educated audiences that appreciated the formality and rhetorical dignity of the speeches. One such piece, *Ministerial Oppression or the Grievances of America*, opened with the news from Lexington, stated the alternative before the colonists—Liberty or Slavery—and closed with Bunker Hill. The dialogues, however, served as background for a plot that centered on the fatal love of Lysander and Cassandra, he the survivor of his family's massacre at Lexington, she the daughter of a leading Boston Tory. Lysander fights and dies at Bunker Hill. Cassandra finds his body, goes mad, and dies. Love must lose in a conflict with Liberty.

John Trumbull and Philip Freneau, devoted to freedom and the muse, turned out easy verse in support of the rebel cause. And young men dizzied by the epic qualities of the war set to work on suitable celebrations—Francis Hopkinson's "Prophecy," Joel Barlow's *Vision of Columbus,* and Timothy Dwight's *Conquest of Canaan.* The labor expended on patriotic poetry, fiction, and drama yielded fruit swollen with bombast and rhetoric. Too many authors believed with David Ramsay "that the talents for great stations" were the same as those "necessary for the proper discharge" of ordinary business. Anyone could do anything. As a result, American literature, at this level, simply transposed to a local setting well-established English themes and techniques. Feelings, even lofty revolutionary feelings, were not enough to evoke genius.

But the writing and speaking of these years did manifest char-

acteristic traits, significant in the lives of readers and listeners.
Sometimes the political verse ran to easily recollected little jin-
gles:

> *It's time to think of raising Hemp & Flax,*
> *If we've a Mind to save a Tax.*

Other lines, in obscure sonority, reached for deeper emotions, as
did those addressed to Oliver Cromwell, who had also defied a
monarch:

> *Ungrateful those, who would no Tears allow*
> *To him who gave them Peace and Empire too!*
> *Princes who fear'd him, griev'd: Concern'd to see*
> *No Pitch of Glory from the Grave is free.*

The language, when free of self-conscious literary pretensions,
drew naturally upon the vocabulary made familiar by the Bible,
Shakespeare, and Milton, but also on the homely metaphors, hy-
perbole, and humor of day-to-day life. On royal corruption: "A
great part of the water, which should go to the King's cistern,
passes through broken pipes." On British delusions about the ease
of reconquering the Americans, a Londoner speaks:

> *Virst, they are to stop all their ports, that is their*
> *rivers, and that will go nigh to drawn em.*
> *Zecondly, they're to dig a ditch in the zea*
> *and that will keep them from running away.*
> *Thirdly, they're to set the air a fire. Vourthly,*
> *they're to let the clouds down upon their heads.*

Americans exploited the capacity of the word to express their
thoughts and emotions, although not in the literary forms to
which ambitious authors aspired.

Overendeavor in music and the plastic arts had more drastic
consequences. Desire was simply not enough; and nothing in the
colonial background had encouraged development of the necessary talent and skill. Music, Robert Carter had said, was (along

with law) the main study for a gentleman; to perfect ability in it was difficult without teachers, and Dr. Rush, for one, argued that the time ought to be spent more usefully. Thomas Jefferson sadly noted in 1778 that music was the favorite passion of his soul, but admitted that fortune had cast his lot in a country where the art was in a state of deplorable barbarism. In Paris he attended concerts and operas, and throughout his life collected sheet music and tinkered with instruments. Most of his countrymen were less fortunate than he.

Here and there wandering entrepreneurs offered every inducement to fee-paying students. Robert Coe thus assured gentlemen hesitant to take up the German flute that a mouthpiece of his own invention made it unnecessary to expend more wind than they could spare or to puff out the face in a vulgar fashion. Settled music masters in the towns and itinerant tutors in the country provided lessons to the ambitious. Jefferson studied the violin for several years, and at Mount Vernon George Washington employed a German, John Stedler, to teach Mrs. Washington and the Custis children. Moreover, local publishers made available little leisure collections of tunes and instruction books, mostly religious. Boston remained supreme in the trade down through the Revolution, although Philadelphia had by then begun to compete with it. Usually music booksellers commissioned job printers to print from blocks to meet immediate local needs, and dealers distributed these volumes in the vicinity. But an occasional musician, such as Andrew Law, spread them more widely. The most prolific single publisher, Daniel Bayley of Newburyport, Massachusetts, issued eleven collections between 1764 and 1778.

Music during worship was the subject of a lively continuing controversy. Everyone agreed that singing prepared the soul for grace and that the pious ought not to become engrossed in the tune at the expense of the text. But agreement was far from unanimous on who should lead or participate and on the use of instruments. Some people regarded choirs as a way of attaching the young to the church and training them in order, obedience, and harmony. Singers who attained a higher level of proficiency than the regular congregation received special seats in the galleries. But those displaced resented it, especially when the choir performed songs too difficult for others to join. Those plain and easy compositions essential to the solemnity of church music, an irate New Hampshire man complained back in 1764, had given way to light, airy, jiggish tunes better "adapted to a Country Dance, than the awful Business of Chanting forth the Praises of the King of Kings." This, another critic wrote, encouraged a "parcel of giddy young folks to sit in the gallery to show off their skill, which is apparently all they care for." Introduction of the bass viol, the devil's fiddle, around 1776 divided churches into catgut and anti-cat camps. Descendants of the Puritans found the organ even more offensive. Boston's First Church purchased one, at the insistence of the congregation and against the wishes of its old minister, Charles Chauncy, who warned his parishioners that instrumental music was not fit for public worship. "The Christian Religion shines brightest in its own dress; and to paint it is but to deform it." The organ arrived in 1785, although diehards retained their ancient prejudices, preferring to "hear this pleasing part of devotion performed by a small number of screaming voices."

Despite their interest in music, Americans could not meet the demands of revolutionary patriotism. Francis Hopkinson's verse and tunes sounded much like their British models, as did the psalms of James Lyon. William Billings' *Singing Master's Assistant* (1778) also showed its debts to English antecedents, as well as to biblical references, popular tunes, and current events. An awkward eccentric, half blind, with one leg and one arm deformed, this Bostonian of many trades refused to yield to rules. Self-confident, he urged the revolutionary sons of harmony to match the fervor of their patriotism with the fervor of song. His *Lamentation Over Boston* expressed the wartime emotions of his countrymen, but did so in a thoroughly archaic mode. So, too, when Benjamin Franklin apparently tried his hand at composing a quartet (in F major, for two violins, viola, and cello) while a guest of Mme Helvetius in Auteuil, he employed the scordatura, an antique seventeenth-century technique that made it possible to play entirely with open strings. A brassy sound was the price of ease of execution; but then the distinguished composer had no musical training to speak of. The transformations that in these decades remade European music scarcely affected the colonies;

not until well after the Revolution did the pianoforte displace
the clavichord and harpsichord, although both Jefferson and the
Carters ordered the new forte-piano from England earlier.

Yet everywhere in the homes and the churches, music sounded
without strain or anxiety. Folksongs, carried from across the Atlantic, passed from generation to generation to convey traditional wisdom, relieve the tedium of tasks, and express emotions
in worship.

Politics enlisted popular melodies on both the Tory and Patriot
sides. *Liberty Song* of 1768, to the tune of the ever-popular
Heart of Oak, contrasted frugal, hardworking Americans with
English pensioners and placemen, each stanza ending in the refrain:

> *In freedom we're born and in freedom we'll live,*
> *our purses are ready,*
> *steady, friends, steady,*
> *not as slaves but as Freemen our Money we'll give.*

Loyalists rejoined, to the same tune:

> *In folly you're born, and in folly you'll live*
> *To madness still ready*
> *and stupidly steady*
> *Not as men, but as monkeys, the tokens you give.*

Only to meet the retort:

> *Come swallow your bumpers, ye Tories, and roar*
> *That the sons of fair Freedom are hamper'd once more;*
> *But know that no cutthroat our spirits can tame*
> *Nor a host of oppressors shall smother the flame.*

The origins of *Yankee Doodle* lay back in the 1740s, when it
poked fun at the victory at Louisburg:

> *Brother Ephraim sold his cow*
> *and bought him a commission*

> *and then he went to Canada*
> *to fight for the nation.*
>
> *But when Ephraim he came home*
> *he proved an errant Coward*
> *He woudn't fight the Frenchmen there*
> *for fear of being devoured.*
>
> *Aminadab is just come Home*
> *His eyes all greased with Bacon*
> *And all the news that he could tell*
> *Is Cape Breton is taken.*

The song became a popular means of burlesque, with various versions touching on colonial holidays, local pride, neighborhood rivalries, harvest frolics, and election escapades.

> *Now husking time is over*
> *They have a deuced frolic*
> *There'll be some as drunk as sots*
> *The rest will have the cholic.*
>
> *Election time is now at hand*
> *We're going to uncle Chace's*
> *There'd be some a drinking round*
> *And some a lapping lasses.*
>
> *Two and two may go to Bed*
> *Two and two together*
> *And if there is not room enough,*
> *Lie one a top o't'other*
>
> *Sheep's Head and Vinegar*
> *Butter Milk and Tansy*
> *Boston is a Yankee Town*
> *Sing Hey Doodle Dandy*
>
> *Heigh ho for our Cape Cod*
> *Heigh ho Nantasket*
> *Do not let the Boston wags*
> *Feel your oyster basket*

Unencumbered by the burden of patriotism, music sprang from the hearts of Americans in ways that reflected their diverse origins and conditions. The Shakers possessed a repertoire of their own tunes that accompanied work in the fields and the shops, as well as services in the meetinghouses. Visitors noted the unearthly effect of the falsetto voices at the Dunker community, Ephrata, and the quick, animated tempo among the Methodists. The fondness of Virginians for music and the skill of their performances surprised a German officer who visited Monticello during the war. Men at the violin, French horn, and flute and women at the spinet or harpsichord spent many an evening in ensemble playing and group singing. His host entertained the Scot John Harrower by playing the fiddle, then asked a slave to perform on a barrafon, an oblong box, holding eleven sticks, beaten rhythmically. Other blacks danced to the banjo—droll music an onlooker found it, generally relating, in a very satirical style and manner, the harsh treatment masters or mistresses gave the bondspeople.

Few musicians thrived solely by their art. Peter Pelham, one of the best-known teachers, received twenty-five dollars a year as public organist of Bruton Church in Williamsburg, while earning forty dollars as jailor. Frequent organ recitals supplemented his income, as did occasional benefit performances; and he did much to encourage the town's musical life. Pelham's report of Franklin's performance on the glass harmonica heard during a trip to New York persuaded Robert Carter to order a special set from England and to learn to play. So, too, John Stevens in Savannah offered concerts while serving as deputy postmaster. Stephen Deblois, who operated Boston's concert hall, one of the town's imposing edifices, kept a store on the ground floor. New York's Ranelagh Garden served food with its outdoor concerts and used fireworks for the finale. Charleston topped off an evening of music with a magician's card tricks.

Music took motion in the dance, by the 1780s even in New England. Gone were the days when Massachusetts law forbade such frolics at weddings and in taverns and when a New York father suggested his daughters master the domestic arts before learning to jig at the dancing school. Girls early took lessons; the arrival of a master often interrupted stern Philip Fithian's classes at Nomini Hall. During the war young women in the Shenandoah area walked seven miles, three times a week, to meet an instructor from France.

Balls were numerous and continued interminably. Washington and Mrs. General Greene were reported to have danced one night for three hours without sitting down, a "pretty frisk," the lady's husband commented. This may have been a healthy exercise, as Dr. Rush suggested, but not when Lucy Carter went to "the ordinary keeper's hop" at Westmoreland Court in Virginia; the windows lacked panes and snow covered the ballroom floor. The Fredericksburg, Virginia, town house, erected by private subscription, set aside a room for dancing. On the South Carolina frontier, Lieutenant Enos Reeves, a northerner, turned up his nose at the couples that "hobbled through the figures without minding the tune." But participation required no precise knowledge of the steps. Dances that bore such names as Old Father George, Cape Breton, High Betty Martin, The President, Priest's House, Leather the Strap, and Constancy called mostly for enthusiastic response to the rhythm. In neither music nor the dance did the Revolution mark a significant change.

A makeshift environment presented its residents with few pleasing visual images. Wealthy Philadelphians in 1769 could secure paper hangings from Plunkett Fleeson in color or gilt, to imitate carvings. Housewives made an art of sweeping the silver sand on their floors into twirls and figures, and the shape of some wooden trenchers reflected a feeling for form. Curiosity brought observers to gawk at the rarities in Dr. Chavet's Philadelphia museum. But few Americans forgot the injunction in the almanac of 1774 to heed "not what may be true, but what is useful."

After the Revolution, as before, they applied the standard of utility to painting and sculpture as to other products. The crude woodcuts and the occasional copper engravings in the almanac had value as a form of instruction, and one could also learn from sculpture—George Washington sent to London for busts of Alexander the Great, Julius Caesar, Frederick the Great of Prussia, Marlborough, and Charles XII of Sweden. Gravestone carvings were manifestly edifying. At a reasonable price a portrait, too, was worth having, and itinerant limners—part-time glaziers and house and sign painters—readily satisfied the demand.

By the 1770s, however, some Americans were willing to pay more for the work of professional painters. Puritan insistence on symmetry and two-dimensionality had eased, as had the disapproval of ornamentation and flattery of the subject. The gentry of the South and of New York and Pennsylvania wanted and got the equivalents of the work they knew from prints by Van Dyck, Holbein, and English court painters—three-dimensional representations of the qualities the sitters most valued in themselves: self-assurance, aristocratic demeanor, fashionableness. Patrons wore elaborate costumes to resemble English ladies and gentlemen and delighted in portraits in which no trace of provincialism showed.

A generation of young painters, described as products of American freedom undebauched by the wickedness of European courts, filled the demand. Charles Willson Peale, a saddlemaker and upholsterer, regarded art as a trade plied like any other, it was to be hoped more remuneratively than most. Two lessons in exchange for a saddle equipped him for a career in Maryland, whence he would move on to London and Philadelphia. On the other hand, John Singleton Copley of Boston, carefully trained by his stepfather and by John Smibert, both professionals, married the daughter of an East India Company agent, purchased a great estate on Beacon Hill, expressed no political opinions, and painted portraits, alike revealing, of Samuel Adams and of the British General Gage's wife. Matthew Pratt in Philadelphia and Henry Benbridge in Charleston were also competent, if not masterly.

The best-known American painter, Benjamin West, had moved to London, not only because commissions were more lucrative there, but also for the opportunity to turn to historical and classical subjects. Copley followed, for he had long aspired to do the same and America offered neither markets nor models for creations of this sort. It was one thing to copy the features of a Boston merchant, another to play philosopher, historian, and moralist expounding on the grand themes of human existence. John

Durand had found no takers for his canvases in 1768 when he offered to put at the service of New Yorkers a "fund of universal and accurate knowledge," including geometry, perspective, anatomy, expressions of passions, and ancient and modern history. A few years later, in Virginia, he was ready to undertake portraits and to paint, gild, and varnish carriages and put coats of arms or ciphers upon them. Success called not merely for imagination, historical knowledge, and psychological insight, but also for exposure, unattainable in the New World, to the work of the great artists of the past.

The Revolution was far from congenial to creative personalities, hence the preference of the ablest artists—West and Copley—for working in London. The adverse effects of the war delayed mastery of techniques such as those Gainsborough explored and kept abroad the most talented practitioners of the generation. Americans saw no need for edifying but expensive national monuments. The decision by Congress in 1783 to commission an equestrian statue of Washington to mark the peace turned into a scabrous joke when Francis Hopkinson proposed that it be large enough to hold private archives of the members in the horse's "intestinum rectum," since the capital might move, and the statue with it.

The level of skill displayed by painters in America, never lofty to begin with, sank with time. The portraits in almanacs and broadsides were sometimes so crude they could not be identified without labels. A variety of devices compensated. Sometimes descriptive verse, snippets of speeches, or brief aphoristic statements made clear the meaning as the drawings alone could not. Often the effort at persuasion turned the picture into an emblem: thus in an almanac of 1769 the English radical politician John Wilkes, crowned with laurels, rested between Britannia, dressed as Minerva, goddess of wisdom, on the one side and Hercules, crushing the serpent Envy, on the other. Hercules appeared in another almanac, of 1770, this time beside a bust of James Otis, while Minerva now bore the liberty cap on a pole. A 1772 drawing showed the patriotic American yeoman leaning on Magna Carta and holding a scroll of John Dickinson's "Farmer's Letters." Words and pictures thus joined in a didactic purpose.

Cartoons, patterned after English models, forcefully delivered political messages. The Stamp Act evoked an elaborate attack. In one instance, a flying figure robed in a sheet holds out a sack of money to a nearby comet marked with a boot, which says, "What a surprising virtue there is in Gold. With it I make the very Stars shed their influence as I please." The allusion was to Lord Bute, the King's Scottish minister who opposed concessions to the colonies. The comet spreads its evil rays on Britannia, another flying figure, behind whom flutter torn pieces of paper marked Magna Ch[art]a. She holds out a Pandora's Box to America, saying, "Take it Daughter its only ye S——p A——t." Loyalty leans against a tree labeled "Liberty Aug. 14, 1765" (the day of the first Boston Stamp Act riot). Clasping a heart to her bosom, she looks at a crown and says, "O tis a horrid blast I fear I shall lose my support." A viper is seen creeping out from under a Scottish thistle, and a dog, its collar inscribed "W. P[it]t's Dog," lifts its leg and douses the thistle.

Another part of the cartoon shows two sailors standing by a cart, one asking, "have ye seen ye S[tam]p M[a]n," the other answering, "there he Drives D——n his eyes," while on the other side of the tree a figure on horseback, in obvious flight, yells, "Fort George Will Save me," alluding to the island in Boston harbor where British troops were stationed. In another corner a group of well-dressed men stands around a gallows labeled "Fit Entertainment of St——p M——n." One complains, "we lose 500 sterling pr. an," another replying, "who would not sell their country for so large a sum?" Beyond, two men bend over an open grave; as one shovels in the dirt, the other asks, "Will you resign?" The stamp collector's voice from down under answers, "Yes, yes. I will." The point of this elaborate caricature, sometimes attributed to Copley, was straightforward: the Stamp Act was the product of an evil, greedy conspiracy; only English favorites in the colonies supported it; and British troops alone could protect the collectors from the wrath of patriots. Whatever the merits of these works by the standard of great art, they communicated with their viewers.

The war interrupted the modest development of provincial architecture. John Hawks, brought from England by North Carolina's Governor William Tryon in 1764, designed a structure to serve both as state house and residence in New Bern, after the model of a country estate at home, though much reduced in size. Public buildings were still derivative; in the absence of trained architects, churches and edifices to house governmental functions followed familiar lines, but often did so gracefully and with attentiveness to the requirements of local materials. Simplicity was the child of necessity. King's Chapel and the Old South Church in Boston, Christ Church in Cambridge and Christ Church in Philadelphia, and St. Paul's Chapel and Trinity Church in New York eschewed ornamentation and embellishment. Funds, when available, went into steeples justified by utility: bells rang for fire, curfew, and funerals, and the vane pointed the direction of the wind. In New England, a change just before the Revolution shifted the meetinghouse entrance from the side to the end, permitting builders to locate the pulpit at the terminus of a long central aisle. But elaborations upon the new floor plan did not come until the end of the eighteenth century, for war interrupted these developments and in some cases destroyed what had already been done.

In architecture, as in the other arts, revolution was an immense diversion. Suddenly carried away by a vast and pompous patriotic pretentiousness, colonists lost any sense of the purpose of their culture and only later slowly staggered to their feet. Rhetoric obscured the genuine wishes of the country. Amid the exciting talk about the future, few Americans noted the mixed effects of the conflict. The damage done by the fighting left the poorly provided parts of the country worse off than before. The only clear gain was exposure of needs that opened the way to subsequent action.

American culture had been at its best when it responded to the restless needs of those it served. The rule of utility demanded by a society of scarce resources was compatible with the general insistence upon rationality and simplicity of style. The Moravians in Bethlehem, Pennsylvania, disturbed the visiting John Adams in one respect: the church—baroque, decorated in strong colors, Italianate in feeling, likely to stir violent passions and not elegant tastes—seemed less appropriate to a virtuous republic than the straight lines and simple forms familiar in New England.

The intractable American environment inhibited some grandiose imitations of European practice, as when Washington planned the ha-ha, or sunken fence, boundary to his garden so as not to break the view from his mansion. The enclosure would be out of sight until closely approached, retaining grazing cattle and sheep at a distance as picturesque parts of the landscape. A few owners of great estates laid out ornamental grounds complete with mazes, rows of flowers, and aisles of trees. But generally English gardening books proved useless, depending as they did on plenty of fertile, worked-over ground, skilled nurserymen, and hothouses. Rocky soil covered with stubble, strange indigenous flora, and extremes of climate posed novel problems, as articles of advice in newspapers, almanacs, and magazines explained. John Randolph's *American Gardener*, written about 1770, emphasized utility: lettuce, nothing more than a "cabbage sort," good only as fodder for rabbits, deserved less effort than artichoke leaves, useful for cleaning pewter. A popular work by Robert Squibb of South Carolina exposed the misleading character of English books and emphasized the necessity of heeding local conditions.

In other respects, necessity compelled Americans to anticipate European theorists. Eighteenth-century British writers, who stressed the moral function of architecture and argued that the artificial product of human labor was always best when it resembled the handiwork of nature, put into words what need put into the practice of Yankee church builders. Philadelphians had long since achieved what John Gwynn advocated for the improvement of London and Westminster in 1766: an urban ground plan composed of straight lines with the streets intersecting each other only at right angles. And war and poverty slowed the transfer to the New World of Old World tastes for chinoiserie and ornate Louis XVI furniture and silver.

When peace released the energies of Americans for rebuilding and new building, they talked grandly of public structures. Little came of the rhetoric. They continued, however, to erect homes to accommodate their various styles of life. Leisure and wealth permitted some to think of elegance. But more usually the simple designs of craftsmen, compelled by limitations of technique and materials to stay within straight lines, flowered after the war in the doors and façades of carpenter-built homes and in the cups and cupboards of silversmiths and cabinetmakers. Great monuments arose in visions; reality more often saw liberty and rebellion trees and displays of civic unity in popular parades and pageants.

Utility was the test of science also. General speculation such as had interested Benjamin Franklin's generation persisted, although in a diffuse form. Lively popular curiosity in 1774 brought audiences in Chestertown, Maryland, to exhibitions of electricity by "Mr. Wall, the comedian." A year later, Mr. Whitehead, a Yorkshireman, profitably displayed a set of pictures and a magic lantern in Virginia. Prospective parents relied on numerology and astrology to determine the sex of their offspring. Manuals that revealed the secrets of human reproduction emphasized omens of all kinds, including sneezing and coughing. Pregnant women marked their children through telepathic operations: a mother's imagination caused a girl to be born hairy or a boy black. Clearly it was unreasonable to believe that the devil could engender when copulating with a woman, since a spirit possessed no seed. But the devil could trap men through the ability to assume a female form. Usefulness was the proof of all these forms of knowledge.

Reason lapped around popular understandings; it did not displace them. At the Sign of the Bottle and Three Boltheads, in Second Street, Philadelphia, the sons of the famous botanist John Bartram practiced pharmacy and medicine. They dispensed the usual chemical and galenical cures and various elixirs and balsams of life; they also sold paints, crucibles, and furniture for doctors' offices and trained apprentices. In 1766 Moses Bartram became a member of the American Society for Promoting Useful Knowledge and proposed two questions for discussion: what became of all the waters pouring into the Mediterranean, and how could men sleepwalk in dangerous places when they could not do so awake? His experiments on silkworms (after an initial failure when his specimen flew out through an open window) concluded that the native were superior to the foreign, yielding more silk and showing no fear of thunder and lightning.

Botany also occupied the attention of female scientists, mostly well-to-do women eager for useful occupations. Jane Colden, daughter of the lieutenant governor of New York, sought to trace the relationship between botany and medicine. Martha Laurens Ramsay applied her scientific knowledge to agriculture and experimented successfully with the growth and preservation of olives in South Carolina, while Martha Daniell Logan wrote a standard book on gardening read in that colony. Also in South Carolina, young Eliza Lucas Pinckney improved the cultivation of indigo and worked on crop rotation, intensive farming, grafting, and fig growing.

In their case, as in that of men, utility was a safer guide than abstract theory. And the war further fixed attention on practical needs, as when a Yale student, David Bushnell, in 1776 built a submarine that worked. The astronomer David Rittenhouse planned fortifications and surveys and experimented with new types of guns. Efforts to produce shot, muskets, cannons, nails, and kettles—all needed when imports ceased—exposed and clarified later problems. Up in Westborough, Massachusetts, for instance, the teenaged Eli Whitney turned his father's tool shed into a two-man nail factory and began to learn something about the industrial problems with which he would deal later. The battlefield also directed attention to medicine. Handbooks described the procedures for treatment in the field; Dr. Rush experimented with a cure for lockjaw; and exposure to the advanced methods of British and French surgeons enlightened local physicians.

In science, as in architecture, music, and literature, little came of inflated rhetoric. Cultural resources were inadequate to carry the revolutionaries to the heights to which they aspired; in the last analysis a society that valued utility supported practical rather than visionary ambitions.

When the eighteenth century drew to a close, enthusiasts still expressed faith in the cultural achievements of the Republic. Optimism had by then become a habit, encouraged by the widening separation from Europe that protected Americans from adverse comparisons. In truth, their achievements lay not in the arts but in the provisional society the Revolution brought into the open.

10

A Provisional Society

For a long time the colonies drifted apart from the mother country—not consciously or deliberately, not by acts of will or choice, but imperceptibly through tiny alterations in habits, manners, and ways of thought. The slow, mincing process of separation made little impression upon people still conscious of their dependence upon the Old World; visitors, able to compare Europe and America, recognized the New World's newness.

The Revolution brought the process of separation into the open and also hastened it. The drama of defiance of authority, and then of war, and finally of victory and independence amazed and exhilarated the actors as well as observers around the world. By the summer of 1776 the change in political temper astonished John Adams. Two years earlier he had not believed it possible so to alter the prejudices, passions, sentiments, and principles of the thirteen little colonies as to make every one of them completely republican. "Idolatry to Monarchs, and servility to Aristocratical Pride was never so totally eradicated, from so many Minds in so short a time." The decision of July 4, he believed, was perhaps the greatest question ever determined among men. The suddenness as well as the resolution with which the people, though addicted to corruption and venality, seized unbounded power surprised Adams.

The citizenry's ability to comprehend the issue outran their leaders' expectations. Americans acted on the basis of no precedent. In all the years of European colonizing experience, never before had a dependent population thrown off the protective guidance of its mother country. These rebels were not exchanging one imperial relationship for another but were rejecting every vestige of tutelage in order to be on their own. Independence would call for toil and blood and treasure. Yet to this cause, laden with uncertainty, the revolutionaries lent their fortunes and their sacred honor.

Separation had its own momentum. Each step required justification by logical argument in press, pamphlets, and sermons, and a wedge of ideas widened the gulf between Old World and New. As the rhetoric changed from preservation of the ancient imperial constitution to independence, its meaning extended from the polity to all other social institutions. The first flags were negative, defensive—*Dont tread on me*, the rattlesnake. Before the fighting ended, union was the emblem. Peace brought no surcease. The American war was over, wrote Benjamin Rush in 1783, but this was "far from being the case with the American Revolution," which would yet extend to government, finance, morals, and manners.

Meanwhile the long, acrimonious war interrupted the transatlantic flow of people, goods, and ideas and increased the need for improvisation. Severance of European ties forced Americans to think and act in new ways. They learned to lead provisional lives: an environment susceptible to frequent change discounted the value of planning and rewarded prompt responses to the unexpected. The need for constant adjustment and readjustment altered the manner in which people regarded government, law, society, one another, and the world about them.

The Continental Congress proved more than a temporary gathering of state emissaries. Its members assembled to voice the colonists' grievances and to explore the means of preserving their place within the empire, an extraordinarily difficult task, involving issues of high principle, subject to prolonged debate. By contrast, the need and the strategy for resistance evoked little controversy. Discussion turned about theory, while in practice Congress began to exercise the powers of government.

Experience had taught the colonists to fend for themselves. The provincial assemblies had enacted charters of incorporation the better to build a library or a school or provide for the needy. But Americans also joined spontaneous societies that, they argued, were not illegal for want of incorporation. Respect for form did not impede action; in the face of necessity they evaded old rules or devised new ones.

Long since, too, practice fostered political participation. Local pressures decisively shaped voting procedures. The great Virginia landowners, subject to the humors of a fickle crowd, had to cajole, fawn, and wheedle for their places; the voters turned out a Carter, among the loftiest of aristocrats, though he "kissed their arses" and servilely accommodated himself to the people. The Hammonds, one of the wealthiest families in Anne Arundel County, Maryland, knew that their political influence depended on the ability to manipulate a mob. In New York City a crusty young gentleman in 1774 observed a horde of tradesmen begin to think and reason. "Poor reptiles! it is with them a vernal morning, they are struggling to cast off their winter's slough, they bask in the sunshine, and ere noon they will bite." A year later he regretted the preference given a herd of mechanics over the best families in the colony. In 1775 the parochial committee that governed Savannah consisted, to Governor Wright's astonishment, of "a Parcel of the Lowest People, chiefly Carpenters, Shoemakers, Blacksmiths etc. with a Jew [Mordecai Sheftall] at their head." Under such circumstances, no group could rely upon an elite position to distinguish its own rational ideas from the opinion of the masses.

The crisis found at hand modes of action, defined by experience. It was certainly not illegal for local committees to correspond with one another and thus pass along news and suggestions for concerted action. William Livingston, among others, had learned that letters sent as if by chance cautioned against insidious enemy acts and shaped popular attitudes. These communications also coordinated the activity of merchants' and workingmen's associations, of clubs and Masonic lodges, and even of children's spinning circles. And while not presuming to exercise the power to govern, the committees of correspondence, in effect, began to rule, sometimes through established agencies, sometimes through conventions, ad hoc assemblies that voiced popular opinion.

The capacity for action explained the summons to the Continental Congress in 1774 and also the subsequent behavior of that body, which assembled again in 1775 and then continued to meet.

Life was hard for the members, as for other Americans. Away from home and family and lodged in expensive quarters, the delegates twice fled Philadelphia when the British advanced. Absences were frequent, so that lack of a quorum often postponed decisions. Certain birds of passage seldom appeared during the winter, discouraged by disorderly debates and useless harangues. Communications from home arrived late or not at all. Oliver Wolcott wryly noted in 1776 that he received as much information from Asia as from Connecticut. William Hooper of North Carolina demanded bluntly of his state legislature, from which he had no word, "Am or am I not a delegate?"

Low pay further exasperated the congressmen. Caesar Rodney was certain that the Delaware general assembly deliberately withheld funds due to him. James Lovell had brought with him only one suit and a hat; these had to serve him for three years, before a desperate letter to the Massachusetts house in 1779 requested more funds. In December 1781 he owed a year's rent and worried about unpaid bills for shoes and stockings. At one point, Roger Sherman and James Madison, stranded in Philadelphia, lacked funds for either a lengthier stay or a journey back home. Nathaniel Scudder of New Jersey complained that he had let his business collapse and had wasted his private fortune for the sake of public virtue. Irrepressible rumors about the ignorance and dishonesty of colleagues fired resentment. Members besieged with requests for favors suspected one another of manipulating loan office certificates issued by Congress in payment for goods and services, and plunged into quarrels over every "plumb pudding." Judgments as often as not rested on whim, fancy, or caprice, as well as on greed and self-interest, so that sometimes it seemed that only the ineptitude of the British Army would save Americans from their inefficient leaders.

Nevertheless, the Congress in practice became a federal legislature, although no formal agreement bound the individual states until ratification of the Articles of Confederation in 1781; and that loose arrangement persisted until the government under the Constitution took office in 1789. Americans, after all, could turn to no ready precedent for a republican federation on so large a scale.

For fifteen years the improvised Congress, always weak and deficient in executive leadership, often incapable of mustering a quorum, plunged the faint-hearted into despair. Unless the government shaped up, Gouverneur Morris predicted in 1781, he had no hope that the Union could subsist except in the form of an absolute monarchy, and that seemed inconsistent with "the Taste and Temper of the People." Yet this group of politicians, sufficiently in agreement to act, negotiated with foreign powers, formed treaties and alliances based on a novel understanding of the rational self-interest of trade, declared war and made peace, commissioned officers, brought an army into being, and took steps toward developing a navy. It assumed active charge of the war, appointed and dismissed commanders, and influenced military strategy. Pressed by the need to resolve interstate conflicts over prizes taken at sea, it established a Court of Appeals in Case of Capture in 1780.

Congress also exercised powers within the country. To finance the war, it printed money that served, however feebly, as a circulating medium. It disposed of a vast public domain in the West and began, though cautiously, to shape a national economic policy. The delegates in Philadelphia acquired these powers without forethought or planning. They and their constituents recognized what had to be done because shared assumptions simplified the decisions of leaders and elicited the obedience of followers.

The same process operated on the local scale. Each province

became an independent state. In Connecticut and Rhode Island, where ties to England had always been fragile, government continued without essential change or interruption. Pennsylvania and Maryland simply abolished their proprietorships. Each of the other colonies passed through an interregnum of greater or lesser length. In the absence of legitimate authority, provincial congresses analogous to the continental one exercised interim authority, while the leaders tried to draft constitutions that would secure the consent of the voters, for, as George Mason noted in 1778, they were determined to do nothing without the approbation of the people.

Agreement among the population was partial, and internal conflicts were frequent. Apart from the outright defenders of the King's prerogative, many Americans, though hostile to the Crown and resentful of the English connection, nevertheless resisted precipitate action. They did not wish to go too far; the liberty all cherished in principle, in practice evoked differences in depth of commitment. Some all along preferred to leave politics to abler heads. Others, like John Ross of Philadelphia, who loved ease and his glass of Madeira, shrugged it all off: let who would, be king; Ross well knew he would still be subject. Why fight? "Tyranny is Tyranny let it come from whom it may"—that slogan gave pause to people fearful of being cheated by promises of liberty.

Each hint of excitement blew the undecided now one way, now another. In New York City the crowd that assembled to greet General Washington, just appointed commander in chief of the American Army, in 1775, soon after turned around and hailed Governor Tryon, disembarking from a British man-of-war in the harbor. Judge Thomas Jones, observing the swift changes in allegiances, could only mutter, "What a farce. What cursed hypocrisy." For quite different reasons, Friends, even those sympathetic to the colonial cause, refused to support the war out of religious scruples, although young Philadelphians formed a company called the Quaker Blues.

Then, too, calculations of interest were complex. In Maryland, small farmers feared that independence would enslave the poor by putting all power into the hands of the rich, while some great landowners feared that removal of royal authority would open the way to anarchy and slave and tenant revolts. Other planters welcomed the separation that would free them from the obligation to repay debts to British merchants. Traders bemoaned the loss of international contacts, and the unpredictable upheavals of war frightened all.

In many places, opportunists held back, waiting to see which way the wind blew before choosing a flag. The wife of a Hessian officer visited the Van Horn family in New Jersey and on each occasion noted a drastic shift in opinion. Fair-weather patriots, perhaps, but the choice of allegiances at the time was not as clear as would appear in retrospect. Ordinary men and women weighed the threats of future retribution from London—whence came warnings that outlawries, confiscations, and executions would be the reward of rebellion—against the certainty of present reprisals for lukewarm patriotism. Concerned for their skins and possessions, they followed the dominant opinion of the district in order to be on the winning side.

The revolutionary zeal of 1774 and 1775, the first heady, manifesto-laden years, subsided. In 1776 enthusiasm flickered and morale slumped, depleting the ranks of the regiments as short-term enlistments expired and desertions rose. Once the meager results of early efforts revealed that victory would not come easily, farmers and artisans preferred their own hearths and families to the discomforts of camp or the hazards of the battlefield. Those better off also wearied of war, not having allowed enough for disasters in the field or foreseen the domestic chagrins that inevitably followed upon a dissolution of the old power. Rumors —of the impending arrival of 50,000 Russian Cossacks hired as British mercenaries, of a plot to arm Catholics, Indians, and slaves against the colonists, of the defection of Georgia and Connecticut—all found ready listeners among people who faced an incomprehensible situation. When only a blurred line separated fact from fiction, tales of a world turned upside down seemed entirely credible.

Angry men did not understand moderation and branded as Tories all those less violent and bigoted than themselves, sometimes whipping dissenters into line or carting them out of town after a tar-and-feather treatment. Moses Dunbar's patriotic father offered to furnish the hemp for a halter with which to hang his loyalist son, who was actually executed in Connecticut in 1777. His blood boiled, a Philadelphian wrote, whenever he met a British sympathizer in the street or the coffee house. "In every place, and in every company, they spread their damnable doctrines." An unrelenting blast of words in newspapers, pamphlets, sermons, and orations attempted to keep fervor alive. Nevertheless, in time, people blocked out the din; and after the initial persecution, well-behaved law-abiding Tories lived undisturbed.

Neither violence nor propaganda drew Americans together in the common cause. Nor was it simply pride, ambition, and vainglory, pounded in the mortar of discord and distilled into falsehood, envy, and malice, as the British charged. Complex personal and social elements fused to release the powerful forces of national patriotism.

Upstarts and outsiders who acquired power and consequence as a result of revolution had a stake in its success, and they suffered from their share of human failings. Fine uniforms and epaulets, easily acquired military titles, and the sense of rank made many a gentleman who had never been one before. Though its purchasing power shrank steadily, paper money spread the feel of wealth. The spruce officer, his pocket stuffed with continental dollars, his head full of grandiose strategies, his days half idle, half occupied with drill, had little cause to regret the daily drudgery of agricultural or mechanic labor he had left in civilian life.

Those who discovered opportunities for profit in independence and war also rejoiced. No eighteenth-century conflict lacked a commercial angle, in the opportunity to provision the fighting men, in prizes taken at sea, in the erratic financial dealings of governments pressed by unusual needs. Before 1774 royal officials dealt out the privileges, and the governors' favorites who took the healthiest shares were or became the established merchants. The new dispensation made room for outsiders as contractors, privateers, brokers. The old-timers, if not Tories, were at best lukewarm patriots and cautious in taking risks on behalf of the Republic. The politicians in the assemblies and congresses who now made the decisions turned to new people with little to lose, daring out of genuine devotion to the cause or out of willingness to gamble for big prizes. They, too, were staunch in allegiance.

The unsettling effects of war exploded in ostentatious living. The will to sacrifice subsided once the initial outburst of patriotism passed, and prosperity created new, ever-escalating demands. A class of merchants and purveyors emerged eager to satisfy their customers. Travelers observed an almost universal increase of expenditures on clothes. Boston ladies wore silk as often as possible and came to church to display their attire rather than to express their piety. Rebecca Franks in 1778 had no shortage of partners at the dance to which she wore a dress "more ridiculous and pretty than anything" she had ever seen— "great quantities of different colored feathers on the head at a time, besides a thousand other things; the hair dressed very high."

The newly rich slipped casually into extravagance. The convulsion having brought the dregs to the top, men who formerly could not feed their children now lived in unfamiliar splendor. Wives of cobblers, tailors, and day laborers in Rhode Island wore chintz and muslin every day, and women in more remote communities, where there were few possible admirers, spent as much on elaborate costumes as their urban counterparts. Expensive dinners, dancing, gaming, and carousing and imports of carriages, wine, and silverware made a mockery of the commitment to a plain and simple life.

Extravagance boded ill for the future of the Republic, the moralists explained. Samuel Adams thundered against citizens who indulged in "superfluity of Dress and Ornament when it is as much as they can bear to support the Expenses of cloathing a naked army." Governor William Livingston of New Jersey protested against domestic and foreign luxury. The war seemed to turn many contented yeomen and honest townsfolk into heedless wastrels. The transformation—ironic but not surprising, since yeomen had never been quite contented and townsfolk never altogether dedicated to virtue—spurred Americans on in the desire for achievement, fame, and improvement, through independence.

But for the leaders, and certainly for the vast majority who went along, more was at stake than expectation of advantage. Young men not influenced by the hope of pecuniary reward wished to be useful by serving the public good. Foreign visitors invariably commented upon the spirit of the Americans both in the ranks and at home. The ragged soldiers, wretchedly equipped, undernourished, and often unpaid, hung on; that many deserted in the long periods of inaction was less significant than the willingness of many more to enlist and reenlist when the need arose. In battle they fought with passion—not, in the eighteenth-century fashion, looking for the chance to live another day but ready to be killed in order to kill. The British complained that concealed villains refused to fight in the open, but shot murderously from ambush in a "sneaking, cowardly manner" and in deadly seriousness.

A positive vision held Americans together; they battled not merely against the trespasses of the Crown and Parliament but, even more, to create a political system in accord with their understanding of a just society. They struggled not to destroy something bad but to create something good—hence the unfolding discovery that resistance to tyranny was an opportunity to fashion a virtuous Republic by achieving independence. John Adams spoke for many in the belief that they had been "sent into life at a time when the greatest law givers of antiquity would have wished to live." His countrymen had the chance to "establish the wisest and happiest government" that human wisdom could contrive.

The people who seized, held, and used power were therefore not content to rule by naked force. Knowing that the descent to revolution was easy, the attempt to rise again difficult, they wished to legitimize force by involving the politically active population; otherwise, they feared, violence would become an end in itself. As they understood it, the severance of ties to the Crown had left Americans in a state of nature. They would emerge from that pristine condition not by passive acceptance of an act by a sovereign but only by their own decisions about the terms of consent, for self-government was their birthright.

The appropriate method for establishing a polity presented more theoretical than practical problems. For a long time, Americans left many critical questions unanswered: Who were the citizens entitled to subscribe to the social contract? What procedures guaranteed that their consent was voluntary? To what extent were the decisions of some binding on all? These and other problems would occupy politicians and philosophers for decades to come. But "consent of the governed" had a simpler meaning for people with generations of experience settling the wilderness. It referred to the pacts, compacts, covenants, and understandings by which they had always formed communities. Legitimacy was not the product of a charter handed down to subjects; it resided in popular willingness to obey.

Firm control sometimes muted controversy and permitted the holders of power to assert their authority in the name of the people, and the provinces thereupon became states. When Governor Wentworth's flight in 1775 left New Hampshire with neither an executive nor a legislature, the provincial congress, with the approval of the Continental Congress, proclaimed itself the ruling body in order to preserve peace and good order and to secure the lives and properties of the inhabitants. South Carolina improvised a government in much the same manner, and Georgia adopted its *Rules and Regulations* in 1776. Virginians, worried about this rough and ready procedure, devised a more formal fundamental charter that systematically allocated powers and made clear the rights the people reserved to themselves. Other states followed, although in Massachusetts and Pennsylvania the process stretched over years, envenomed by bitter disagreement.

Americans insisted upon putting authority within legitimate forms: otherwise society would slip into the anarchy that all abhorred. They harbored no illusions about human nature and knew that power corrupted—anyone, everyone, even themselves, and particularly the lawyers among them. Few disagreed with the Pennsylvania lawyer who confessed the need to put a guard upon his virtue. Being "habituated to exercise one's ingenuity in inventing arguments on the wrong side, at least warps the Judgment, & will in time corrupt the heart, unless constantly opposed by an active virtuous principle." A written constitution alone could protect "posterity against the wanton exercise of power" likely to follow from "the strong bias of human nature to tyranny and despotism."

Earlier the colonists defined the word "constitution," as Englishmen did, as the accumulation of statutes and precedents that described the structure and operations of government. In that sense they referred to the ancient constitution of Britain, having in mind not a single document but the historic antecedents of current practice. Yet after 1774 the meaning of the term changed. A constitution was a written frame of government ratified by the people, and that was the expression of consent which Americans desired. In time almost all the states passed through the process that gave them legitimacy.

The similarities among the schemes devised outweighed the differences. Pennsylvania's first effort, including its unicameral assembly, reflected the distinctiveness of its history and of its population mix, but before long it fell into line. For all the other states a single chief executive, a bicameral legislature, an independent judiciary, a bill of rights, and a large measure of local authority were the products of a century's shared political experience. Clumsily contrived, these arrangements nevertheless proved durable, sustained as they were by roots deep in the past. Tinkering with forms sometimes impeded actions demanded by the crisis, but not for long and not in essentials.

Massachusetts went to an extreme in insisting that a constitution was a social contract valid only when composed by a convention specifically elected for the purpose and then accepted by a direct vote of the people. Similar although less rigid propositions made sense to other Americans, for they stemmed from commonly held views about the importance of law and about the nature of personal rights.

Life in the wilderness or close to its edge bred a deep respect for law. The colonists knew the corrosive effects on society of any weakening of restraints. In July 1776, while Congress considered the grand theme of independence, John Adams wanted to know about the opening of the courts back home. What business did they do? he asked his wife. Were the grand juries and petit juries sworn? Did they try any criminal or civil actions? How were people affected by the reappearance of courts? How were the judges treated, with respect or cold neglect? These were important questions.

The concern with legality, reason, and equity was an element in the most destructive revolutionary incidents. The same John Adams defended the rights of the British soldiers accused of the Boston massacre. And the managed crowds that attacked royal officials or dumped overboard the East India Company tea nevertheless voted that they abhorred and detested all petty mobs, riots, breaking windows, and destroying private property. They acted not as self-constituted bands but as surrogates for communities, shackled for the moment by despotic officials.

The solicitude for proper procedures was neither just a cloak for resisting Britain nor simply a maneuver that created legal fictions to justify the use of power. After 1776 as before, the search for legitimacy and the desire to create a righteous government emanated from an enduring respect for the law, which to Americans meant not the precise provisions of ancient statutes or judges' opinions but rather the articulation of their own sense of good and evil, justice and injustice. To political philosophers and lawyers those vague terms left authority dangerously unbounded by orderly rules. But the people in rebellion confidently knew their meaning of the law without the jurist's definition.

American law, locally administered, shaped, and legislated, sharply diverged from the English. The colonists had established equal treatment as a measure of its validity. When Virginia judges in 1766 allowed Colonel Chiswell bail after he had stabbed a respectable merchant in a drunken tavern brawl, it did not quiet protests to cite supporting English cases. Virginia did not, however, have to follow the defective British law; before the trial commenced, Chiswell died of "an uneasiness of mind" which produced "nervous fits," leading to the rumor that he had committed suicide. Local control through monthly courts of common pleas and through quarterly sessions were also means of ensuring communal oversight of justice.

By the 1770s the law had become an instrument by which colonists frustrated the exercise of authority, a standard by which to judge parliamentary regulations, and the basis for evolving constitutional ideas. The sense of what was right depended upon no phrases in books. People knew there was something wrong with inflation, whatever the statutes said. Farmer Sharp, a character in the satire *A Little Teatable Chitchat* (1781), made his fortune by clearing his debts in paper, then progressed to the state legislature, where he drafted a bill to abolish Christianity—no more maintenance for ministers, no more punishment for murder, and no more censure for attempted suicide.

As they knew right from wrong, so, too, Americans knew that privileges were "but titles of servitude." Men and women enjoyed rights not by grace of a gift from some superior but because the Creator had so designed the nature of humans. Flaming lists of those natural rights accompanied many a political or constitutional statement; but however persuasive as rhetoric, these enumerations were neither clear nor complete. No bill of rights mentioned privacy, for instance, or the freedom to move, or the definition of citizenship—issues of vital importance, taken for granted. Assurance of trial by jury was commonplace but left crucial questions unanswered. Although the guarantee was silent in these matters, people understood it to mean indictment by a grand as well as trial by a petit jury and a unanimous decision by a body of twelve. Supporting that understanding was a change, already well under way in 1775, in the nature of the proceedings, from an inquest to seek out the guilty to a method of establishing innocence. Significantly, defendants secured the right to counsel in the United States well before they did in England; colonial petit juries arrogated to themselves the privilege of passing on matters of law as well as of fact; and grand juries became weapons with which to foil royal prosecutors by refusing to indict. When residents of Albany in 1765 tore down the army barracks on land the town desired, the court responded to a demand for punishment by declaring them a "posse comitatus," law-abiding inhabitants assisting in law enforcement. The meaning of law in New York was not identical to that in London.

The sovereign citizens of the Republic, secure in the protection of their rights by law they themselves defined, casually used key terms without precision. The people were sovereign, each state was sovereign, and the United States was sovereign; and all the tangled issues of federalism remained in abeyance until 1787. Nevertheless, Americans expected that government would be an instrument to serve the citizens' purposes. Their history had shown the necessity of cooperation and communal effort. Log rolling and house raising, cornhusking, and quiltmaking belonged to the tradition of neighborly rural assistance, as useful on the frontier as in areas long settled. So, too, with fire companies and libraries in town. Now the people in power turned to the state as the mechanism for joint endeavors. Whatever Americans knew about the experience of Europe indicated the desirability of doing so.

Yet between 1774 and 1783 little came of that certitude. Government was weak; lacking authority and financial resources, it could not heed the heavy calls upon it. Nor did citizens heed its calls upon them. Again and again expectations proved delusive; the people who now held political control blithely believed that they could accomplish what domination from Britain had prevented before the Revolution. Alas, they discovered that the state, though now their creature, was effective only in a limited sphere. In the final analysis the initiative lay with individuals, as alone as ever, taking chances as before.

For decades the colonists had longed to form banks that would issue paper money as the Bank of England did. Often enough, one assembly or another had authorized the creation of such institutions, which farmers and merchants regarded as the means of economic salvation, hoping thus to solve their currency problems. Few people knew just how these financial organizations operated, and some wanted reserves based on silver, while others preferred land. But royal intransigence undid every scheme. Only Parliament could grant such charters, and it showed no inclination to do so.

When independence removed this obstacle, another, less visible but as formidable, appeared. No one knew how to go about organizing and managing the business. The Continental Congress chartered a Bank of North America; but soon the states created institutions of their own, often more than one, all competing with one another, so that before the century ended, these were well on the way to becoming individual business enterprises. Meanwhile many merchants resorted to private devices, issuing scrip and writing bills that sometimes also spiraled out of control, but in any case rested upon speculative faith.

Other cooperative ventures followed the same course. For years the fertile colonial schemes for improvement of wharves, markets, and other urban amenities, for insurance against fire and other disasters, and for education and philanthropy had depended upon means of assembling capital and providing management in evasion of the English insistence that assemblies could not issue charters of incorporation. Once independent, legislatures could do so. But having the right, they discovered the same problem: want of knowledge and of experience. At the same time, insistence that everyone have a chance and the feebleness of political control took the heart out of monopoly, licensing, and other traditional means of directing the economy. Again speculation filled the gap, as venturesome individuals reached for opportunity.

The Republic could not pull together the resources to intervene successfully in any aspect of life. Americans did what had to be done on their own, at their own risk, and often inadequately. Taking chances furthered expansion and rewarded the daring. But the absence of communal undergirding left the cautious and the weak exposed to the privations of a hard life.

Prolonged war called attention to the roles and rights of the dependent. The alteration of habits, practices, and conventions deeply rooted in the past and firmly grown into colonial life would have been difficult under the most propitious of circumstances. But circumstances were not propitious, and Americans lacked the intellectual resources to confront the problems of children, women, delinquents, and servants. What they could not solve the citizens preferred to evade or postpone for the future.

Many children in country and town drifted on their own in the confusion of the fighting. Already in 1776 an observer noted poor youngsters wholly neglected and left to range the streets without schools, without business, given up to all evil. Although sixteen was the legal age for enlistment, boys of fifteen, fourteen, or even thirteen took up arms and slipped away from control. Meanwhile the replacement of apprenticeship and indentured servitude by purely temporary, contractual employment weakened the most usual methods of education and acculturation. Yet for decades Americans failed to respond to the challenge, hoping that it would somehow disappear, through restoration of the traditional household or in some other, as yet unforeseeable, fashion.

Revolution and speculations about the Republic's destiny exposed the deficiencies of the schools. To rule themselves, citizens needed knowledge; ignorant men and women remained slaves. Every youth should know intimately every detail of the country's geography, John Adams wrote in August 1776. Yet that was far from the case. His wife, Abigail, complained that the deficiency was even worse for girls than for boys, and hoped that the new constitution would do something to advance the knowledge and virtue of all. If the country wished to have heroes, statesmen, and philosophers, it required learned mothers to raise them, since much depended on early education.

Experience demonstrated the utility of better training than in the past, not only in usual "female accomplishments" and the domestic arts, but also in spelling, grammar, arithmetic, French, history, and geography. Benjamin Franklin enthusiastically supported these efforts. Widowhood, he thought, was so common that most women sooner or later shouldered business responsibilities. Taxpaying fathers of girls argued the injustice of educating boys only and the desirability of enhancing the intelligence of mothers. Others, however, maintained that female schooling was wasteful, that it would spoil housekeepers (they would read too many novels), teach servants to write love letters while neglecting their duties, and delude wives into defiance of their husbands.

However communities settled these disputes, there were no means of executing the most admirable intentions. Pennsylvania's constitution obliged the legislature to establish schools in each county with salaries sufficiently high to enable the masters to instruct youth at low cost. It was, however, easier to frame such a provision than to find appropriate teachers. The colleges also suffered. In those that still functioned, public business took up the professors' time, to the great detriment of complaining students. War had destroyed or damaged other institutions, such as that in Providence. Pennsylvania, Yale, and Columbia fended off charges of disloyalty and aristocracy, suspect as they were of training part of the citizens "to cheat the rest of their liberties."

The meager response did not staunch the flow of words about education at all levels, but the talk described visions only, not reality. In the postwar decade, college enrollments failed to regain their prewar level. Presbyterian and Congregational missionary impulses sometimes stressed the importance of frontier schools; and a few new academies staggered into being, although neither the number of students nor the quality of teachers encouraged their promoters. Walker Maury's troubles were symptomatic. This well-connected graduate of William and Mary set up a school in Orange County, Virginia, and welcomed to it in 1782 three Randolph children, Richard, Theodorick, and John. The boys believed themselves exiled, "tyrannized over and tortured by the most peevish and ill-tempered of pedagogues," and thrown in with boorish, sloppy, and poor pupils. "A more vicious and profligate crew never got together." The other lads hated and mistreated the few gentlemen's sons.

A year later Maury moved to Williamsburg, hoping to expand his institution through affiliation with the college. From a tractable and shy boy, Theodorick turned into an insolent youth, and repeated floggings failed to bring him to terms. He refused to go to church three Sundays in a row, on the pretense of not having any clean clothing, and won the support of his brother Richard, who also believed that the well-born should not appear in public without suitable attire. Maury never doubted that he did his duty; the pupils were there to obey and he to dictate, for without discipline the boys would come to a bad end. He discharged Theodorick but refused to return the fees paid in advance. He then gave up the academy and accepted a headmastership in Norfolk, Virginia.

The temporary expansion of women's roles ended with the war. It had drawn them into the world outside their homes and had raised their value as helpmates and supports, but had not altered men's view of them or their own consciousness of themselves and of their position in society. Once husbands came back, wives willingly returned to their former roles. Those able by birth, marriage, or exceptional intelligence to raise the banner of female discontent asked primarily for recognition of the importance of their own sphere, motherhood. No one called for a drastic reshaping of roles. Indeed, the trials of war fortified the older images. Women who had suffered the hardships of years when they had to handle all challenges on their own welcomed the return to domesticity. Postwar prosperity permitted them to withdraw into homes where increasing wealth indulged more sheltered lives. Wartime organizations disbanded, while fears about social stability focused attention on political issues.

Caution also inhibited change in the status of other dependent groups. The basic irrationality of imprisonment for debt had long troubled colonists. Massachusetts laws since the seventeenth century allowed an imprisoned debtor who swore that he was unable to support himself in jail and that he had no hidden property to work "in the prison or dependencys thereof." Creditors notified of the oath and unable to prove it false had to pay the debtor's board or let him go free. In most places by the time of the Revolution, debtors, kept apart from criminals, enjoyed some freedom of movement. Nevertheless corrupt and brutal jailors and inadequate facilities showed the need to reform a type of incarceration with no purpose. With the expansion of the economy and of credit, an increasing number of substantial merchants found themselves in debt and in danger of prison. Many patriotic citizens, the *Boston Gazette* wrote in 1784, suffered in jail because they had impoverished themselves as a result of loans to their government during the war. Dishonest debtors would always take advantage of innocent creditors, but their number was small and ought not to determine the fate of those who suffered because of the accidental sinking of a ship, sickness, or other misfortune beyond their control.

The Pennsylvania constitution limited the practice, as did

Massachusetts by legislation. But an inherited suspicion of debt perpetuated imprisonment. Debt was an evil, and failure to repay a sin, the result of idleness and ill husbandry. Like the thief, the borrower took what was not his and deserved punishment, fear of which would restrain absconders and prevent the willful concealment of assets. Americans suppressed awareness of the quiet contradiction between that attitude and their pervasive borrowing, urban and rural, and jails continued to receive the victims of unlucky risks. Efforts at more general penal reform for the moment yielded equally modest results. Only in reducing the number of capital crimes did the revolutionary spirit bear fruit.

Every argument that the colonists urged in favor of their own liberty operated, they knew, with equal force in favor of that of the slaves. Since freedom was an inherent right of the human species, blacks had the identical claim to it as others. Observing a North Carolina auction in 1782, Lieutenant Enos Reeves wondered, "Is this Liberty?—is this the Land of Liberty I've been fighting for these six years?" Americans understood that they could not contend for the rights of some while withholding them from others. Taking ultimate abolition for granted, they were, however, uncertain when it would come, or how.

Well before 1776 doubts about the propriety of bondage had intruded upon the consciousness of the colonists and had modified accepted practices, baleful to virtue. Jefferson's *Summary View* in 1774 called for the abolition of the institution, introduced in the country's infant state; and although opposition from Georgia and South Carolina softened the statement in the draft Declaration of Independence, his *Notes on the State of Virginia* still advocated gradual uncompensated emancipation, and migration.

The impetus to reach that goal came not from occasional acts of resistance, rebellion, or escape but from the dawning awareness of the slave's humanity. John Tabor Kemp, attorney general of New York, seeking release of a Negro spirited aboard a ship bound for South Carolina, argued in 1763 that a black man "ought to be protected in his liberty as much as a white man." In the next decade, petitions for freedom began to reach the Massachusetts assembly and the Virginia courts. When the Baptists gathered a church at Broad Creek, Delaware, they counted two Negroes members. The Fincastle, Virginia, court in 1774 allowed Roma, a slave, to testify in self-defense and found her not guilty of an attempt to kill her master, treating her as a person, not property. That year the astonished Bob Carter, a Virginia planter's son, listening to his tutor read the *Monthly Review* on the writings of the black slave poet Phillis Wheatley, asked to see her—did she know grammar and Latin?—then suddenly exclaimed, "Good God, I wish I was in heaven!" Perhaps the thought crossed his mind that she would not be a slave in a better order. The auctioneer in Philadelphia, prodding the salable girls from pens to block and getting the bids raised by erotic descriptions, shocked John Hancock. A Negro from Maryland preached near Christopher Marshall's orchard in Pennsylvania— speaking well to sundry people for nearly an hour.

Quakers led by Anthony Benezet had by then concluded that slavery was a sin; Philadelphians formed an abolition society; Methodists in Maryland rioted for emancipation; and several groups demanded an end to further imports of slaves. Connecticut, Delaware, Maryland, and Virginia enacted laws to that effect; North Carolina imposed a prohibitory tax; and Pennsylvania provided for gradual liberation. Virginia in 1782 eased the process of manumission. Vermont declared slavery a violation of natural rights, and Massachusetts judges by 1783 held it inconsistent with the state constitution that declared all men to be born free and equal. New Hampshire, Connecticut, and Rhode Island also put an end to bondage.

In the expectation of gaining freedom, five thousand blacks, free and slave, served in the American armed forces; they were a substantial element in the Rhode Island contingent. Others worked on roads and fortifications, acted as guides and spies, or enlisted as privateers. But while the northern states moved toward emancipation, the southern did not. Thousands of slaves in the South had turned to the British, expecting liberation from their rebellious masters. The fugitives followed Cornwallis, eating barren the regions through which they passed, like swarms

of locusts attacking a field. The surrender at Yorktown doomed
them to return to their owners, with no other recompense than
smallpox for their bounty and starvation and death for their
wages.

The inability to imagine the social transition to freedom inhibited emancipation: how could former masters and former
bondsmen efface the memory of past injustices and live together
as equals? The difficulty in answering that question did not
derive from a belief in innate racial characteristics. A Virginian
noted that the "sable skin" of the slaves was but "a pretext for
their unnatural debasement," and mulattoes gave evidence of the
frequency of miscegenation, concubinage, and mixed common-
law marriages. People who believed in the common descent of
all human beings from a single pair of ancestors could not avoid
the conclusion that all differences were the products of environment. Americans, ethnocentric like Englishmen, considered Africans, who spoke "a mixed dialect between the guinea and English," ugly, savage, heathen, promiscuous, and incompetent. But
those traits were the products of circumstances and would, in
time, yield to the beneficent influence of the New World. The in-
feriority ascribed to blacks was more intense than that ascribed
by one group of whites to another, but of the same kind. The
Pennsylvanian who lived near Lancaster, "in a neighborhood of
lumps of mortality, formed in shape of men and women, but so
impolished, so hoggish and selfish, that no good, kind sociability
makes any impression upon their boorish nature," was referring
to the Dutch. Papists were lazy, impertinent, improvident, lying
chatterers.

Revolutionaries escaped the dilemma that an immediate
wrong posed by way of the expectation, hope, or pretext that it
would ultimately disappear. The federal constitution never used
the word "slave," only "person held in servitude," a designation
also applied to indentured servants; many laws used the same
language.

Americans thus evaded the issue. Slaves were not constituent
members of the society, as were the Irish and Germans. Nor did
blacks readily shed the distinctive elements of their culture, as
Joseph Ottolenghe discovered after years of preaching to them

in Savannah. Whites could not suppress the fear, therefore, that social disorder would inevitably follow emancipation. At their most candid, men like Patrick Henry, himself a slave owner, conceded that slavery was repugnant to humanity, inconsistent with the Bible, and destructive to liberty. However culpable his conduct, he would do his duty to virtue by confessing the rectitude of her precepts and lamenting his inability to conform to them. Others, similarly situated, clung to the conceit of time's power to eradicate evil.

The case of the Indians seemed deceptively easier. They appeared to have a free choice. Their friends, like Benezet, argued that the tribes could adopt the white man's faith and ways and live by his side in amity. Or they could retain their identity as separate nations, in which case there was a whole empty continent through which to move, as they vacated savage lands for civilized use. In either event, abundant space and time relieved the Republic of the obligation to act.

Acculturation proceeded equably in some eastern provinces, but frontier experience belied the expectation that it would operate where the tribes were most numerous. It had not been long since Captain Raymond Demere wrote the governor of South Carolina that Indians were "a Commodity that are to be bought and sold." Scalpings on both sides were usual. A Cherokee said it in 1789, "You began it and this is what you get for it." The embittered accusation had by then reverberated throughout the areas in which the two races made contact. Those realities, however, did not weaken the belief that progress would dispose of the problem. There seemed no alternative.

Characteristically, a provisional society looked to the future. Its people, having moved recklessly through war to independence, improvised brilliantly in politics where historic experience guided them. But Americans emerging from the Revolution also approached social issues to which the past held no clue, about which they could think confidently only in terms of ages yet to come. They did so because the future, they knew, had a special place for them as a people.

11

The New World's Newness

When Philip Fithian, on the eve of the Revolution, glimpsed the Natural Bridge in Virginia, he rhapsodized—a work divine. It was beautiful to behold the westward progress of civilization. A few years before, the area was a habitation of cruelty; in 1775 men and women, civilized and religious, by legal purchase had made it a useful settlement. The thought occurred to him that soon, perhaps before a century passed, his countrymen and -women would live in towns overlooking the shores of the Pacific Ocean. Certainty of progress as the special destiny of America suffused the writing and thinking of his contemporaries.

Confidence did not spring from any sense of unique national heritage or from great cultural achievements or from social stability. Candid appraisal would have revealed heterogeneous origins, meager artistic products, and persistent instability. Yet the turbulence of war and independence did not diminish but increased certainty about the future. Loss of a good part of their leadership and the dismantling of much of their institutional apparatus strengthened rather than weakened Americans' sense of identity and their commitment to progress.

Independence stimulated western expansion. The formidable obstacles once presented by Johnson and Stuart and their Iroquois and Cherokee allies vanished. Although the British retained annoying posts in the old northwest and bases in Florida after 1783, they interfered more often with trappers and traders than with settlers. The war removed the old barriers in the way of migration. Laws enacted not by royal ministers but by an elected Congress shaped land policy and decided the fate of the West. Future garrisons consisted of Americans who had already shown an ability to control the Indians. Official sympathies thereafter lay wholeheartedly with the westward flow of population.

Furthermore, the Revolution clarified titles and eased the process of disposing of land to newcomers. Collaboration and confederation forced the rival states to surrender their western claims to the central government, which soon devised a national land system to distribute acreage widely. Speculators remained important and new companies sprouted, but the alternative of purchase in relatively small plots stimulated expansion. Men and women, stubbornly hopeful, trudged through Nashville, Knoxville, and Pittsburgh on the way to yeomen's clearings, while in the flourishing little towns merchants, ministers, tailors, and printers planned ampler futures of their own. The warranty of future expansion offset the dislocations of war.

Loss of the former political and economic leadership therefore caused no concern. The exit of the loyalists removed the uppermost social group in many places. The occupation of New York City by British troops had given false security to numerous prominent families, encouraged to maintain their ties to the Crown and emboldened to express open hostility to rebellion. Once their cause was lost, they departed, leaving behind their possessions and vacating places of power. In Pennsylvania and the neighboring colonies, large merchants with special ties to London stayed for a time in the hope of moderating opinion, then prudently departed at independence.

In New England the division came earlier. Popular sentiment, clearly favorable to the Revolution, showed that the break was inevitable and compelled families loyal to the Crown to flee. Thomas Hutchinson and Peter Oliver of Massachusetts and the Wentworths of New Hampshire left empty the executive and judicial posts they had once filled. In all the northern provinces the flight of the established lawyers with closest connections to the royal government brought to the fore younger practitioners with a less traditional, more popular understanding of justice. The loss of leadership was less striking in the South, where the great planters moved in the vanguard of rebellion. There Scots and others from the backcountry, prolonging their conflict with the eastern gentry, most readily enlisted in the Tory ranks.

The loyalists by no means formed a homogeneous group; many people in humble circumstances joined the eminent in the refusal to rebel. But the flight of the old leaders, the visible personalities accustomed to deference and control, had drastic social consequences. Few patriots mourned their departure; many edged forward to take up the empty places. Some Tories returned after 1783, but meanwhile the possessions left behind slipped into new hands. Great estates confiscated by the revolutionary governments, divided and redistributed, laid the foundations for the fortunes of a new patriot gentry, while the novel opportunities for trade brought wealth to an entirely fresh group of merchants in the seaboard cities.

Americans sensed the chance for a fresh start. As provinces became states, the citizens decided to move their capitals westward or inland. No doubt the gradual shift of the legislative meeting places away from Portsmouth, New York, Philadelphia, Williamsburg, New Bern, Charleston, and Savannah responded to changes in the distribution of power and population. Perhaps also the preference for Exeter, Albany, Lancaster, Richmond, Raleigh, Columbia, and Augusta owed something to the desire for locations away from the coast and accessible to the frontier. Rural suspicions of the big cities, formerly the seats of the royal governors and still identified with unrepublican luxury and vice, also played a part in the transfer. But in addition it expressed the preference for a break in continuity, as if to mark the fact that the Americans were now making an altogether novel departure in the experience of the nation and, indeed, of mankind.

Disestablishment of all existing institutions seemed eminently appropriate, self-evidently desirable, an inescapable although not always recognized feature of republicanism. Americans did not decide to abolish the monarchy. But they hardly noticed the disappearance of the King or of royal authority after 1774. In all the years of controversy that preceded the final separation from Britain, they had repeatedly expressed loyalty to the sovereign, no doubt in a firmly fixed ritual that required no reflection and bore no special sense of affirmation, but that nevertheless expressed a sense of regal deference. Nowhere did the intricate debates of theory and practice argue against the desirability of a patriot king at the apex of government, as the ancient constitution required. No member of the Continental Congress in 1774 voiced such hostility to the Crown as did the Wilkite mobs in Britain. Eighteenth-century thinkers on both sides of the ocean cherished no doctrine more firmly than the one holding that only a small state could operate without a monarch.

Yet with independence once a reality, the faith of kings simply was no more, as Thomas Paine put it. No vote, no formal action of any sort, marked the decision. The very concept of royalty as a possible option vanished. Americans did not do what other revolutionaries in the eighteenth and nineteenth centuries did again and again: find a new monarch to replace the one ousted. No one missed the King, always a remote figure, out of contact, out of sight, out of mind, irrelevant. The United States needed neither a hereditary chief executive nor a source of royal authority to give its government legitimacy. Independence revealed a commitment to republicanism, always there, long silent, now openly trumpeted.

The institutional attributes of aristocracy also vanished. Before the Revolution as after it, masters of great plantations, owners of extensive landed estates, and families of substantial mercantile wealth enjoyed considerable political power. Now and then such individuals lusted for the elegant trappings of their European counterparts. But gestures of imitation only earned the rebuff of sensitive, censorious neighbors, as did John Hancock's every effort at display while governor of Massachusetts. No one ventured to suggest the award of titles of nobility, despite the deference colonists had shown the occasional duke or lord among them before 1775. The hint of hereditary distinction in the Society of the Cincinnati aroused a furor because any symbol of establishment was incompatible with republicanism.

The Church of England presented a ready target for disestablishment; Virginia and Maryland dissenters had already resisted the fees paid to support its parsons. At independence the tie to the Crown ceased to be an asset and became a liability. With Britian now an enemy, privileges that had rested upon old imperial connections faded away. Congregationalism, by contrast, sustained by association with the patriot cause, retained vestigial links to the state into the nineteenth century, though even there modifications prevented discrimination against other sects. Remnants of old Puritan associations with the government lingered for a half century more, diminishing in strength year by year in the face of growing hostility to special favors. The long battle of the Baptists and of other groups, first for toleration, then for equality, drew to a victorious conclusion.

Constitution makers and legislators often groped for means of ensuring both liberty of conscience and support of public worship. Some states at first thought it enough to bar ministers from civil positions; others proceeded to offer equal protection to all Protestants, or to every denomination of Christian; a few protected every faith "not repugnant to the peace and safety of the State." In several places, moreover, particular qualifying oaths limited election to office. But the Virginia Statute for Establishing Religious Freedom (1786), drafted by Jefferson and supported by Madison, finally proclaimed that any attempt by rulers to influence the mind or to hinge the rights of citizens upon opinions begot habits of hypocrisy and departed from the plan of Almighty God, who chose not to propagate religion by coercion. The measure, a model for many other states, erected a wall between the conscience of believers and the power of government. Blasphemy, public prayer, and Sunday observance long remained troubling issues. But the general principle was clear. The polity could neither interfere with nor support the citizens' preferences of worship. A church would survive not by state recognition but by the will of its own members freely expressed.

Educational, philanthropical, and cultural institutions of every sort passed through a similar transformation. Not a charter or patronage but concerned members gave life to colleges, hospitals, orphanages, and libraries.

The departure of the loyalists, the loss of the King, and disestablishment unsettled society, but also strengthened and stabilized it. Aristocracy, the establishment, and the Crown well before 1775 had become superficial protuberances, easily amputated and forgotten. The flight of the loyalists meant little to a society that did not depend for leadership on a hereditary upper class. Even the gentry were of relatively recent vintage in America, where the volatile environment encouraged movement to the topmost ranks. The vacuum at the apex of society did not long endure; new people quickly occupied the vacated places.

Nor did disestablishment have grave consequences in a society accustomed to making do for itself. For years the colonists had learned how to manage without privilege in voluntary associations. After independence the same habits and practices extended to every sphere of social action. Even the Episcopal Church did not suffer by disestablishment but in time gained strength. Paradoxically, the appointment of bishops, once viewed as a dangerous threat to liberty, evoked no controversy under the Republic. Jonathan Mayhew's grandson became an Anglican bishop, as did the fierce Tory Samuel Seabury, who had actually served in the British Army.

Old habits were out; in personal as in political life people longed for rebirth. "An entirely new scene will open itself," wrote Mordecai Sheftall at the end of the war, "and we have the world to begin again." In 1777 a Middlesex County, Massachusetts, jury acquitted a girl accused of murdering her illegitimate child on the ground that the offense complained of had occurred before the Declaration of Independence; what had happened under the King did not count. In the same year the daughter of a respectable Boston family discovered that the stranger she married was a sot who had arrived in Massachusetts having abandoned a wife and five children; that did not faze a free woman convinced that a fresh start was the right of every citizen.

The rapidity of change and the diversity of places and times bred continuing concern lest the fragile alliance of war crumble and the separate states float apart. At their initial encounters, delegates from the eastern provinces had sniffed suspiciously at southerners, remote in social background and in habits. A long history of conflict between Yankees and Yorkers left a legacy of wariness and latent hostility; the last will of Lewis Morris in 1760 provided for the education of his son Gouverneur anywhere except Connecticut. The solicitous father had feared the influence on a youth of "that low craft and cunning so incident in the people of that country," although "many of them under the sanctified garb of religion have endeavoured to impose themselves on the world for honest men." The reputation of Yankees as "a set of low, dirty, griping, cowardly, lying rascals" lasted for decades. Rivalry among the Germans, English, Irish, and Scotch-Irish, among the Quakers, Catholics, Presbyterians, and Anglicans in Pennsylvania, extended into politics as well as religion.

Hence it seemed to Thomas Hutchinson that the preface to the Declaration of Independence rested on a false premise: that the colonies were "one *distinct people* and the kingdom another, connected by *political* bands." The former governor of Massachusetts, by November 1776 a Tory exile in London, argued in a pamphlet entitled *Strictures upon the Declaration of a Congress at Philadelphia* that the proposition had never been true. Events had passed him by. A poem on liberty in *The Virginia Almanack* for 1771 hailed Britannia's sons; *The Lancaster Almanack* for 1775 reprinted the verse but substituted the word "Americans." In becoming Americans the colonists became a people.

More than the resonance of Jefferson's words demonstrated the existence of a national identity, commemoration of which came, appropriately, on July 4, the date of the Declaration's adoption. That Yankees and Yorkers, Dutch and Quakers frequently quarreled was less surprising than that they more often worked and acted in unity, without compulsion or formal agreement, almost reflexively.

Cautious, timid patriots feared that though the threat from a common enemy for the moment abated regional and group hostilities, in the long run only a pervasive continental national spirit would prevent the appearance of competing sovereignties within the nation. To that end John Jay argued in 1787 that Providence had given this one connected country to one united people, descended from the same ancestors, speaking the same language, professing the same religion, and very similar in their manners and customs. Jay of course knew that his own ancestors were French, and he was privately solicitous about the positions of Americans not of English ancestry, including the African slaves. Not far from his home, villagers still spoke Dutch, while Gaelic, Welsh, and German might greet him in his travels. But he imagined that belief in common origins would strengthen the national spirit.

He was wrong. It was not merely the need for confederation and union that forced citizens of the Republic to accept variations of regional types as the price of the ability to work together. Christopher Gadsden's exhortation to erase the distinctions that made some New Englanders and others Virginians remained unheeded, but people did not need the reminder of this patriotic South Carolinian that all were Americans, who recognized and accepted one another's differences.

To justify independence and the war, rebels stressed the non-English aspects of their culture. Rebellion was not really a form of matricide because Britain was not really the mother country. Observations in London in January 1775 convinced Boston's Josiah Quincy "more and more every day that the commonalty in this country are no more like the commonalty in America than if they were two utterly distinct people."

Europe and not England was the parent country, explained *Common Sense*. "This new world hath been the asylum for the persecuted lovers of civil liberty from every part" of the Old World. The nation about to achieve independence derived its strength from numerous sources, for Americans traced their ancestry to all the peoples of Europe. The Frenchman who called himself "An American Farmer" explained that the peculiar combination of heritages had created a new species of man. Americans appropriated all world history as a prelude to the establishment of their nation. And the Revolution hardened the determination to preserve cultural distance from Britain. Noah Webster's speller and reader in 1783 and 1785 pointed out that Americans spoke a language decidedly different from English

and argued for uniform speech patterns and orthography for all
the states.

Practical experience was more persuasive than rhetoric. A
committee of the Congress advised General Washington not to
exchange German prisoners, who would remain, if they could, to
settle when they observed how their countrymen, having arrived
without a farthing, acquired plentiful fortunes by care and industry. A petition to the Pennsylvania legislature in 1781 explained that the German settlements had greatly contributed to
the wealth and strength of the states and urged the government
to encourage continued immigration.

Improved communications began to knit the country together.
To regularize the distribution of mail, Congress in 1785 contracted with stagecoach proprietors to carry the post on a route
that stretched from Maine to Georgia, thus replacing the private
carriers who had done business on their own. The stagecoaches,
however, paid more regard to the convenience of passengers
than to the needs of correspondents and insisted on early morning departures and late night arrivals. Merchants and clerks
forced to write at night complained, and the federal postal establishment tried to employ cheaper, more adaptable postriders. On
horseback or on wheels, the mail got through with growing de-
pendability.

Eagerly Americans sought evidence of unity in their vast, diverse country. At a Philadelphia fete in 1782 Benjamin Rush
"saw the world in miniature. All the ranks, parties and professions in the city, and all the officers of government were fully
represented." Old as well as new families, doctors and ministers
of the gospel, the learned faculty of the college and people who
knew not whether Cicero spoke Latin or Greek, painters, musicians, and poets and men never moved by beauty, harmony, or
rhyme, merchants, tradesmen, Whigs, former Tories, and folk of
all national origins conversed with one another like the children
of one father, evidence of their Union.

After the Revolution, as before it, rapid change and a fluid society encouraged social mobility. The availability of land, the
willingness to move, and expansion of the frontier assured every-

234 A Restless People

one but the slave some degree of independence in agriculture. The demand for skilled labor left the crafts open; inability to enforce strict licensing did the same for the professions; and since trade fell within no controlled lines, new merchants again and again reached for wealth. The departure of the Tories; the formation of governments open to fresh influences; and the speculative atmosphere bred by war, shortages, and inflation made new people affluent, kept society off balance, and inhibited any tendency toward stratification. Neither in theory nor in practice were the rebels levelers; they lusted for rank and privileges as avidly as other eighteenth-century people. The patriot general traveled with guards, attendants, and wagonloads of baggage, as the enemy did. The elected governors and judges prized titles and perquisites as had those formerly appointed by the Crown. But place was earned, not inherited, and was held—and could be lost —not by the grace of God or the King, but by consent and merit. That much was actuality, not merely rhetoric.

There was no discounting the effect of opportunity. This, "An American Farmer" said, was every person's country, knowing, properly speaking, no strangers. Leaving the overstocked Old World, Europeans no sooner breathed the air of the New than they formed schemes, embarked on designs inconceivable back home, and thus became Americans. Just before the Revolution, Edmund Burke had exclaimed, "There is America," which for the moment "serves for little more than to amuse you with stories of savage men and uncouth manners; yet shall, before you taste of death, show itself equal to the whole of that commerce which now attracts the envy of the world."

Not common descent, nor yet common language, religion, or culture, but a common situation made Americans one people. For all their eloquence in political discussion, the revolutionaries never defined what they meant by the word "Union." Although the Articles of Confederation dangled unratified until 1781, the Union was already long since perpetual and became more perfect in the federal constitution of 1787. The word referred to more than a set of governmental arrangements; it encompassed also the emotion Rush felt in 1782 at sight of differences counterpoised by common purposes and common destiny.

Union was more than political; the tie expressed the identity, as a nation, of men and women who shared the unremitting insecurity of freedom. Exposed at the unstable edge of a continent, habituated to hazards in every aspect of life, ever in motion, ever probing opportunity, Americans joined one another in the republican experiment, hoping that the consent of citizens would permit all to live together without constraints upon any.

Euphoric enthusiasts celebrated the virtues and beneficial effects of republicanism. Some hoped that the social requirements of the new nation would enlarge and redefine the female domain by emphasizing the importance of motherhood in the nurture of future citizens. Domestic behavior and child raising, which affected the very survival of the nation, were bound to improve. Since environment determined health, the blessings of liberty would certainly eradicate plagues. The biblical Jews, Benjamin Rush knew, under a democratic form of government lived without diseases except those sent by God as punishment. Countries where people enjoyed the products of their labor suffered less from epidemic illnesses than those where despotic, feudal methods prevailed. Patriots were healthier than loyalists; the war cured hysteria in women who had supported the American cause; and many a barren marriage produced offspring in the wake of independence. By contrast, observers noted, the Tories suffered physical and mental breakdowns, due to excessive concern for the safety of their persons and property, to loss of power, and to dietary changes caused by inflation and oppression. A wholesome society would escape artificial illness. And if the plague struck, as it did in Philadelphia in 1793, the outbreak was providential, Jefferson explained, since it would discourage undue concentrations of population in cities.

The buoyant expressions of confidence never fully blew away the clouds of doubt that darkened horizons for the most optimistic patriots. Again and again gloomy news reminded Americans of Tory and British predictions that rebellion would plunge the country into misery, that independence would lead to anarchy with the contending leaderless mobs breaking their necks, one by one. "America has seen its best days," Pennsylvanian James Allen moaned in 1775. The country could not escape ruin, whoever won; and if it fell, "Liberty no longer continues an inhabitant of this Globe." Never again, Thomas Hutchinson wrote, would Massachusetts inhabitants enjoy so great a share of natural liberty as if they had remained a colony. Instead of advancing in opulence and strength, the loyalist John F. D. Smyth explained, the states would decline in population and sink into poverty, victimized by "riots, confusion, and every kind of culpable and criminal violence and excess," so that people before long would wish "for the restoration of that government" they had so lately overturned.

Mutual dependence sharpened the vision of citizens who scrutinized the performance of their neighbors. Expecting much of one another, they promptly detected shortcomings. Alexander Hamilton condemned his countrymen for the "folly of the ass and all the passiveness of the sheep." They were, he believed, "determined not to be free," and he almost wished for universal ruin to hide the disgrace. George Washington, generally a man of serene faith, toward the end of 1776 thought the game pretty near up. And Thomas Jefferson, though usually sanguine, in 1781 expressed anxiety: with the conclusion of the war, the country would go downhill, its rulers corrupt, its people careless and absorbed in making money, until their rights either revived or expired in a convulsion. That year the French consul, writing from Richmond, concluded that Virginia could not long remain democratic. Yankee farmers, Pennsylvania woodsmen, and Carolina planters, knowing the fallibility of human nature and the power of greed, passion, and ignorance, had long since learned that the trail followed to reach a clearing might lead only to the edge of a precipice.

For reassurance they could recall Benjamin Franklin's affirmation in the _Pennsylvania Gazette,_ thirty years before independence: when a whole people arrived at a judgment, especially a free people, they were likely to be infallible. The citizens had to believe that they were a whole people, for they knew that people made a state, not walls, or ships devoid of people. Those uneasy about present hardships drew comfort from the promises of the future; and the past, as commonly understood, underwrote those promises. They had pitched in a place Providence had made their country and their fortress.

A few years back, they had been loyal subjects of the Crown. Now they were independent. How had that happened?

People with faith in progress could answer. They acted as they did because they moved in the vanguard of a procession that embraced all mankind, marching in the same direction. The heritage of the concept of mission reinforced that certainty. Since the days of John Winthrop, Americans had learned that they were building a city upon a hill for the emulation of the whole world, a task that imbued the destiny of the United States with universal significance. The test of times to come was the ultimate assurance. In the intimacy of a religious "relation," Joseph Terry in 1771 blessed God that he "was born and brought up in a Land of gospel Light." Even a loyalist, James Murray of North Carolina, conceded in 1775 that colonial union was "a Step in the Scheme of Providence for fixing in Time an Empire in America." The Revolution, *Common Sense* announced, was "not the concern of a day, a year, or an age," but of posterity even to the end of time. America, that unwieldy mass of earth whose exuberant bosom nourished a wise and gigantic people now flourishing in learning and arts, evoked deep reverence. It was not rash to assert, a journal entry noted in 1775, that their "Commerce, & Wealth, & Power" were "Yet to rule the Globe!" For "what visible purpose could Nature have formed these vast lakes," asked the poet Philip Freneau in 1782, "if this new world was not to become at some time or another the receptacle of numerous civilized nations?" Americans were the western pilgrims, carrying along the arts, sciences, vigor, and industry which began long since in the East. They would close the great circle. Millennialism—anticipation of the early arrival of an era of general righteousness and happiness—became an integral part of religion in the United States; and already John Ledyard's wanderings across Europe, Asia, and Africa provided a foretaste of the visionary zeal that later carried merchants and missionaries around the world.

History spelled out the message. What England had achieved
in seventeen hundred years, Burke explained, Americans had ac-
complished in the course of a single lifetime. A grand design,
which some knew as Divine Providence, others as progress,
marked the path toward future salvation, redemption, perfection,
and the improvement of mankind whether through affliction,
judgments, or gradual enlightenment.

Other nations mingled good and evil qualities: France, luxury
and Papism; Sweden, private industry and public profligacy;
Denmark, slavish loyalty to a race of good-natured kings; Switzerland, liberty and self-containment; Holland, patriotism but
swollen with wealth; and Italy, an unweeded garden. Once Britain had led the way to regeneration; but such corruption of manners and government as *The Beggar's Opera* described and as
the plots of George III's Ministry exemplified proved its un-
worthiness for the role. In an almanac for 1772 an American visitor informs the guide through the ruins of Westminster Abbey in
1994 that while the issue of rights was in dispute, "your ministers were running horses at Newmarket. These, with many
other acts of dissipation, intemperance, injustice, violence, ignorance, and despotism," were the causes of the Kingdom's
wretched condition. Franklin warned in 1775 that bribery, prodi-
gality, and corruption in the old rotten state might poison his
own rising country. England having given freedom her warning
to depart, Asia and Africa having long since expelled her, and
Europe treating her as a stranger, there remained but one asylum for the fugitive. Leadership passed to the New World republic, not for its sake alone but for that of all mankind. Soon
unfolding epics from Timothy Dwight's *Conquest of Canaan*
(1785) to Joel Barlow's *Columbiad* (1807) recounted the glorious story.

Americans had never considered themselves detached, apart—
and not only because ties of commerce, migration, and culture
linked them to other parts of the world. What was as important
was a sense of common destiny that animated the curious engravings and accounts in almanacs and books of strange folk in
New Zealand, Asia, and Africa. All had places in the grand universal procession toward freedom. The Massachusetts assembly

in 1769 toasted the Briton Isaac Barré; Dr. Charles Lucas, the Irish patriot; the brave Corsicans; the cantons of Switzerland; the distressed Poles; and the seven united provinces of the Netherlands. That year one of the leading Sons of Liberty named his son Pascal Paoli in honor of the gallant Corsican, whose birthday Bostonians celebrated. And Europeans identified with the hopes of the New World future—not only intellectuals who wrote of noble savages, unspoiled nature, and free yeomen, but also the Scottish peasants of Skye who called a dance "America," because it kept them ever "going, setting and wheeling round each other."

After the assembly of the French States-General in 1789, therefore, Americans watched events in Europe with more intense interest. In the winter of 1792–93 "Friends of the Rights of Man" everywhere in the United States honored the "late triumph of liberty over despotism in France" by overeating and drinking republican toasts. Civic feasts marked the occasion, and citizens of all ranks paraded to banquets at which sympathy for the poor and oppressed flowed as freely as the punch. The Philadelphia festivities after the beheading of Louis XVI in 1793 heard a toast proclaim that the world would soon become "one great democratic society comprehending the human race," and a hopeful Bostonian looked forward to the day when all distinctions of race, nationality, and language would disappear and the Rights of Man, as defined by Thomas Paine, would prevail. Since people everywhere descended from a single pair of progenitors not more than four thousand years past, the physical, cultural, and moral differences among them were responses to diverse environmental conditions and would fade in time.

Deflation of these extravagant hopes, a few years later, followed upon discovery that what the French termed "revolution" was not identical with what Americans did. In the Old World the word meant the process—the overthrow of an existing government by force; in the New World it meant the product—formation of a virtuous republic. The corrupt French Directory, ruling by force and subverting the law, did not accord with American concepts.

In the centuries that followed, expectations revived and disappointments followed. Universality was a necessary condition of the nationalism of a people, diverse in origins, oriented toward freedom, and directed toward future progress. But the world as it was never was what it should have been, and though nineteenth-century European revolutionaries looked to the United States for a model, they could not replicate a republic that sprang from the experience of restless men and women loose in the great spaces of a promised land. And after 1917 another model, which valued neither law nor consent nor rights, proved more attractive.

Yet though from time to time Americans momentarily turned their sights inward, they could not long escape their heritage as a New World people, probing the frontier of human experience and the conditions of freedom. The stability, sense of tradition, ease, and personal gratification for which they often longed remained out of reach. A restless people found itself ever confronting new challenges and, generation after generation, recklessly abandoned inherited assumptions to explore new ways of life. That was its heritage from the eighteenth century.

Notes for Further Reading

Few subjects have received as extensive treatment as the American Revolution. That event cast its shadow across the future, generating worldwide shock waves as people everywhere sought analogies to it and tried to learn from it, to find relevance in it.

But shadows obscured reality. For two hundred years, generation after generation in reexamining the Revolution distorted it, casting shadow upon shadow and burying the past actuality.

Every interpretation expressed the need of the interpreter at a given time and place. People who turned to the past when they were about to act did not seek knowledge: they behaved out of interest, prejudice, ignorance, emotion, and faith. In history, they sought a belief that would help them act with unity and determination; that is, they sought a myth, whether it conformed to reality or not. The accretion of such interpretations made it ever more difficult to perceive reality.

Some myths about the Revolution dissolved with relative ease. The cluster of attitudes in the early nineteenth century that aimed to strengthen nationality, develop patriotism, and counter divisive forces led to exaggerated veneration of the Founding Fathers. To develop a national outlook, Parson Weems and George Bancroft provided the country with a legend buttressed by history: a united, homogeneous, and moral people guided by heroic leaders had thrown off a tyrant's yoke and founded the Republic. One need only comment that the Founding Fathers were men subject to passion, emotion, self-interest, error, and stupidity, operating in a society torn by dissent, conflict, and insecurities; to say that does not diminish but rather enhances their achievements.

An alternative set of myths prevailed in the 1970s. In that time of denigration the descendants of the 1920s debunkers peeped beneath the togas and discovered feet of clay, or at least of flesh; then, like Gore Vidal, they compensated for lack of knowledge by exploiting the sensational—even if it had to be invented.

Neither myth, however, was likely to deceive any historian familiar with the sources. The characters in the drama of independence were neither divine nor doltish, but men and women of all degrees who struggled in novel circumstances, with only incomplete awareness of what they were doing, for a new definition of themselves as a nation. Documentary sources, scrupulously collected and preserved, and printed in numerous publications of high value, provide the means of cutting through to the truth.

There is no dearth of material, either primary or secondary, for students willing to seek it. These notes comment on the more important and most readable sources. More elaborate listings include John Shy, comp., *The American Revolution* (Northbrook, Ill., 1973), and Frank Freidel, ed., *Harvard Guide to American History* (Cambridge, Mass., 1974), Sections 35, 36. Dwight La Verne Smith, *Era of the American Revolution* (Santa Barbara, Calif., 1975), is a broad but unselective bibliography.

The earliest systematic effort to treat the subjects here considered was James Schouler, *Americans of 1776* (New York, 1906). Evarts Boutell Greene, *The Revolutionary Generation 1763–1790* (New York, 1958), shared the virtues and the faults of the *History of American Life Series* of which it was Volume IV. Arthur M. Schlesinger, *Birth of the Nation* (New York, 1968), and Richard Hofstadter, *America at 1750* (New York, 1971), also dealt with the period.

Numerous collections of papers, letters, and journals, both of famous statesmen and of humbler people in all walks of life, deserve sampling. Among the more useful are James Allen, "Diary," *Pennsylvania Magazine of History* IX (1885); Ann Eliza Bleecker, *Posthumous Works* (New York, 1793); John Carroll, *Papers*, Thomas O'Brien Hanley, ed. (Notre Dame, Ind., 1976); Landon Carter, *Diary*, Jack P. Greene, ed. (Charlottesville, Va., 1965); François Jean, Marquis de Chastellux, *Travels in North America in the Years 1780, 1781, 1782*, Howard C. Rice, Jr., trans. and ed. (Chapel Hill, N.C., 1963); Baron Ludwig von Closen, *The Revolutionary Journal*, Evelyn M. Acomb, trans. and ed. (Chapel Hill, N.C., 1958); Nicholas Cresswell, *Journal, 1774–1777* (New York, 1928); Samuel Cooper, "Diary," *American Historical Review* VI (Jan. 1901); Amos Farnsworth, "Diary," *Proceedings of the Massachusetts Historical Society* II (Dec. 1897–Jan. 1898); Philip Vickers Fithian, *Journals and Letters*, Hunter D. Farish, ed. (Williamsburg, 1957); Alexander Graydon, *Memoirs* (Harrisburg, 1811); Jeremiah Greenman, *Military Journal*, Robert C. Bray and Paul E. Bushnell, eds. (De Kalb, Ill., 1978); John Harrower, *Journal*, Edward Miles Riley, ed. (Williamsburg, 1963); Ann Hulton, *Letters of a Loyalist Lady* (Cambridge, Mass., 1927); Christopher Marshall, *Extracts from the Diary*, William Duane, ed. (Albany, N.Y., 1877); Henry Melchior Mühlenberg, *Journals*, T. G. Tappert and J. W. Doberstein, eds. (Philadelphia, 1942); James Murray, *Letters*, N. M. Tiffany and S. I. Leslay, eds. (Boston, 1901); Peter Oliver, *Origin and Progress of the American Revolution*, Douglas Adair and J. A. Schutz, eds. (San Marino, Calif., 1961); Enos Reeves, "Letter-Books," *Pennsylvania Magazine of History* XXI (1897); Benjamin Rush, *Autobiography, Travels Through Life and Commonplace Books*, George W. Corner, ed. (Princeton, 1948); Janet Shaw, *Journal*, Charles M. Andrews, ed. (New Haven, 1921); J. F. D. Smyth, *A Tour in the United States of America* (London, 1784); John Tudor, *Diary*, William Tudor, ed. (Boston, 1896); Albigence Waldo, "Diary," *Pennsylvania Magazine of History and Biography* XXI (1897); Charles Woodmason, *The Carolina Backcountry on the Eve of the Revolution —Journal and Other Writings*, Richard J. Hooker, ed. (Chapel Hill, N.C., 1953). Fithian was tutor in the home of a southern planter, as was Harrower, a Scottish indentured servant. Hulton, Murray, Oliver, and Smyth viewed the revolutionary events with pungent Tory dismay. The magisterial collections of the writings of Washington, Adams, Jefferson, Hamilton, and Franklin and of the members of the Continental Congress make a wealth of information available to any reader.

An abundant secondary literature survives the continuing efforts to interpret the Revolution, reflecting every fashion in historiography, politics, and ideology. Later books did not always supplant earlier ones, and quality, to say nothing of readability, had little to do with time or the bias of the authors. Any selection is therefore idiosyncratic. General surveys include Douglas Adair, *Fame and the Founding Fathers* (New York, 1974); David Ammerman, *In the Common Cause: American Responses to the Coercive Act of 1774* (Charlottesville, Va., 1974); Larry R. Gerlach, ed., *Legacies of the American Revolution* (Logan, Utah, 1978); David Freeman Hawke, *Honorable Treason: The Declaration of Independence and the Men Who Signed It* (New York, 1976); Michael Kammen, *A Season of Youth: The American Revolution and the Historical Revolution* (New York, 1978); Stanley N. Katz, ed., *Colonial America: Essays in Politics and Social Development* (Boston, 1976); Benjamin Woods Labaree, *The Boston Tea Party* (New York, 1964); Jackson Turner Maine, *The Social Structure of Revolutionary America* (Princeton, 1966); Edmund S. Morgan, *The Challenge of the American Revolution* (New York, 1976).

The divergence in their early history and in the approach to independence, as well as the separate organization of their archives and other source materials, made the individual states logical subjects of historical research and interpretation. Some of the most thoughtful accounts took this form. Among them are Christopher Collier, *Connecticut and the Continental Congress* (Chester, Conn., 1973); Richard L. Bushman, *From Puritan to Yankee: Character and Social Order in Connecticut 1690–1765* (Cambridge, Mass., 1965); J. Leitch Wright, *Florida in the American Revolution* (Gainesville, Fla., 1975); Barton J. Starr, *Tories, Dons and Rebels* (Gainesville, Fla., 1976); Kenneth Coleman, *The American Revolution in Georgia 1763–1789* (Athens,

Ga., 1958); Harold E. Davis, *The Fledgling Province: Social and Cultural Life in Colonial Georgia* (Chapel Hill, N.C., 1976); Philip A. Crowl, *Maryland During and After the Revolution* (Baltimore, 1943); Ronald Hoffman, *A Spirit of Dissension: Economics, Politics and the Revolution in Maryland* (Baltimore, 1973); Richard D. Brown, *Revolutionary Politics in Massachusetts* (Cambridge, Mass., 1970); Robert E. Brown, *Middle Class Democracy and the Revolution in Massachusetts* (Ithaca, N.Y., 1955); Oscar and Mary F. Handlin, eds., *Popular Sources of Political Authority* (Cambridge, Mass., 1966), on Massachusetts; R. F. Upton, *Revolutionary New Hampshire* (Hanover, N.H., 1936); Thomas J. Archdeacon, *New Jersey Society in the Revolutionary Era* (Trenton, 1975); Andrew C. Mellick, Jr., *The Story of an Old Farm: Life in New Jersey in the Eighteenth Century* (Somerville, N.J., 1889)—interesting though inaccurate in detail; Carl L. Becker, *History of Political Parties in the Province of New York* (Madison, Wis., 1909); Patricia U. Bonomi, *A Factious People: Political Parties in the Province of New York* (New York, 1971); Hugh T. Lefler and William S. Powell, *Colonial North Carolina: A History* (New York, 1973); Harry R. Merrens, *Colonial North Carolina in the Eighteenth Century* (Chapel Hill, N.C., 1964); Richard A. Ryerson, *The Revolution Is Now Begun* (Philadelphia, 1978), and James T. Lemon, *The Best Poor Man's Country* (Baltimore, 1972), on Pennsylvania; Sidney V. James, *Colonial Rhode Island: A History* (New York, 1975); David S. Lovejoy, *Rhode Island Politics and the American Revolution* (Providence, 1958); Richard M. Brown, *The South Carolina Regulators* (Cambridge, Mass., 1963); M. Eugene Sirmans, *Colonial South Carolina* (Chapel Hill, N.C., 1966); Chilton Williamson, *Vermont in Quandary* (Montpelier, Vt., 1949); and Robert E. and B. Katherine Brown, *Virginia 1705–1786: Democracy or Aristocracy* (East Lansing, Mich., 1964).

Except for the West, regional approaches have been less successful, but there is useful material in John R. Alden, *The First South* (Baton Rouge, 1961); Donald B. Chidsey, *The War in the South* (New York, 1969); Jeffrey J. Crow and Larry E. Tise, *The Southern Experience in the American Revolution* (Chapel Hill, N.C., 1978); John A. Neuenschwander, *The Middle Colonies and*

the Coming of the American Revolution (Port Washington, N.Y.,
1974); and James Truslow Adams, Revolutionary New England
(Boston, 1923).

Biographies are abundant, with statesmen the most usual sub-
jects. The following is a selection of the clearest and soundest:
Charles W. Akers, Abigail Adams: An American Woman (Bos-
ton, 1979); Peter Shaw, The Character of John Adams (Chapel
Hill, N.C., 1976); William G. McLoughlin, Isaac Backus and the
American Pietistic Tradition (Boston, 1967); Anne Zimmer, Jon-
athan Boucher: Loyalist in Exile (Detroit, 1978); Louis Morton,
Robert Carter of Nomini Hall (Williamsburg, 1941); Louis
Leonard Tucker, Puritan Protagonist: President Thomas Clap of
Yale College (Chapel Hill, N.C., 1962); Verner W. Crane, Ben-
jamin Franklin (Boston, 1954); Claude-Anne Lopez, Mon Cher
Papa: Franklin and the Ladies of Paris (New Haven, 1966);
Herbert S. Allan, John Hancock (New York, 1948); Richard R.
Beeman, Patrick Henry (New York, 1974); Bernard Bailyn, The
Ordeal of Thomas Hutchinson (Cambridge, Mass., 1975); Roger
J. Champagne, Alexander McDougall and the American Revolu-
tion in New York (Schenectady, N.Y., 1975); Irving Brant, James
Madison (Indianapolis, 1941–50); Helen Hill Miller, George
Mason (Chapel Hill, N.C., 1975); Charles W. Akers, Called
Unto Liberty: A Life of Jonathan Mayhew (Cambridge, Mass.,
1964); Don Higginbotham, Daniel Morgan, Revolutionary Rifle-
man (Chapel Hill, N.C., 1961); Max N. Mintz, Gouverneur
Morris (Norman, Okla., 1970); Emory G. Evans, Thomas Nelson
of Yorktown (Williamsburg, 1975); David Freeman Hawke,
Benjamin Rush (Indianapolis, 1971); Christopher Collier, Roger
Sherman's Connecticut (Middletown, Conn., 1971); Burke Davis,
George Washington and the American Revolution (New York,
1975); James Thomas Flexner, George Washington in the American Revolution (Boston, 1968).

Each chapter of this volume draws upon the original sources
but also upon a wealth of monographic material, some of it in
books, some in journal articles. A brief selection follows to help
the reader through the literature.

Chapter 1. The standard accounts of agriculture are Lewis C.
Gray, History of Agriculture in the Southern United States to

1860 (Washington, D.C., 1933); P. W. Bidwell and J. I. Falconer, *History of Agriculture in the Northern United States, 1620–1860* (Washington, D.C., 1925). Jerome E. Brooks, *The Mighty Leaf: Tobacco Through the Centuries* (Boston, 1952), and two insightful essays by Aubrey C. Land—"Economic Behavior in a Planting Society," *Journal of Southern History* XXXIII (Nov. 1967), and "The Tobacco Staple and the Planter's Problems," *Agricultural History* XLIII (Jan. 1969)—throw light on the plantation. Emory G. Evans, "Private Indebtedness and the Revolution in Virginia," *William and Mary Quarterly* XXVIII (July 1971), examines an important subject. On the complex issue of tenantry, David C. Skaggs, *Roots of Maryland Democracy* (Westport, Conn., 1973), is less persuasive than Gregory A. Stiverson, *Poverty in a Land of Plenty* (Baltimore, 1977); and Sung Bok Kim, *Landlord and Tenant in Colonial New York* (Williamsburg, 1978), is excellent. D. Alan Williams, "The Small Farmer in Eighteenth Century Virginia Politics," *Agricultural History* XLIII (Jan. 1969), and Robert Zemsky, *Merchants, Farmers and River Gods* (Boston, 1971), treat aspects of government in the southern and northern provinces. Merrill Jensen, "The American Revolution and American Agriculture," *Agricultural History* XLIII (Jan. 1969), deals with the effects of war. L. J. Greene, *The Negro in Colonial New England* (New York, 1942); Edmund S. Morgan, *American Slavery, American Freedom* (New York, 1975); Gerald W. Mullin, *Flight and Rebellion: Slave Resistance in Eighteenth Century Virginia* (New York, 1972); and Peter H. Wood, *Black Majority* (New York, 1974), contain material on slavery. Chester E. Eisinger, "The Freehold Concept in Eighteenth Century American Letters," *William and Mary Quarterly* IV (Jan. 1947); Howard Mumford Jones, *The Pursuit of Happiness* (Cambridge, Mass., 1953); Caroline Robbins, *The Pursuit of Happiness* (Washington, D.C., 1974); and Arthur M. Schlesinger, "The Lost Meaning of 'The Pursuit of Happiness,'" *William and Mary Quarterly* XXI (July 1964), touch on the ideas of property and the yeoman.

Chapter 2. The general problems of cities are the subjects of Carl Bridenbaugh, *Cities in Revolt: Urban Life in America*

1743–1776 (New York, 1964); Carville Earle and Ronald Hoffman, "Urban Development in the Eighteenth Century South," *Perspectives in American History* X (1976); and Sylvia Doughty Fries, *The Urban Idea in Colonial America* (Philadelphia, 1977). Pauline Maier, *From Resistance to Revolution* (New York, 1973), treats the recourse to violence. By asking the wrong questions, Dirk Hoerder, *Society and Governments 1760–1780: The Power Structure in Massachusetts Townships* (Berlin, West Germany, 1972), is doomed to give the wrong answers.

Philadelphia, then the largest American city, has received extensive treatment in Carl and Jessica Bridenbaugh, *Rebels and Gentlemen: Philadelphia in the Age of Franklin* (New York, 1942); Stephen Brobeck, "Revolutionary Change in Colonial Philadelphia," *William and Mary Quarterly* XXXV (July 1976); William Bell Clark, "The Sea Captain's Club," *Pennsylvania Magazine of History* LXXXI (Jan. 1957); Darlene Emmet Fischer, "Social Life in Philadelphia during the British Occupation," *Pennsylvania History* XXXVII (July 1970); James H. Hutson, "An Investigation of the Inarticulate, Philadelphia's White Oaks," *William and Mary Quarterly* XXVIII (Jan. 1971); and Charles S. Olton, "Philadelphia's First Environmental Crisis," *Pennsylvania Magazine of History* XCVIII (Jan. 1974). John F. Watson, *Annals of Philadelphia* (Philadelphia, 1857), is anecdotal but interesting when used with caution.

New York City is the subject of Oscar T. Barck, *New York City During the War of Independence* (New York, 1931); Don R. Gerlach, *Philip Schuyler and the American Revolution in New York 1773–1777* (Lincoln, Nebr., 1964); Frank Monaghan and Marvin Lowenthal, *This Was New York* (New York, 1943); Esther Singleton, *Social New York Under the Georges* (New York, 1902); and Thomas J. Wertenbaker, *Father Knickerbocker Rebels: New York City During the Revolution* (New York, 1948).

Oliver M. Dickerson, *Boston Under Military Rule 1768–1769* (New York, 1970), is a valuable collection of contemporary materials. G. B. Warden, *Boston 1689–1776* (Boston, 1970), and his "The Distribution of Property in Boston 1692–1775," *Perspec-*

tives in American History X (1976), are useful modern accounts. Justin Winsor, *The Memorial History of Boston* (Boston, 1880), is old but still interesting. Robert A. Gross, *The Minutemen and Their World* (New York, 1976), examines the town of Concord, Massachusetts.

Mechanics, merchants, artisans, and other groups are the subjects of Carl Bridenbaugh, *The Colonial Craftsman* (New York, 1950); Arthur Cole, "The Tempo of Mercantile Life in Colonial America," *Business History Review* XXXIII (autumn 1959); William W. Condit, "Christopher Ludwick, Patriotic Gingerbread Baker," *Pennsylvania Magazine of History* LXXXI (Oct. 1957); Virginia D. Harrington, *The New York Merchants on the Eve of the Revolution* (New York, 1935); Benjamin W. Labaree, *Patriots and Partisans: The Merchants of Newburyport 1764–1815* (Cambridge, Mass., 1962); Staughton Lynd, "The Mechanics in New York Politics 1774–1788," *Labor History* V (fall 1964); Thomas Eliot Norton, *The Fur Trade in Colonial New York 1686–1776* (Madison, Wis., 1974); Charles S. Olton, *Artisans for Independence: Philadelphia Mechanics and the American Revolution* (Syracuse, N.Y., 1975); Frederick B. Tolles, *Meeting House and Counting House: The Quaker Merchants of Colonial Philadelphia* (Chapel Hill, N.C., 1948); and Richard Walsh, *Charleston's Sons of Liberty: A Study of the Artisans 1763–1789* (Columbus, S.C., 1959).

Gary B. Nash, *The Urban Crucible* (Cambridge, Mass., 1979), summarizes a version of town life sharply at variance with that presented in this volume, one that appears also in James A. Henretta, "Economic Development and Social Structure in Colonial Boston," *William and Mary Quarterly* XXII (Jan. 1965); Jesse Lemish, "Jack Tar in the Streets," *William and Mary Quarterly* XXV (July 1968); and Allan Kulikoff, "The Progress of Inequality in Revolutionary Boston," *William and Mary Quarterly* XXVIII (July 1971). These historians find a developing radical consciousness that produced "a mental breakthrough" and that ended the politics of deference in the towns of the revolutionary era. Increasing poverty, they claim, led to a growing awareness of class interests among the laboring groups. Apart from their flawed factual basis, these fanciful works share a common misun-

derstanding of what workingmen and -women were actually like
in the 1770s.

Chapter 3. Alice Hanson Jones, *American Colonial Wealth*
(New York, 1977), is an indispensable array of the data further
analyzed in her summary volume *Wealth of a Nation to Be*
(New York, 1980).

Daniel H. Calhoun, *Professional Lives in America: Structure
and Aspiration 1750–1850* (Cambridge, Mass., 1965), and Donald Scott, *From Office to Profession* (Philadelphia, 1978), treat
the ministers' position.

Most accounts of the status of physicians also cover health and
the healing arts, which are treated separately in this book. Richard H. Shryock's *Medicine and Society in America 1660–1860*
(New York, 1960), is the most extensive survey. Also useful are
Otho T. Beall, Jr., "Aristotle's Masterpiece in America," *William
and Mary Quarterly* XX (Apr. 1963); Whitfield J. Bell, "Medical
Practice in Colonial America," *Bulletin of the History of Medi-
cine* XXXI (Sept.–Oct. 1957); Wyndham B. Blanton, *Medicine in
Virginia in the Eighteenth Century* (Richmond, 1931); Cath-
erine M. Scholten, "On the Importance of the Obstetrick Art,"
William and Mary Quarterly XXXIV (July 1977); and Robert
Cumming Wilson, *Drugs and Pharmacy in the Life of Georgia*
(Atlanta, 1959). Courtney R. Hall, "Jefferson on the Medical
Theory and Practice of His Day," *Bulletin of the History of
Medicine* XXXI (May–June 1957), and George Rosen, "Political
Order and Human Health in Jefferson's Thought," *Bulletin of the
History of Medicine* XXVI (Jan.–Feb. 1952), consider views of
medicine in the revolutionary era.

The biographies of attorneys who entered politics touch inci-
dentally on the legal profession, as do Maxwell Bloomfield,
American Lawyers in a Changing Society 1776–1876 (Cam-
bridge, Mass., 1976); Milton M. Klein, "The Rise of the New
York Bar, the Legal Career of William Livingston," *William and
Mary Quarterly* XV (July 1958); Charles R. McKirdy, "A Bar
Divided, the Lawyers of Massachusetts and the American Revo-
lution," *American Journal of Legal History* XVI (July 1972); and
Edwin C. Surrency, "The Lawyer in the Revolution," *American*

Journal of Legal History VIII (Apr. 1964). On teachers, see R. F. Seybolt, "Schoolmasters of Colonial Philadelphia," *Pennsylvania Magazine of History* LII (1928).

General accounts of printing include Lawrence C. Wroth, *The Colonial Printer* (Portland, Maine, 1938); Frank Luther Mott, *A History of American Magazines 1741–1850* (Cambridge, Mass., 1939); Lyon N. Richardson, *A History of Early American Magazines, 1741–1789* (New York, 1931); Stephen Botein, "Meer Mechanics and an Open Press," *Perspectives in American History* IX (1975); Leonard W. Levy, *Freedom of Speech and Press in Early American History* (New York, 1963); and Marion Barber Stowell, *Early American Almanacs* (New York, 1977).

Among the helpful treatments of particular persons and places are Hennig Cohen, *The South Carolina Gazette 1732–1775* (Columbia, S.C., 1953); Richard F. Hixson, *The Press in Revolutionary New Jersey* (Trenton, 1975); Peter J. Parker, "The Philadelphia Printer," *Business History Review* XL (spring 1966); Dwight L. Teeter, "Benjamin Towne," *Pennsylvania Magazine of History* LXXXIX (July 1965).

On the relation to revolutionary issues, see Bernard Bailyn and John B. Hench, eds. *The Press and the Revolution* (Worcester, Mass., 1980); Carl Berger, *Broadsides and Bayonets: The Propaganda War of the American Revolution* (Philadelphia, 1961); Philip Davidson, *Propaganda and the American Revolution 1763–1783* (Chapel Hill, N.C., 1941).

Chapter 4. On these subjects, early works tended to be anecdotal, later ones ideological. Both types contain material of interest. Alice Morse Earle, *Customs and Fashions in Old New England* (New York, 1893), and her *Home Life in Colonial Days* (New York, 1898); Sydney G. Fischer, *Men, Women and Manners in Colonial Times* (Philadelphia, 1898); and Paton Yoder, "Private Hospitality in the South," *Mississippi Valley Historical Review* XLVII (Dec. 1960), are useful. Edmund S. Morgan, *Virginians at Home* (Williamsburg, 1952), is modern in approach. Mary Cable, *The Little Darlings* (New York, 1975); Arthur W. Calhoun, *A Social History of the American Family* (Cleveland, 1917); Oscar and Mary F. Handlin, *Facing Life* (Boston, 1971);

Peter Gregg Slater, *Children in the New England Mind* (Hamden, Conn., 1977); and Daniel Scott Smith, "Parental Power and Marriage Patterns," *Journal of Marriage and Family* XXXV (Aug. 1973), describe the role of children.

James Axtell, *The School Upon a Hill: Education and Society in Colonial New England* (New Haven, 1974); Edward P. Cheney, *History of the University of Pennsylvania* (Philadelphia, 1940); Lawrence A. Cremin, *American Education: The Colonial Experience* (New York, 1970); J. William Frost, *Connecticut Education in the Revolutionary Era* (Chester, Conn., 1974); Howard Miller, *The Revolutionary College: American Presbyterian Higher Education 1707–1837* (New York, 1976); Samuel E. Morison, *Three Centuries of Harvard College* (Cambridge, Mass., 1936); Leon B. Richardson, *History of Dartmouth College* (Hanover, N.H., 1932); Douglas Slone, *Education in New Jersey in the Revolutionary Era* (Trenton, 1975); Louis Leonard Tucker, *Connecticut's Seminary of Sedition, Yale College* (Chester, Conn., 1974); and Thomas J. Wertenbaker, *Princeton 1746–1896* (Princeton, 1946), deal with various levels of schooling.

General works on eighteenth-century women include Mary Sumner Benson, *Women in Eighteenth Century America* (New York, 1935); Barbara Cunningham, "An Eighteenth Century View of Femininity," *Pennsylvania History* XLIII (July 1976); Elizabeth Dexter, *Colonial Women of Affairs* (Boston, 1924); Richard W. Hogeland, ed., *Women and Womanhood in America* (Lexington, Ky., 1973); Carl Holliday, *Woman's Life in Colonial Days* (Boston, 1922); Herbert Moller, "Sex Composition and Correlated Culture Patterns of Colonial America," *William and Mary Quarterly* II (Apr. 1945); and Julia C. Spruill, *Women's Life and Work in the Southern Colonies* (Chapel Hill, N.C., 1938). Linda Grant DePauw, *Founding Mothers* (Boston, 1975), and Elizabeth Evans, *Weathering the Storm* (New York, 1975), examine women in the revolutionary decade. Mary Beth Norton, *Liberty's Daughters* (Boston, 1980), deals with the experience of American women in the half century after 1750, more adequately for the earlier than for the later decades.

Nancy F. Cott, "Divorce and the Changing Status of Women

in Eighteenth Century Massachusetts," *William and Mary Quarterly* XXXIII (Oct. 1977); Herman R. Lantz, "Marital Incompatibility and Social Change in Early America," *Sage Research Papers in the Social Sciences* (London, 1976); Thomas R. Meehan, "Not Made Out of Levity," *Pennsylvania Magazine of History* XCII (Oct. 1968); and James S. Van Ness, "On Untieing the Knot," *Maryland Historical Magazine* LXVII (summer 1972), treat divorce in various provinces.

Chapter 5. Many of the works on manners and the family mentioned under Chapter 4 are also helpful on the subjects treated in Chapter 5.

Accounts of various aspects of health include George A. Billias, "Pox and Politics in Marblehead, 1773–1774," *Essex Institute Historical Collections* XCII (Jan. 1956); Newton C. Brainard, "Smallpox Hospitals in Saybrook," *Connecticut Historical Society Bulletin* XXIX (Apr. 1964); Vern L. Bullough, "An Early American Sex Manual," *Early American Literature* VII (winter 1974); Patrick Henderson, "Small Pox, Patriotism and the Norfolk Riots, 1768–1769," *Virginia Magazine of History* LXXIII (Oct. 1965); and E. E. Hume, "Surgeon John Jones," *Bulletin of the History of Medicine* XIII (Jan. 1943).

Richard J. Hooker, "The American Revolution Seen Through a Wine Glass," *William and Mary Quarterly* XI (Jan. 1954); Marie Kimball, "Some Genial Old Drinking Customs," *William and Mary Quarterly* II (Oct. 1945); Samuel A. Drake, *Old Boston Taverns and Tavern Clubs* (Boston, 1917); and Alice M. Earle, *Stage Coach and Tavern Days* (New York, 1900), contain information on drinking.

Chapter 6. The most comprehensive work on the relation of the frontier to the Revolution is still Thomas Perkins Abernethy, *Western Lands and the American Revolution* (New York, 1937), to be supplemented by Richard Morton, *Colonial Virginia, Westward Expansion and Prelude to Revolution* (Chapel Hill, N.C., 1960); Richard Slotkin, *Regeneration Through Violence* (Middletown, Conn., 1973); and Jack M. Sosin, *The Revolutionary Frontier, 1763–1783* (New York, 1967). Mann Butler, "Details of

Frontier Life," *Register of the Kentucky Historical Society* LXII (July 1964), and Lowell H. Harrison, "A Virginian Moves to Kentucky," *William and Mary Quarterly* XV (Apr. 1958), examine frontier life; and biographies of frontiersmen contain a wealth of information about personality and society, among them Charles A. Jellison, *Ethan Allen, Frontier Rebel* (Syracuse, N.Y., 1969); John Bakeless, *Daniel Boone* (Harrisburg, Pa., 1965); and Nicholas B. Wainwright, *George Croghan, Wilderness Diplomat* (Chapel Hill, N.C., 1959). British agents are the subjects of John R. Alden, *John Stuart and the Southern Colonial Frontier* (London, 1949), and James T. Flexner, *Mohawk Baronet: Sir William Johnson of New York* (New York, 1959). Competent works on the Indians include Allen Trelease, *Indian Affairs in Colonial New York* (Ithaca, N.Y., 1960); Louis De Vorsey, *The Indian Boundary in the Southern Colonies 1763–1765* (Chapel Hill, N.C., 1966); Robert S. Cotterill, *The Southern Indians* (Norman, Okla., 1954); Barbara Graymont, *The Iroquois in the American Revolution* (Syracuse, N.Y., 1972); and Georgiana C. Nammack, *Fraud, Politics and the Dispossession of the Indians* (Norman, Okla., 1969). Bernard W. Sheehan, "Indian-White Relations in Early America," *William and Mary Quarterly* XXVI (Apr. 1969), surveys the literature judiciously. Ian C. C. Graham, *Colonists from Scotland* (Ithaca, N.Y., 1956), and Catherine S. Crary, "The Humble Immigrant and the American Dream," *Mississippi Valley Historical Review* XLVI (June 1959), describe migration; and Freeman H. Hart, *The Valley of Virginia in the American Revolution* (Chapel Hill, N.C., 1942), deals with the war.

Chapter 7. General treatments include Rodney Atwood, *The Hessians* (Cambridge, England, 1980); Walter H. Blumenthal, *Women Camp Followers of the American Revolution* (Philadelphia, 1952); Charles K. Bolton, *The Common Soldier under Washington* (New York, 1902); Thomas Fleming, *1776: Year of Illusion* (New York, 1975); Don Higginbotham, *War of American Independence* (New York, 1971); Arnold Pavlovsky, "Between Hawk and Buzzard," *Pennsylvania Magazine of History,* CI (July 1977); Jonathan Rossie, *The Politics of Command in* the *American Revolution* (Syracuse, N.Y., 1975); John Shy, *A People Numerous and Armed* (New York, 1976); John J. Stoudt, *Ordeal at Valley Forge* (Philadelphia, 1963); Neil Stout, *The Perfect Crisis: The Beginning of the Revolutionary War* (New York, 1976); and Willard M. Wallace, *Appeal to Arms* (New York, 1951). Steven T. Charles, "John Jones, American Surgeon and Conservative Patriot," *Bulletin of the History of Medicine* XXIX (Sept.–Oct. 1965); John Cochrane, "Medical Department of the Revolution," *Magazine of American History* XII (Sept. 1884); David L. Cowen, *Medicine in Revolutionary New Jersey* (Trenton, 1975); Donald J. D'Elia, "Dr. Benjamin Rush and the American Medical Revolution," *Proceedings of the American Philosophical Society* CX (Aug. 1966); and James E. Gibson, *Dr. Bodo Otto* (Baltimore, 1937), treat medicine during the war. On gambling, see T. H. Breen, "Horses and Gentlemen," *William and Mary Quarterly* XXXIV (Apr. 1977), and Jane Carson, *Colonial Virginians at Play* (Williamsburg, 1965).

Chapter 8. Treatments of religion are abundant. Among the best are Charles W. Akers, "Religion and the American Revolution: Samuel Cooper," *William and Mary Quarterly* XXXV (July 1978); Carl Bridenbaugh, *Mitre and Sceptre* (New York, 1962); Evarts B. Greene, *Religion and the State* (New York, 1941); Joan R. Gunderson, "Anthony Gavin's A Master Key to Popery," *Virginia Magazine of History* LXXXII (Jan. 1974); Sydney V. James, *A People Among Peoples: Quaker Benevolence in Eighteenth-Century America* (Cambridge, Mass., 1963); William G. McLoughlin, *New England Dissent 1630–1833* (Cambridge, Mass., 1971); Herbert M. Morais, *Deism in Eighteenth Century America* (New York, 1934); and Harold E. Taussig, "Deism in Philadelphia during the Age of Franklin," *Pennsylvania History* XXVII (July 1970). Herbert Leventhal, *In the Shadow of the Enlightenment* (New York, 1976), considers changing folk beliefs. Gladys Bryson, *Man and Society: The Scottish Inquiry of the Eighteenth Century* (Princeton, 1945), examines an important influence on American thought. Garry Wills, *Inventing America: Jefferson's Declaration of Independence* (Garden City, N.Y., 1978), a trendy work aimed at the popular market, has no scholarly merit and casually misreads the document it treats.

Chapter 9. Among the useful surveys are Kenneth Silverman, *Cultural History of the American Revolution* (New York, 1976); Everett Emerson, ed., *American Literature 1764–1789* (Madison, Wis., 1977); and George F. Dow, *The Arts and Crafts of New England, 1704–1775* (Topsfield, Mass., 1927). Lawrence C. Wroth, *An American Bookshelf* (Philadelphia, 1934), reconstructs works likely to be known in the colonies at the start of the revolutionary era.

Among useful works on the theater are Richard Moody, *America Takes the Stage* (Bloomington, Ind., 1955) and *Dramas from the American Theatre, 1762–1909* (Cleveland, 1966); George C. D. Odell, *Annals of the New York Stage* (New York, 1927); Thomas Clark Pollock, *The Philadelphia Theater* (London, 1933); Hugh F. Rankin, *The Theater in Colonial America* (Chapel Hill, N.C., 1965); George O. Willard, *History of the Providence Stage 1762–1891* (Providence, 1891); and Eola Willis, *The Charleston Stage* (Columbia, S.C., 1924). E. P. Richardson, *Painting in America* (New York, 1956) and "The Stamp Act Cartoon in the Colonies," *Pennsylvania Magazine of History* XCVI (July 1972); Anna Wells Rutledge, *Artists in the Life of Charleston* (Philadelphia, 1949); Charles Coleman Sellers, *Charles Willson Peale* (New York, 1969); Henry Wilder Foote, *John Smibert, Painter* (Cambridge, Mass., 1950); and Grose Evans, *Benjamin West and the Taste of His Times* (Carbondale, Ill., 1959), deal with aspects of colonial art.

Useful treatments of music include Edward D. Andrews, *The Gift to Be Simple: Songs, Dances and Rituals of the American Shakers* (New York, 1940); Samuel E. Barney, *Songs of the Revolution* (New Haven, 1893); Gilbert Chase, *America's Music from the Pilgrims to the Present* (New York, 1966); Helen Cripe, *Thomas Jefferson and Music* (Charlottesville, Va., 1974); Arthur Paler Hudson, "Songs of the North Carolina Regulators," *William and Mary Quarterly* IV (Oct. 1947); Charles Kaufman, *The Music of Eighteenth Century New Jersey* (Trenton, 1975); J. A. Leo Lemay, "The American Origins of 'Yankee Doodle,'" *Wil-*

liam and Mary Quarterly XXXIII (July 1977); Frank Moore, *Songs and Ballads of the Revolution* (Port Washington, N.Y., 1964); and Charles D. Platt, *Ballads of New Jersey in the Revolution* (Port Washington, N.Y., 1972).

On science, see Brooke Hindle, *The Pursuit of Science in Revolutionary America 1735–1789* (Chapel Hill, N.C., 1956), and Raymond Phineas Stearns, *Science in the British Colonies of America* (Chicago, 1970).

Chapter 10. Studies of politics are abundant. Allan Nevins, *The American States during and after the American Revolution, 1775–1789* (New York, 1924), and Jackson Turner Maine, *The Sovereign States, 1775–1783* (New York, 1973), deal with internal politics; the later book does not supplant the earlier. Jack P. Greene, *The Quest for Power* (Chapel Hill, N.C., 1963), traces the development of the colonial assemblies. Charles Sydnor, *Gentlemen Freeholders: Political Practices in Washington's Virginia* (Chapel Hill, N.C., 1952), is a lucid account. Elisha P. Douglass, *Rebels and Democrats* (Chapel Hill, N.C., 1955), examines the struggle for majority rule. Chilton Williamson, *American Suffrage* (Princeton, 1960), and Robert J. Dinkin, *Voting in Provincial America* (Westport, Conn., 1977), present the material on that privilege.

Helpful studies of the law include George A. Billias, ed., *Law and Authority in Colonial America* (Barre, Mass., 1965); Henry J. Bourguignon, *The First Federal Court* (Philadelphia, 1977); David H. Flaherty, *Privacy in Colonial New England* (Charlottesville, Va., 1972); and Douglas Greenberg, *Crime and Law Enforcement in the Colony of New York* (Ithaca, N.Y., 1976); and William E. Nelson, *The Americanization of the Common Law* (Cambridge, Mass., 1975). John Phillip Reid, *In a Defiant Stance* (University Park, Pa., 1977), offers an interesting comparison with Ireland. Aspects of the relation to the economy emerge in Robert A. Feer, "Imprisonment for Debt in Massachusetts Before 1800," *Mississippi Valley Historical Review* XLVIII (Sept. 1961), and Oliver W. Holmes, "Shall Stagecoaches Carry the Mail?," *William and Mary Quarterly* XX (Oct. 1963). Bernard Bailyn, *The Ideological Origins of the American Revolution*

(Cambridge, Mass., 1967); and Gordon Wood, *The Creation of the American Republic* (Chapel Hill, N.C., 1969), probe the relation to ideas.

The literature on slavery is large and mediocre. The best works are David Brion Davis, *The Problem of Slavery in the Age of Revolution, 1770–1823* (Ithaca, N.Y., 1975), and Duncan J. MacLeod, *Slavery, Race and the American Revolution* (New York, 1974). James Hugo Johnston, *Race Relations in Virginia* (Amherst, Mass., 1970), is one of the few books to approach, though imperfectly, the question of miscegenation.

Chapter 11. On the loyalists the standard accounts now are Robert M. Calhoon, *The Loyalists in Revolutionary America* (New York, 1973), and William N. Nelson, *The American Tory* (Oxford, England, 1961). But there are still elements of interest in Claude H. Van Tyne, *The Loyalists in the American Revolution* (New York, 1902). For American thinking with reference to the rest of the world, there are useful materials in Nathan O. Hatch, *The Sacred Cause of Liberty* (New Haven, 1977). James West Davidson, *The Logic of Millennial Thought* (New Haven, 1977), stresses the continuities in New England thought, while Ernest L. Tuveson, *Redeemer Nation* (Chicago, 1968), points to the change at the Revolution. See also Oscar Handlin, *One World* (Oxford, England, 1974).

Index